A Northeast Gardener's Year

A

NORTHEAST

GARDENER'S

YEAR

LEE REICH

Addison-Wesley Publishing Co., Inc.

Reading, Massachusetts   Menlo Park, California   New York

Don Mills, Ontario   Wokingham, England   Amsterdam   Bonn

Sydney   Singapore   Tokyo   Madrid   San Juan   Paris

Seoul   Milan   Mexico City   Taipei

Grateful acknowledgment is made for permission to reprint portions
of the following:

"Two Tramps in Mud Time" from The Poetry of Robert Frost, *ed. Edward*
Connery Lathem. Copyright 1936 by Robert Frost. Copyright © 1964 by Lesley
Frost Ballantine. Copyright © 1969 by Holt, Rinehart, and Winston.
Reprinted by permission of Henry Holt and Company, Inc.

Library of Congress Cataloging-in-Publication Data

Reich, Lee.
  A Northeast gardener's year / Lee Reich.
    p. cm.
  Includes index.
  ISBN 0-201-55050-4
  1. Gardening—Northeastern States. I. Title.
SB453.2.N82R45   1992
635'.0974—dc20   *91-34574*
                                          CIP

Jacket and text design by Cynthia Krupat
Jacket illustration by Vicki Herzfeld Arlein
Set in 10.5-point Monticello by DEKR Corporation

3 4 5 6 7 8 9-MW-95949392
Third printing, July 1992

Contents

Acknowledgments

TWO PEOPLE who I would like to thank for their careful reading and useful criticism of my manuscript are Nancy Miller, my editor at Addison-Wesley Publishing Company, and Joseph Reich, my father.

I would also like to acknowledge the work of anonymous artists of a century ago, represented by the engravings interspersed throughout the text.

Preface

A H A ! You have stumbled upon me back near the blackberries, pitchfork in hand, turning over my compost pile. But come along, let's wander about the garden. During our coming year together, a particular activity or aroma — perhaps a flower that catches my eye — may prompt me to set aside what I am doing and take up pen and paper. There will be no orderly system to what I write, except as dictated by the progress of the seasons, which we will follow month by month.

I have chosen to divide the gardening year into monthly chapters because of the distinctive ambience and set of activities I associate with each month in the garden. And whereas the Julian year begins in January, my gardening year gets under way in March. I will begin each chapter by setting the tone for the month with a few lines of borrowed poetry, then follow with a short description of what is going on plantwise. From there, we are left to the whims and vagaries of the weather and the weeds, the unfolding of blossoms and the ripening of fruits, perhaps the cry of a plant begging to be repotted as it pushes its roots through the holes in the bottom of its container. This book is not meant to be encyclopedic — there are plenty of good encyclopedias for that (my favorite is *The Standard Cyclopedia of Horticulture* [1927], by Liberty Hyde Bailey). Consider this book a figurative stroll through one man's garden.

I have gardened as far west as Wisconsin, as far south as Delaware, and as far north as New York. This book is applicable to at least that range, and any reader could stretch the range a bit more — to include the whole of what we generally call the Northeast — by adding or subtracting a few days on either side of the outdoor growing season.

Although the terrain in the Northeast ranges from flat, river bottom land to rolling hills to craggy mountains, perhaps the most defining feature of the Northeast is dramatic seasonal changes. Our cold winters can nip back or kill tender plants, and our humid summers favor plant diseases. But these potential hardships are more than offset by equable proportions of rainfall and bright, sunny skies through the growing season. Spectacular autumns, often with protracted, warmish Indian summers, prepare both plants and gardeners for cold weather. And at least from the gardener's standpoint, if a winter happens to be particularly bitter, the breath of spring is just that much sweeter when it finally arrives. Each season has its beauty and rewards in the garden.

My present garden — the inspiration for this book — lies in New York. Here, winter lows drop to minus 20 degrees Fahrenheit and summer highs reach 95 degrees Fahrenheit. On average, spring frost is finally chased out of my garden by the end of May and autumn frost makes its debut the first week in October. Most garden sites have their inherent merits and faults, and in my case they are good soil and bad air. I live in a river valley where the soil is all that any gardener could hope for — a deep, well-drained silt loam with no rocks at all. But cold air that settles in this low spot brings late spring frosts that nip overeager flowers and charges the air on summer nights with an extra dose of moisture.

I define my garden loosely, not only by the fence within which I grow the bulk of my vegetables and a few flowers. A sugar maple that I planted on my property five years ago is part of my "garden," as is a distant neighbor's tree, whose view I enjoy and "cultivate" with a frame of two shrubs on my property — borrowed scenery, as the Japanese call it. Anyone familiar with the climate of the Northeast may wonder about the possibility of *year-round* gardening. In the dead of winter, I pretty much ignore that fenced-in area for vegetables, but turn my attention to other parts of the "garden": branches of Nanking cherry glistening in sunlight; herb plants growing indoors in pots on a windowsill; dreams spurred on by plant catalogs.

So join me as I meander about in the coming months. This is not a book to be read at one sitting, but month by month, as it was written. I hope each month's offerings will guide, entertain, and, most of all, inspire.

Lee Reich
New Paltz, New York
March 1991

A Northeast Gardener's Year

MARCH

Ah, March! We know thou art
Kind-hearted, spite of ugly looks and threats,
And, out of sight, art nursing April's violets!

Helen Hunt Jackson, *"Verses. March"*

IN EARLY MARCH the garden cannot help but appear disheveled, with patches of snow and battered remains of last year's plants here and there, and trees and shrubs in need of pruning. The new season begins slowly, as days that grow longer and warmer convince buds on woody plants to swell and green sprigs of herbaceous plants to poke cautiously through the ground. Overwintered spinach and *mâche* offer a few tender leaves for salad.

This slow beginning is like that of a roller coaster ride: all of a sudden, things bump into gear and I am swept onward and upward at an increasingly rapid pace. By the end of the month, I have cleared away old plants, straightened posts heaved awry by frost, and finished the bulk of the pruning. I will wait until bloom time to prune my peach tree (when I can assess winter damage), and until bloom is past to prune lilac, forsythia, and other spring flowering shrubs. Indoors, I have sown hardy annuals — petunias, cabbages, snapdragons, and the like — and those tender annuals, such as impatiens, whose seeds germinate slowly. As seeds germinate, windows and cold frames become stocked with seedling flats.

Another season of gardening is under way!

Wild Tulips — I cannot decide if the unfurling leaves poking up through the ground are attractive or just interesting. The outer side of each leaf is commonplace enough — green, with subtle maroon shading. But the inner sides are velvety maroon with olive-green stripes tracing from each leaf's tip to its still-buried base. Whether pretty or just interesting, these leaves are welcome. They promise radiant flowers, for they are leaves of wild tulips.

Wild tulips? Isn't this a contradiction in terms? After all, what plant is more genteel than the tulip? The flowers are perched high, away from the "dirt," on stalks so straight that they seem to have responded to the yell of "Attention!" from some flower sergeant.

But this image of a formal flower portrays "garden tulips," complex hybrids so called because they are the tulips most commonly planted. Garden tulips are the result of centuries of breeding that began in 1554 when Busbequius, the Austrian ambassador to Turkey, admired tulips in a garden in Constantinople and paid dearly for some seeds that he then brought back to Europe. The resulting hybrids, a rainbow of colors in shapes ranging from those as dainty as columbines to those as corpulent as peonies, are far removed from their wild ancestors.

I prefer to trace this aristocratic line back to its humbler beginnings; it is the wild tulips whose cheery blossoms I now await. The same mail-order catalogs whose pages are ablaze with garden tulips often devote a half-page to wild tulips, sometimes called species, or botanical, tulips. The color range of wild tulips does not match that of garden tulips, but how many colors does a garden need? My *Tulipa greigeii* 'Red

Riding Hood' has vivid, scarlet blossoms, each cradling a black blotch in its center. And for a waterlily out of water, I am growing *T. kaufmanniana*, commonly known as the waterlily tulip. The creamy yellow petals, brushed on their outside with rose, open to a flat star with a deep-yellow, sunny center. Not bad for wildings, eh? (And these are only two of the 150 or so *Tulipa* species.)

My affection for wild tulips also has a practical side. 'Red Riding Hood' and waterlily tulips bear their pert blossoms atop short, sturdy stems, so are less apt to flop over from rain or wind than are their high-bred relatives. (The short stems also look less gawky to me.) And wild tulips are truly perennial, so each bulb I planted keeps multiplying and blooming for years. Garden tulips have become so aristocratic that even with coddling they lose steam after a couple of years, and are best grown as annuals.

The needs of wild tulips are as modest as is their lineage: a soil that is well drained and moderately fertile, and a site in full, or almost full, sunlight. Some of my wild tulips are growing up through a carpet of creeping thyme beneath a clove currant bush. Others I have planted in a drift at the feet of dwarf apple trees growing in an *allée*.

If these tulips have a defect, it is one they share with garden tulips. In a couple of months, the paddlelike leaves will have lost their lush exuberance of spring and each day will fade a little more until they eventually brown and die. Yet these leaves, no matter how unsightly, must be left to ripen in order to nourish the bulbs below ground for blossoms next year.

No need to jump ahead, though, for now I watch the succulent, young leaves (but are they pretty?) push upward on warm days and sit still and wait out cold days. Watching my wild tulips is a paradigm for March in the garden: Although the plants will not bloom for a month or more, I revel even in waiting, because the steady progress of the season assures me that the merry reds and yellows are on their way.

Potting Soil — The tulips begin the season by themselves; my part in this beginning takes place, officially, on the garage floor, for it is here that I mix up potting soil that will nourish seedlings for the garden. And why make, rather than buy, potting soil? Why bake bread?

There is no magic to making potting soil. My basic ingredients are garden soil, mineral aggregate, and organic matter. Gardening books of a hundred years ago specified "loam" as the soil to use in potting mixes. But you did not just go out and dig up a few shovelfuls of loamy soil; you found a rich, loamy pasture, then dug squares of turf one shovel blade deep and stacked them upside down in a neat pile a few feet high to decompose for a few months. I disregard tradition for this ingredient and just skim some soil from my garden.

Garden soil adds nutrients and weight to a potting mix, and helps buffer it against drastic changes in nutrients or acidity. But used alone, garden soil is too dense for plants in containers. It does not absorb water quickly enough, and once water does get into it, it holds so much that waterlogging results. (Store-bought potting mixes usually do not contain any real soil and are more finicky about being properly watered and fertilized. The main reason these mixes are soil-less is because soil is hard to find on a commercial scale and even then, it is an inconsistent material.)

The mineral aggregate I use — perlite, a lightweight material made by "popping" volcanic rock — makes the final mix less dense, so water flows readily into it, through it, and out the bottom of the container. Some gardeners instead use vermiculite, a type of mica baked hot enough to separate the thin plates. I prefer perlite because those accordion layers of vermiculite collapse if the potting soil is compressed, and because vermiculite decomposes over time.

Organic matter, the third basic ingredient of my potting mix, helps the mix hold water. (I am not being contradictory in first trying to get water to drain out of my potting soil by adding mineral aggregate, then adding organic matter to help the mix hold water. Roots need air and water: without aggregate in the mix, they get only the latter; without organic matter, only the former.) Organic matter also buffers soils against drastic changes in acidity and clings to nutrients that later are slowly released to the plants.

Peat moss and compost are the organic materials I use. Peat moss is partially decomposed bog plants, and the best peat for potting mixes is Canadian peat or Michigan peat. So-called peat humus is so decomposed that it has little water-holding capacity. Sometimes I substitute sphagnum moss for all or part of the peat moss. Sphagnum moss is dried (not decomposed) sphagnum plants and has the added benefit of inhibiting the growth of damping-off fungi, which rot the stems of young seedlings.

Some gardeners might cringe at the thought of all the microorganisms living in the unsterilized compost and garden soil in my potting mix. But I fear not — most microorganisms in soils and composts are beneficial. I did take precautions once for a mix in which I sowed cyclamen seeds, which I knew would take months to germinate. In all that time, there would be too much opportunity for unfriendly microorganisms to get the upper hand and gobble up my precious seeds . . . or so I surmised.

If a potting mix does need heating to kill off some unsavory inhabitants, pasteurization, rather than sterilization, is in order. The lower temperature of pasteurization leaves enough "good guys" to keep any interloping "bad guys" in check. For those cyclamen seeds, I pasteurized the potting mix by burying a potato in it in a baking pan, then putting the pan in a moderately hot oven. Using this method, the soil is heated sufficiently by the time the potato is cooked.

Once the ingredients are gathered together, I am ready to mix. My ritual opening of the gardening season begins as I sweep clean an area in the center of my garage floor, then pile on two gallons each of garden soil, peat moss (or sphagnum moss), perlite, and compost. For additional nutrients, I sprinkle on top of the mound a cup of lime, a half-cup each of bone meal and soybean meal, and, if I have it handy, a few sprinklings of kelp and ground rock powders such as greensand and rock phosphate. This is a mixed bag of ingredients, but I reason that plants, like humans, benefit from a varied diet.

I slide my garden shovel underneath the pile and turn it over, sprinkling on some water and working around the perimeter until the whole mass is thoroughly mixed and slightly damp. Finally, I rub the mix through a half-inch sieve and recite a few incantations to finish off the brew.

March 6

Old Seeds — I asked my friend Judy if she had ordered her garden seeds yet. "I have plenty saved from previous seasons," she told me. My eyebrow went up as I thought of the wasted effort in planting dead seeds. Seeds are living, albeit dormant, embryonic plants that do not remain viable forever. The viability of seeds in new packets is assured by government standards, which set minimum germination percentages for each type of seed. The packing date and the germination percentage often are stamped on the packets.

Judy's old, dog-eared seed packets may or may not be worth using this coming season, depending on where she kept them and what kinds of seeds they are. Conditions that slow biological and chemical reactions also slow aging of seeds: low temperature, low humidity, and low oxygen. My seeds find their low-temperature, low-humidity home in tightly closed canning jars on the back shelf of my refrigerator during spring and summer, then in my unheated garage in fall and winter. A convenient way to keep the humidity low is to sprinkle powdered milk, from a freshly opened box, in the bottom of the jars. Renew the powdered milk each year. (There is no practical way for any backyard gardener to store seeds in a low-oxygen atmosphere.)

So how long should Judy keep dipping into her old seed packets? Even with the best storage conditions, sowing parsnip or salsify seeds after they are more than one year old is not worth the risk. Two years of sowings can be expected from packets of carrot, onion, and sweet corn seed; three years from peas and beans, peppers, radishes, and beets; and four or five years from cabbage, broccoli, brussels sprouts, cucumbers, melons, and lettuce.

Among flower seeds, the shortest-lived are delphinium, aster, candytuft, and phlox. Packets of alyssum, Shasta daisy, calendula, sweet pea, poppy, and marigold can be reused for five or ten years.

I will suggest to Judy that instead of blindly sowing her old seeds, she test the germination of each packet. All that she has to do is to count out twenty seeds, spread them between two moist paper towels on a plate, invert another plate over the first to seal in moisture, and keep the plates warm, around 75 degrees Fahrenheit. After one to two weeks, she can peel apart the paper towels and count the number of seeds with little white root "tails." Any packet whose germination is very low should be tossed into the wastebasket. Knowing the germination percentage of seeds worth saving will allow her to adjust her sowing rate accordingly.

The record life span for seed longevity is held by a species of lupine, *Lupinus arcticus*, whose seeds germinated after ten thousand years. But such lengthy seed survival is rare; in this case, the lupine seeds were unearthed from the silt within lemming burrows in Arctic permafrost. Stories of plants growing from thousand-year-old seeds found buried in ancient Egyptian tombs are spurious. In the 1930s, T. Becquerel studied the viability of seeds that had been held in storage with the National Museum of Paris — the oldest seeds to germinate were 221-year-old *Mimosa glomerata* seeds. At the other extreme in longevity are seeds such as those of the swamp maple (*Acer saccharinum*), which retain their capacity to germinate for only about a week.

Sensitive Plant — With a belated seed order, quickly sent off today to Pinetree Garden Seeds of New Gloucester, Maine, I included a request for a seed packet of "sensitive plant," a plant that is both inedible and homely. I want to grow this plant so that it can entertain me and others with its response to being touched (thigmotropism). Part of the joy in growing plants is watching them respond, albeit slowly, to water, fertilizer, and other environmental stimuli. With sensitive plant,

response is rapid — at least to touch, which causes quick and temporary collapse of the leaves.

This touch response is the result of both an electrical stimulus — much like that generated in animal nerves — and a chemical stimulus. The substance, known as Ricca's factor (after Ubaldo Ricca, who first noted the chemical response in 1916), has been extracted from plants, although never identified chemically. The stimulus travels through the plant at two centimeters per second, so you can watch leaves of a large plant collapse in a wave of motion after one leaf is touched.

Response to touch is not uncommon in the plant kingdom. In a couple of months out in the garden, pea tendrils will be pulling my pea vines up a chicken-wire fence. A month or so later, bean stems flopping loosely in the air will close in tight spirals on encountering the poles I have set out for them. And how about the Venus's-flytrap, which closes its hinged leaf around an unwitting fly?

Plants are discriminating about what they will move

(thigmotrope?) for. Venus's-flytrap can distinguish somewhat between living and dead prey by closing only if two different sensing hairs within its "jaws" are touched in succession, or one hair is touched twice. Tendrils can distinguish between different types of surfaces, responding more quickly to rough or textured surfaces than to smooth or soft surfaces. (The practical implications in the garden are obvious.) Some plants bend toward what touches them, other plants bend away. Beans are less discreet; no matter where they are touched, they move in the same direction, clockwise or counterclock-wise, depending on the type of bean.

I said that touch response in plants "is not really uncom-mon," so you may be thinking, "There aren't *that* many plants with tendrils, twining stems, or with leaves that collapse or close when touched." You are right. But *all* plants, some more than others, are dwarfer and stockier when repeatedly touched (or shaken or bruised). This is one reason why indoor and greenhouse plants, which are not exposed to wind, are more leggy than outdoor plants. This is why a pine tree growing on the windswept edge of a craggy cliff is so small and tough looking compared with its svelte counterpart sheltered within the forest. Scientists have found that even repeatedly holding a ruler against a leaf to take measurements for experiments influences leaf size.

Tendrils and twining stems obviously are useful for get-ting plants up off the ground. Leaves that close around a fly help nourish the Venus's-flytrap. And stocky growth in re-sponse to shaking makes a plant at a windy site better able to withstand the force of wind.

But what use could "fainting" be to a sensitive plant? Rapid collapse of the leaves could help the plant conserve water in drying winds. Or, if a large animal nibbled even one leaf, the plant's lushness would evanesce, leaving an unappe-tizing skeleton of stems. Rapid collapse might also startle, then scare away, a hungry insect. Perhaps the reason for thigmotropism in this plant is to be found in the plant's scientific name — *Mimosa pudica. Pudica* is the Latin word for bashful. Sensitive plant is an entertaining plant, but one that I will not touch too much in an outward show of affection, for fear of collapsing it.

March 12

Indoor Sowing — Look around the home of any inveterate gardener from now through the next couple of months, and you will find seed flats in all sorts of odd places — atop the hot water heater or the pilot light of the stove, snuggled up near the wood stove, blocking hot air vents, and, of course, perched on sunny windowsills. These warm spots are appropriate places for seed flats. Most seeds germinate quickest between 65 to 85 degrees Fahrenheit. "Gentle bottom heat" is what old gardening books instructed.

Sixty-five to eighty-five degrees Fahrenheit is a rather broad range, and each type of seed has its own preference within this temperature spectrum. Snapdragon and pansy, for example, germinate best at 65 degrees; lettuce and endive at 75 degrees; and cucumber and okra at 90 degrees. I germinate my seeds by setting planted flats on a thermostatically controlled heating mat made especially for this purpose (it is waterproof, among other things). Although I can adjust the temperature to within a couple of degrees of whatever temperature I want, this precision is wasted. In a given week, I may be germinating zinnia seeds (optimum temperature 70 degrees) and broccoli seeds (optimum temperature 85 degrees), for example, so the best I can do is to set the mat at about 80 degrees and put the broccoli flat right on the mat and elevate the zinnia flat slightly above the mat. Germination still takes place — albeit more slowly — at temperatures either above or below the optima. For all the technology, "gentle bottom heat" is what I strive for.

In addition to gentle bottom heat, some seeds need light in order to germinate. This phenomenon was first discovered about a century ago by a botanist who tested the effect of light on 964 species of predominantly wild plants. Germination of 70 percent of those plants was promoted by light, and germination of 27 percent was inhibited by light. The remaining 3 percent were unfazed either way.

Decades later, a chemical called phytochrome was isolated from plants and found to be responsible for this phenomenon. When exposed to red light, phytochrome changes to a form that promotes seed germination. In the dark, it gradually changes back to its original form, which inhibits germination.

Only a small amount of light is needed to induce germination. A few feet away from a fluorescent light is adequate. You might think incandescent light would be better, because it casts a redder light. But incandescent light also includes a large proportion of wavelengths longer than red, such as those found in the dark (including infrared, or heat). These wavelengths put phytochrome in the form that inhibits germination. Incandescent light still is effective, although less so than fluorescent light.

Fortunately, garden plants generally are not as affected by light as were the seeds of the wild plants in the study mentioned previously. Still, many vegetables, together with coleus, impatiens, petunia, lobelia, hollyhock, and snapdragon, germinate better with light. Usually it is tiny seeds that need light to germinate. This natural protection mechanism keeps small seeds from germinating while they are deep within the soil, where they would use up food reserves before the emerging shoots reached light. (This has practical implications outside in the garden. Digging or rototilling the soil keeps bringing up — sowing, you might say — weeds by exposing their seeds to the germination-promoting effect of light.)

Calendula and nasturtium are examples of seeds whose germination is inhibited by light. Such big seeds need lots of water to germinate, a condition most often found deep in the soil, and — you guessed it — darkness. Small seeds of pansy and portulaca also germinate best in darkness. But pansy thrives where there is moisture and shade, so it behooves the seeds to remain dormant until they have been transported to a suitable habitat. And portulaca seeds, like those of other dry land plants, are better off if germination is delayed unless they are deep in moist soil, where it is dark.

With seed flats sown, watered, and sited, I watch and wait for germination. I have grown seedlings for my garden for years, but I still get a tingle of excitement when that first green leaf shows against the background of brown sphagnum moss. Once those seeds germinate, the flats need "growing on" (to use another term from old gardening books) conditions, which usually means cooler temperatures and abundant light.

March 14

Celeriac — I just checked my basement and saw that celeriac I put down there for storage last fall is still in perfect condition. And here I am, already sowing it again for this season. Celeriac? The word sounds like celery, and celeriac and celery are even in the same genus and species: *Apium graveolens*. But celeriac is a root crop, a knobby root that by summer's end is riding up out of the soil as if deciding whether its place is in or out of the ground. The flavor of the root is similar to celery, but smoother — delicious raw in salad, or cooked in soup (especially pea soup) or stew. Anyone who believes celeriac to be a mere vulgar relative of celery should check the price in the grocery store.

The high price tag on celeriac belies the ease with which it can be grown. Celeriac culture is similar to that of celery, except that celeriac is more forgiving and does not need blanching. The plant needs a long growing season (about 120 days), so I start it indoors this month in order to harvest roots the size of softballs by autumn. A few different varieties are available, but all the ones I have grown — 'Prague', 'Alabaster', 'Balder', 'Zwindra', and 'Jose' — have yielded large, good-tasting roots, actually indistinguishable to me from one variety to the next.

Anyone who wants to grow celeriac must grow transplants, because they are rarely available for purchase. The special requirement in growing these transplants is patience:

Seedlings do not poke through the soil until two or three weeks after sowing, and then their initial growth is slow. I scatter the seeds thinly over a flat filled with potting soil, then sprinkle on an additional light covering of soil. Once the seedlings are large enough to handle, I transplant them to another seed flat, spacing plants two inches apart each way or sticking one plant in each cell of plastic cell packs.

I do not transplant celeriac outdoors until the end of May. If transplanted too early, the plants allegedly are shocked by cold and ruined as they put their energy into growing seed stalks rather than roots. (This also is, allegedly, a problem with celery, but I have never had even one celeriac or celery plant do this.) Celeria plants require full sun and rich soil, with about an eight-inch spacing.

Except for weeding, plants need no further care. Few pests bother celeriac — none that I ever had to do anything about. Some old books talk about periodically cutting off the

lateral roots near the soil surface to get a cleaner and larger "knob" on knob celery (another name for celeriac), but this practice is probably for naught or worse.

Celeriac is edible as soon as the root grows large enough

to eat. Small roots hardly seem worth harvesting, considering the time spent germinating and transplanting each plant, so I leave the bulk of the harvest in the ground until cold weather settles in autumn. Then I lift plants out of the soil and shake some of the dirt from the roots. After cutting the leaves off right at the crown, I put the roots in a plastic bucket in a cold, humid place — just where they are on this March day, as firm and tasty as the day I harvested them.

March 15

Garden Planning — I am a little tense, because sometime soon I have to sit down and map out this year's vegetable garden. Ideas have been bouncing around inside my head for the past few weeks, but the day must come (before I plant peas) when procrastination will bow to action.

Then I will gather together on the kitchen table some clean white paper, a sharpened pencil, a ruler, and notes and plans of gardens past; I will take a deep breath and begin with the first order of business — planning for crop rotation. The theory: Plant no vegetable in the same spot more often than every fourth year. The rationale: A garden pest might survive the winter to bother the same plant the following year . . . unless the plant happens to be growing elsewhere, in which case the pest starves and dies. Pests often are equally fond of all plants in a plant family, so I will not grow tomatoes, peppers, eggplants, or potatoes (nightshade family) at the same location without waiting three years. Ditto for cabbage, broccoli, cauliflower, or brussels sprouts (cole family), beans or peas (legume family), and carrots, celery, celeriac, or parsley (umbellifer family). Of course, in the years before I replant tomatoes, I might grow carrots, then beans, then cabbages at that spot.

I also rotate plants according to how they affect nutrient balance in the soil. Leafy vegetables (spinach, lettuce, cabbage) take a lot of nitrogen from the soil, beans and peas add nitrogen to the soil, fruiting vegetables (tomato, pepper, eggplant) soak up phosphorus, and root vegetables (carrots, radishes, turnips) use a disproportionate amount of potassium. In the bed right near the garden gate, I might grow a leafy vegetable one year, then a fruiting vegetable, then a root vegetable, then a pea or bean, and finally back to the leafy. I follow the same rotation in the adjacent bed, beginning perhaps with a fruiting vegetable. And so on around the garden.

So much for theory. In practice, I am always tucking lettuce, radishes, onions, sometimes even cabbages, in among other plants helter-skelter throughout the garden. And how can I resist using the fence around my garden to support peas — every year! I find some consolation for my sloppiness knowing that crop rotation is to no avail when dealing with a pest such as the striped cucumber beetle, which has no trouble flying thirty feet across the garden from where last year's cucumbers were to where this year's cucumbers are. I am diligent, though, about rotating tomatoes to avoid leaf-spotting diseases, which can defoliate plants by summer's end.

Because I always try to eke the most from every square foot of garden space, I factor another scheme — succession cropping — into my garden planning. The theory: few vegetables are in the garden from the time the soil first thaws in spring until the first frost in autumn, so a given spot in the garden could have more than one crop back to back during the same year. Looking over my notes, I see that in previous years I have successfully cropped autumn spinach following spring peas, late carrots following early lettuce, autumn broccoli following early bush beans following extra-early radishes, and autumn Chinese cabbage following summer cucumbers.

My final cropping scheme — again to maximize use of space — is called intercropping. The theory: Until large plants fill out their leafy canopy, there's room between them for smaller plants. I stick onion sets, to be harvested as scallions, between early lettuces, between cabbages, around tomatoes, all through the garden, in fact. Lettuce goes between pole beans, tomatoes, or broccolis, and a few radish seeds here and there in a carrot row are up and out of the way by the time the carrots build up steam.

Are you beginning to see why my nerves get edgy when it is time to plan the garden? And I have not yet mentioned one other cropping scheme I sometimes factor in. This scheme, called companion planting, is a wrinkle on intercropping. Rather than intercrop just any two plants that physically can be accommodated in a given space, it seems that some plants are finicky about their neighbors, which inhibit or promote growth, or attract or repel pests. Carrot and onion, corn and squash, and tomato and cabbage are examples of beneficial associations.

Years ago, it was at this point in garden planning that I was ready to throw up my hands. How was I to factor all these cropping schemes into a harmonious, productive garden? Wasn't gardening supposed to be a relaxing hobby? A pastoral diversion?

Over the years, my planning has become increasingly calm. I have accumulated a pile of previous seasons' notes to guide me. I mostly ignore companion planting (much of it is unproven). And, most important, I now abide by this principle: never delay planting for lack of a plan.

March 16

Paths — Walking around the back of my garden yesterday, after dumping kitchen trimmings on the compost pile, I recognized a major design flaw in the landscape. My garden is functional enough, producing an abundance of fruits, flowers, and vegetables. But like so many backyards, the garden per se is aesthetically disjunct from the house, separated by a breadth of lawn. Over the years, I have dressed up the garden with a pair of dwarf cherry trees flanking the garden gate, rows of pot marigolds to stare over to the house, and mounds of allysum to brighten the ground beneath the gooseberry bushes. Still, something has been lacking.

Yesterday, as I cast my gaze through the garden back

toward the house, I imagined a path running from the living room right across the lawn, then right into and through the garden. Suddenly, the whole landscape was knit together. The coherence I envisaged was more than just aesthetic. My path would create a physical and psychological connection between house and garden (psychological because a path can lead the imagination, even if the feet stay in place). There is no time like late winter, with the garden devoid of lush, green foliage and splashes of flower color, to reveal the unadorned essentials of the landscape.

My path is going to be a straight shot right from the living room to and through the garden. Since the present garden gate is out of this proposed line, I did briefly consider curving a path from the back of the house over to this gate. A curved path would be more informal than a straight path, but I figured that the backdrop of woods behind the garden was rusticity enough — a bit of formality was needed. I also could get over to the present garden gate with a straight path having an abrupt jag in it. The jag and curve also are ways to slow down feet and imagination along a path. But I want to make the connection between the garden proper and the back of my house as intimate as possible. I can always invite a more leisurely pace by making the path wider. And I will slow down the pace within the garden with a path running perpendicular to the path from the house. These paths will divide the garden in quarters, their intersection creating a point for reflection (and perhaps a sundial).

So my plan is to move the gate, and then make it visually jump even closer to the house with some adornment: a cedar arbor with clematis vines clambering up the sides and over the top, and a rhododendron on either side. Once again, a formal air will be created by the mirror-image planting on either side of the axis. But not too formal: the cedar posts will be unfinished trunks, their bark still peeling, and there is no way, even if I wanted, to press clematis into formal attire.

I have to think of something — perhaps a garden bench or a bird bath — for the terminus of the proposed path from my house. I can't let this straight path dissolve in the woods or, worse yet, leave in place the doghouse now in that line of sight. If you can see the end of a path, something worth seeing or going to should be there. In an informal garden, a path can disappear out of sight as it curves, drawing footsteps or imagination to an unseen lure.

What about paving? Paving on any path should harmonize with the landscape. A path that is too obtrusive, either because of gaudy paving or largesse, draws attention away from the landscape. On the other hand, commonality between paving outdoors and flooring indoors brings the garden and house even closer. Commonality might be achieved with the use of similar materials (terra-cotta indoors and brick outdoors, for example), similar colors (wood floor indoors and

crushed stone of similar color outdoors), or similar paving patterns (the same parquet pattern on wood indoors and brick outdoors). Decisions! Decisions! Decisions!

It is especially nice this time of year, when the weather

sometimes prevents going outside, to be able to look out a window and not only enjoy the landscape but feel part of it. A well-placed path can do this. A well-placed path also provides firm, dry ground on which to trod out to the garden to drop the first seeds of the season into warm ground.

March 21

Digging — Spring soil preparation separates gardeners into two camps: the diggers and the nondiggers. I belong to the latter school, so let me first make short work of the former.

What are the rationales for turning over the soil with a rototiller, spade, or garden fork? Digging aerates the soil, especially if quantities of organic materials such as leaves, sawdust, or manure are mixed in. There also is a psychological benefit to digging the garden each spring. The hard work stirs the blood as well as the soil. And a freshly prepared seedbed is like a clean slate, with last year's mistakes erased.

I offer two rules for diggers: not too much, and not too soon.

"Not too much": The objective in digging the soil is *not* to reduce it to a fine powder. Soil particles bind together into aggregates, called peds, which have a good spectrum of pore sizes for the air and water needed by plant roots. Especially with a power rototiller, it is too easy to pulverize the peds. Control the urge to run the tiller up and down the rows until the soil is like dust. Nothing beats tillage with a shovel, followed by raking, for exercise and for tempering the tendency to overwork the soil.

"Not too soon": Wait for the soil to dry out a little before tilling. Working a wet soil, especially one that is clayey, ruins its crystalline structure. The soil becomes good for sculpture, but poor for plant growth. On the other hand, digging a bone-dry soil leaves large, rock-hard clods. Squeeze a handful of soil. If it crumbles apart easily, it is ready to till; if it wads up, it needs to dry out some more. When the soil has just the right amount of water in it, a shovel or spading fork slides in easily. As a clod is lifted and turned, it breaks from its own

[21]

weight along fault lines of the peds. Following spadework, gentle coaxing with a garden rake easily crumbles larger clods into smaller aggregates for a seedbed.

Turning the soil is an age-old tradition that dies hard. Edward Faulkner laid the first serious challenge to this annual ritual in his book *Plowman's Folly* (1944). Ruth Stout further popularized the concept of no-digging in her book *How to Have a Green Thumb Without an Aching Back* (1955), a title that suggested a most obvious reason not to dig the soil.

The facts speak for themselves: Churning the soil charges it with oxygen, which rapidly burns up valuable organic matter. Churning the soil also destroys channels left by earthworms and old roots, and upsets capillary connections. These large and small pores move air and water throughout a soil. Admire the lush growth along roadsides and in pastures, where the soil is undisturbed; even midsummer's heat hardly causes these plants to flag. Digging also brings to the surface dormant weed seeds, which are just waiting for a bit of light and perhaps a bit more air to infuse them with life. And finally, those of us who forgo digging need not delay spring planting until the soil dries.

So what do you do if you do not dig? My garden is in permanent beds — never dug, of course — which are three feet wide with eighteen-inch-wide paths between them. I keep the beds in the same place every year, and the soil in the beds never gets compacted because I plant, weed, and harvest from the paths alongside the beds. These are not raised beds, which are useful only where drainage is poor but otherwise tend to dry out too readily in summer. I keep weeds out of the paths between the beds by dumping whatever organic materials I have at hand: wood chips one year, sawdust another year, leaves yet another year, even a few layers of newspaper topped by leaves, sawdust, or chips.

Each spring I blanket the beds with a two-inch dressing of compost, occasionally supplemented with a sprinkling of soybean meal, wood ash, limestone, or ground rock powders for extra nutrients. The weed-free compost smothers most small weeds. I dig out large weeds individually, roots and all, and cut the tops off any small weeds that do grow by skimming the soil surface with a sharp, hand-held hoe. After a few years, weeds are few enough so weeding is a pleasant divertissement rather than an incessant chore.

Starting a no-dig garden is simple, but you need sufficient organic materials. Begin by mowing the proposed garden area, then covering it with a sprinkling of fertilizer and a few layers of newspaper. The newspaper effectively smothers existing vegetation, and eventually decomposes to form humus. On top of the newspaper, lay down a few inches of leaves, manure, and/or straw; and top this organic mat with a couple of inches of weed-free compost. Then plant. Keep the planting beds in the same location every year, and maintain paths from which you can reach inside the beds. Sandy soils can tolerate being walked on, but if you must walk on beds in other soils, first lay down a wide board to distribute your weight.

I sometimes miss that neat, smooth expanse of fluffy, dark soil that remains just after tilling a garden. Then again, by the time I would be admiring that view, my seeds are already in the undug ground.

March 28

Pea Planting — Hold your horses, garden mavens, it's still too early to plant peas! As I watch and talk to other gardeners, I note that too many of you already have planted your peas. It makes me worry that I have waited too long to plant *my* peas.

Early sowing is important with peas, because they love cool spring weather. Peas must be up and harvested before hot weather turns the pods tough and tasteless. And in some gardening circles, a gardener's worth is measured by how soon the first mess of fresh peas is on the table.

But rushing the season may not advance the harvest, because pea seeds will not germinate in soil that is colder than 40 degrees Fahrenheit. And if the seeds do not germinate, they are liable to rot. Although I have heard of gardeners drilling holes in frozen ground in midwinter for peas, I like to plant mine so they sprout as soon as they hit the dirt.

Sowing too early also does not give a good return in terms of early harvest. Competitive spirit aside, a one-week difference in sowing date might give only a day or two difference in harvest date. Growth is slow during cool spring weather, and not much happens in the one week that the earlier planted peas sit in the soil.

If peas are sown too early and the seedlings do emerge, cold weather might strike them down. Even though traces of winter linger after my later-sown peas show their heads, the weather is rarely severe enough to cause damage. I did get a scare a few years ago when a late snow covered my inch-high pea seedlings, but they were left unscathed.

Now that I have rationalized my tardiness in sowing early peas, just when am I going to plant them? Most years I play the averages and plant according to the calendar date. My day for pea sowing is April 1. If the weather is warm in late March, early sowers will get their first peas ahead of me.

However, if the weather is cold and wet at that time, early sowers will have to resow. At any rate, all of us pea growers will be enjoying fresh garden peas by June, give or take a few days.

APRIL

The sun was warm but the wind was chill.
You know how it is with an April day
When the sun is out and the wind is still,
You're one month on in the middle of May.
But if you so much as dare to speak,
A cloud comes over the sunlit arch,
A wind comes off a frozen peak,
And you're two months back in the middle of March.

Robert Frost, "Two Tramps in Mud Time"

IN SPITE OF curtain calls by Ol' Man Winter, perhaps even a late snowfall, plant growth progresses steadily, in step with the likewise steady warming of air and soil. The first seeds I planted outside have barely broken through the ground (okay, so I scratched away some dirt to check on them). After the grays and browns of winter, the fresh, green leaves of bulbs are a welcome sight even before their flowers appear. And I forgot all about the anemones I had planted in a bed of vinca — what a pleasant surprise!

There is much to do. Warmth finally defrosts the compost pile, and I spread the rich, brown stuff over the garden. Through the month, I resolutely plant indoors and out. Sweet pea, cleome, radish, lettuce, and other hardy seeds go directly into the still-cool soil outside; indoors, I sow tomato, marigold, pepper, and other tender seeds needing a jump on the season. The cold frame demands my close attention, needing venting on warmish, sunny days and closing up on frosty nights.

Blossoms on trees and shrubs are most welcome — except for those on apricot, peach, and plum trees. I would like to see swelling buds on these plants open as late as possible, or not at all, this month. One calm, cloudless, cold night when the blossoms are open could mean no fruit from these trees this year. Oh well, there are always grapes, pears, and persimmons, all of which bloom sufficiently late to escape spring frosts.

April 1

When to Plant — It's hard for me to keep my wits about me when it comes to planting annual flowers and vegetables this time of year. On balmy days, I am sure that I have delayed planting too long. Cool days reassure me that I have plenty of time to plant. But any colder than cool, and an icy chill goes right down my spine, as I fear I have planted too soon.

I curb my planting whims to some degree by watching the blossoms developing on trees and shrubs. They respond to the general, rather than day-to-day, warming trend and therefore are good barometers of when and what to plant. For example, forsythia and daffodil do not bloom on exactly the same date each year, but when they do bloom, the weather finally has warmed enough to sow the *hardiest seeds* outdoors. Crunchy radishes, tender peas, fragrant sweet-pea flowers, and delicate poppies are on the way as soon as forsythia and daffodil give me the go-ahead to plant those seeds. Other vegetable seeds I sow to the accompaniment of forsythia blossoms are carrot, chard, lettuce, and spinach. Other flowers are calendula, allysum, cornflower, and baby's breath.

The next blossoms I keep an eye out for are those of the shadbushes (juneberries), and the flowering quinces and cherries. This will also be the one time when the common lilac earns its keep, in the form of fragrant lavender or white blossoms. Quick on the heels of lilac blossoms will be the creamy white or salmon-pink dogwood blossoms. As these blossoms unfold, I start planting out *cold-hardy seedlings* that have been growing indoors. Vegetable transplants that will tolerate the frequent freezing nights that still occur with all these blossoms are cabbage, broccoli, onion, and leek. And I must not forget the flowers: snapdragon, dusty-miller, salvia, pansy, and lark-spur.

Looking forward to the month of May, I will keep an eye out for blossoms on spirea, wisteria, and wild cherry, which herald the planting of *cold-tender seeds* of annual flowers and vegetables. Although the air temperature might dip oc-casionally at this time, the ground will have sufficiently warmed by then to remain so. Oak leaves will be the "size of mouse ears," the traditional time when the American Indians planted their corn. Besides corn, I also will plant seeds of beans, okra, and the curcurbits (melons, squashes, and cucum-bers). The soil also will be warm enough to sow nasturtium, cockscomb, morning glory, sunflower, and the big three of American gardens: marigold, zinnia, and petunia.

Finally, toward the end of May, I will look along road-sides for creamy white blossoms dangling from wild black locust trees and the white mounds of Vanhoutte spireas in front yards. These blossoms are the natural signal that all danger of frost should be past and *cold-tender plants* can be set in the garden. Garden centers and nurseries will be over-flowing with zinnias, marigolds, tomatoes, and peppers, neatly lined up in plastic trays. Squash and cucumber plants can be set out then.

Nature sometimes leads me momentarily astray. Even when spireas and locusts are in bloom, late frost, which could spell death for tender transplants, is not impossible. A simple covering of practically anything — newspapers, towels, in-verted flower pots — will ward off any light frosts that occur.

When catalpas burst into bloom and the fragrance of mock orange fills the air, the door finally will have closed on the last vestiges of Ol' Man Winter. Yet even these late blossoms will be a timely sign to sow seeds — in this case, cabbages and broccolis for the fall garden.

April 9

Cold Frames and Cloches — I always seem to be trying to extend some boundary. Like that of the garden's edge. Or weather that says: "You can't grow a fig tree this far north" or "Cold is sure to linger for at least another month." Well, cold might linger, but I can hasten along that first harvest from the vegetable garden. Merely covering plants with some sort of translucent shelter hastens plant growth by retaining warmth and providing protection from winds.

A "cold frame" is a clear plastic or glass topped box set directly on the ground, functioning in the garden as a miniature greenhouse. My simplest cold frame is made from four pieces of scrap pine boards nailed together into a three-foot by twelve-foot rectangle. The covering is two pieces of quarter-inch clear plastic, each of whose previous incarnation was as a floor runner beneath an office chair. My most elaborate cold frame is a purchased structure, looking much like a miniature barn with a double-wall, polycarbonate plastic roof that folds open or closed along tracks in the eaves.

The traditional form for a cold frame is a box with a sloping roof. The roof is highest along its north edge and slopes down an inch or two for every foot from back to front, with the lowest point no less than a foot high. The larger the cold frame, the more even temperatures remain inside, but the cold frame must be small enough that you can reach plants and soil while standing outside the frame — after all, this is a cold frame, not a greenhouse. A common size is some multiple of six feet by three feet.

The traditional covering for a cold frame is glass, valuable for its clarity and permanence. Glass is readily available because people always seem to be discarding old window frames (often conveniently six by three feet in size). But glass breaks easily: I once had a cat that constantly walked — perhaps he pounced — on my glass frames and broke them.

Partly because of that cat, I now prefer plastic for covering my cold frames. Plastics are lightweight and easily cut to fit makeshift frames. The light weight of plastic is a debatable advantage, as I learned one blustery spring morning when I found my cold frame's plastic cover in my neighbor's yard. Plastic also deteriorates with age, becoming less transparent to light, although this problem is mitigated by storing the covers in the garage for the summer.

A stick of wood eighteen inches long by three inches wide by one inch thick props open the plastic cover of my homemade cold frame when needed. I use the full eighteen-inch length for ventilating on hot days later in the season, or when I harvest, sow seeds, or water. Depending on wind and temperature, I slide the one-inch edge or the three-inch edge of the lumber beneath the lid to prop it open just a crack on sunny, cold days. The lid is not attached to the cold frame, but is kept from sliding when propped by a couple of wooden cleats attached at the rear of the frame. The cleats also make it easy to lift off the frame completely once summer weather arrives or if I want to let rainfall do a thorough watering for me.

The ideal site for a cold frame is a well-drained soil with a slope facing east or southeast. At the very least, the site must receive full sun in winter. A cold frame will stay even warmer in winter if it is snuggled near a fence, wall, or dense evergreen shrub on its north side.

For all its use, a cold frame has a limited area; the way

to extend the principle — with a less permanent structure — right out on the garden rows is with temporary coverings, called cloches (pronounced like *closes,* with a *sh* instead of an *s* sound on the first *s*). *Cloche* is French for bell jar, and is used because the original cloches were large bell jars that French market gardeners set over plants to act as miniature

greenhouses. At one time, acres and acres of bell-jar-covered fields surrounded Paris and supplied out-of-season vegetables to the city's households and restaurants.

There now are modern versions of the traditional cloche. One is the Hotkap, a waxed-paper hat anchored in place with soil on its brim. A gallon plastic milk jug, with its bottom cut off, can lead a useful afterlife as a cloche. I have used one-gallon glass jugs, whose bottoms I cut off with a bottle cutter. New types of cloches, such as tepees of water-filled tubes, fiberglass boxes, and plastic A-frames, are always coming on the market.

The limited air volume within cloches has a tendency to overheat on warm, sunny days. Here is where the homemade jug cloches are handy; just unscrew the cap for venting. Hot-kaps are vented by tearing the wax paper progressively open as the season progresses.

Where a whole row of similar plants needs protection, one long tunnel cloche makes more sense than do individual cloches over each plant. A tunnel cloche is more like a min-iature greenhouse, and the temperature of the large volume of air underneath does not plunge as low at night, nor soar as high on sunny days, as under individual cloches. The cool summer climate of England, where cloches often are necessary to assure a crop of tomatoes, has prompted innovation in cloche design. There you find glass tents made from panes of glass held together by the tension of wires and set end to end along garden rows.

More modern tunnel cloches are fashioned from clear plastic film held aloft with a series of metal hoops kept in place with their ends stuck into the soil. The edges of the plastic are anchored with a covering of soil, or the plastic is sandwiched in place by couplets of hoops, one inside the plastic and the other on the outside, at intervals along the length of the cloche. A covering that does not need venting is clear plastic with slits, which demands less attention, but of course will not protect against as much cold as an unvented covering. The main problem with these tunnel cloches in my garden was that they collapsed each winter under the first heavy snowfall.

"Floating row covers" are lightweight woven or spun-bonded fabrics that drape loosely onto the garden rows and "float up" as growing plants push on them. Sunlight, rain, and sprays pass right through. The temperature under floating row covers is only about 6 degrees Fahrenheit higher than the temperature outside, but no venting is needed. Insects cannot penetrate the tiny holes of floating row covers, so they have potential use for insect control. One year I covered my eggplant seedlings with one of these fabrics, and effectively brought the plants through their critical young stage when flea beetles do irreparable damage. I now rarely use floating row covers, not because they are ineffective, but because I like seeing the garden covered with green plants and brown dirt, not gauzy white film.

Off-season storage of cloches can be a problem for those of us whose garages already are overflowing with shovels, seed flats, potting soil, rakes, and other garden-related items. Fortunately, I don't have to ponder where to put a gardenful of bell jars. Hotkaps are useful for only one season, and panes of glass stack when glass tent cloches are carefully disassembled (although I have found annual attrition of a certain number of panes unavoidable). Water-filled cloches collapse when drained. Clear plastic can be folded for reuse perhaps one more season. Diaphanous floating row covers are the easiest to store; the covering for a whole row crushes into a ball small enough to carry around in my pocket from one season to the next.

April 10

Enough but Not Too Much — How much kohlrabi do I expect to eat this year? According to *Gardening for Food and Fun* (U.S. Department of Agriculture *Yearbook of Agriculture, 1977*), twelve pounds of kohlrabi satisfies one person for one year. Fifteen feet of garden row will yield this twelve pounds, so unless I am a kohlrabi fanatic, I should not plant fifty feet of this vegetable.

The point is: Plant vegetables according to expected consumption. Vegetables are easy to grow; the hard part is to grow just the right amount. The "excess zucchini syndrome" of late summer is apparent in more insidious ways with other vegetables from the garden. Witness the sighs from family members as broccoli is sneaked into yet another recipe, after two weeks of different broccoli dishes every meal. Isn't zucchini bread yet another way of disposing of zucchini?

Too much of any one vegetable can easily kill anyone's taste for it. One spring I decided that it would be nice to have fresh parsnips all winter. Parsnips store well in the ground under mulch, or in a root cellar. So I planted . . . and planted . . . and planted . . . and still have not recovered. In the fifteen years since that planting, I have grown parsnips again only once. And that was a short row.

Root crops such as parsnips, carrots, and beets yield about one pound per foot of row. The average person supposedly eats about twenty pounds of any of these each year, so only a twenty-foot row is needed. Obviously, some adjustments should be made for personal preferences and lacks thereof. A two-foot row of parsnips still yields too much for my taste!

Broccoli often gets overplanted. I once saw a garden that, as far as I recall, was only broccoli — an especially striking sight because it was winter and the leafless, frozen, brown stalks still stood, lined up like soldiers. On the average, five broccoli plants will satisfy one broccoli eater, with an additional five plants to provide frozen broccoli through the winter.

Each spring, I balance in my mind the delectable flavor of home-grown melons against the fact that they take up a lot of space and require a long season to ripen. A half-dozen or so plants will keep one person in melons for the summer.

Squashes also are greedy for garden space. If each person planted only three or four plants, there would be no zucchinis found orphaned on doorsteps and in unlocked cars this summer. Everybody could double that amount if they were planning to freeze squash for the winter.

The first few years that I grew my own tomato seedlings, I grew twice as many as I needed, in case I lost some. I was so careful that usually they all survived. Because I ended up with all those transplants, I figured I might as well plant them. What if pests or cold zapped any of them in the garden? Once again, I nurtured the plants carefully and usually all of them thrived. Fortunately, such antics did not kill my taste for tomatoes. Five tomato plants will supply fresh tomatoes for one person; another five or ten will provide pizza topping, tomato juice, and stewed tomatoes throughout the winter.

Here are more guidelines for the average amount of other vegetables to plant for one person for fresh eating, and the additional amount needed for storage:

VEGETABLE	FRESH	STORAGE
Bush snap beans	15 feet	15 feet
Pole snap beans	6 feet	10 feet
Pole lima beans	10 feet	15 feet
Cabbage	4 plants	8 plants
Eggplant	3 plants	3 plants
Peppers	4 plants	4 plants
Okra	6 feet	6 feet

Vegetables such as leaf lettuce, radishes, and mustard greens grow quickly, so I seed them directly in the garden rather than grow them as transplants. They do not require a great investment in garden space or growing time, so I do not care if they are in excess. I tuck them in among other vegetables.

Incidentally, I do not like kohlrabi, so even though fifteen feet of row provides enough for most people for a year, I never plant it.

April 13

Volunteers — Every year I expect some volunteers in my garden. Before you steer your car in my direction with an offer of assistance, note that these volunteers are plants, not people. Volunteer plants are annuals that replant themselves every year in the garden, thus saving the gardener the trouble of planting.

And where do these volunteers come from? Most come from seeds ripened and dropped on the soil last fall and winter. Dill, borage, and ground cherries (*Physalis* spp.) are notorious for this habit — I planted them just once and have never had to again. Annual flowers that self-sow include alyssum, calendula, cornflower, cleome, cosmos, California poppy, morning glory, petunia, and nicotiana.

Other volunteers are inadvertently sown as I spread compost over the garden. Tomatoes and ground cherries are seeds most likely to survive the heat of my compost pile. Sunflower, melon, squash, and pumpkin seeds are large enough to be able to burst forth from a compost pile's innards, or grow wherever the compost is spread. Occasionally, they appear where an overlooked fruit rotted on the ground the previous season.

To encourage volunteers, I must not be over meticulous in the garden. If I harvest all the dill when it is young and green, no plants will be left to sow seeds. If I cover the whole garden with a three-inch blanket of leaf mulch, small-seeded volunteers will smother before reaching light. Overzealous weeding is another habit that will take with it some potentially valuable volunteers.

On the other hand, I cannot give volunteers free reign in the garden. Weeds have been defined as "plants out of place," and there is a fine line between a welcome volunteer and an unwelcome trespasser. An exuberant pumpkin vine is out of place in a bed of carrots. Most of twenty-five tomato plants popping up right next to each other are, by definition, weeds. I do not allow any garlic chives to volunteer in my garden — the plant is just too ambitious and is very hard to weed out.

Nature makes the choices when it comes to volunteer plants. With volunteers, I never fear that seeds have germinated too early in the spring. And I can rest assured that wherever volunteers appear, they have found suitable conditions with respect to sun and soil. Of course, volunteers do not always show up where I want them to.

Unfortunately, most civilized plants cannot be relied on to perpetuate themselves by volunteering. Corn, for example, is ineffective at self-sowing. As the kernels from a fallen, ripe cob germinate, they tangle together and crowd each other out. One of corn's probable ancestors, teosinte, does disperse its ripe seeds (but we humans prefer to bite into a cob full of intact kernels).

Nonetheless, among those garden plants that are capable of self-sowing, I do let some capable volunteers work in the garden.

April 14

Tomatoes — Today I received a call for help from a thousand miles away. My friend Kit telephoned to ask how to grow the ultimate tomato. He was hoping this season for *more* than just a "homegrown" tomato; he wanted one tomato with a juicy, sweet yet tangy pulp, and a skin so tender as to barely be able to contain that pulp. I advised him to choose his varieties carefully. And because such varieties probably are not available as transplants, I told him to plan on raising his own from seeds.

Besides standard round, red tomatoes, I have grown white tomatoes, yellow pear-shaped tomatoes, red pear-shaped tomatoes, and red plum-shaped tomatoes. I no longer grow the white or yellow varieties (except 'Lemon Boy'), because they lack the tartness that I happen to like in tomatoes. For unabashed flavor, my choices for the best-tasting varieties are 'Gardener's Delight', 'Belgian Giant', and 'Sweet 100'. Just about as good are 'Nepal', 'Valencia', 'Pruden's Purple', and 'Lemon Boy'.

Admittedly, flavor is not the only criterion in choosing a tomato variety. Apartment dwellers who cannot squeeze even one 'Belgian Giant' plant onto a small balcony surely have enough space for the diminutive 'Tiny Tim' tomato. With plenty of sunlight, a fifteen-inch-high plant will be loaded with red, cherry-sized tomatoes. Gardeners who want to impress neighbors with the first ripe tomato on the block should grow a variety such as 'Sub-Arctic Cherry', which is cold resistant and ripens its first fruits only forty-five days after transplanting. I found 'Sub-Arctic Cherry' to be insipid, but it was early. If I were going to vie for the record for growing the world's largest tomato, I would choose 'Delicious'. Each 'Delicious' tomato usually weighs over a pound, but over six and a half pounds is needed to beat the record, which was set with this variety.

Kit called me in the nick of time, because tomato seeds must be sown indoors now. Tomato plants require a long, warm season to ripen their fruits. By growing plants indoors for a month or so, the plants will ripen their first fruits by July (rather than by September, which would occur if the seed were sown outdoors).

Given a good potting mix, warmth, and adequate, but not excessive, moisture, tomato seeds germinate readily. The ideal tomato plant, when transplanted, has lush, green leaves and a stocky stem. This ideal is achieved by giving plants as much light as possible, without excessive warmth, and by keeping the plants slightly thirsty and hungry, although never to the point of allowing the leaves to wilt or turn pale. Most potting soils have enough nutrients to sustain plants for a month or two. If the leaves do begin to yellow, I feed the plants a little liquid fertilizer as per directions. (Very important, those last three words.)

It is hard to imagine, but only in the past 150 years have tomatoes found a place in the vegetable garden. Tomatoes were grown centuries ago by the Aztecs, whose *xitomate* gave us the word and the genes for the present-day tomato. But when first brought over to Europe, love apples, as tomatoes were called, were believed to be poisonous and were grown only as ornamentals. Among Europeans, the Italians first realized the value of the *pomodoro*, this "golden apple." Now

the tomato is the number-one favorite vegetable in American gardens. Kit is right to want to grow the best.

April 20

Garden "Lemons" — "Grow a cauliflower big enough to sit in a chair!" "Grow a fifty-pound cabbage!"

These are lines of exaggeration from old-time seed

catalogs, but times have not changed much. The plant business, like any other business, still sometimes resorts to a bit
of exaggeration to promote its wares. Garden catalogs are
filled with page after page of enticing fruits, vegetables, and

flowers. Nestled in the pages among the many plants worthy
of cultivation are a few "lemons."

My gardening enthusiasm makes me easy prey to such
enticements, and, indeed, over the years I have been lured to
grow some horticultural "lemons." A general rule I now follow
is: If an edible plant is touted as being "great for pickles," it
may not be good for much else.

The list of "lemons" that follows will, hopefully, spare
fellow gardeners some garden space, effort, and shattered
expectations.

Celtuce. "Grow this vegetable and you will have celery
and lettuce in one plant." It sounded like a good idea, especially since I have never grown celery to my satisfaction.
Unfortunately, celtuce tastes like bad celery and bad lettuce.
Are you familiar with the leafy stalks that shoot up from old
lettuce when the days get hot? That, essentially, is celtuce,
the stalk being the "celery" and the leaves being the lettuce.

Tree Tomato. In cold northern climates, this small tropical
tree must be grown in a large pot, outdoors in the summer

and indoors in the winter. The tree tomato is supposed to bear delicious, tomatolike fruits. Perhaps it does. I never did get mine to fruit. I followed the directions, and the plant quickly grew to six feet. I wrestled the plant through doorways in the fall; I waged a never-ending battle with aphids; and I endured the plant's putrid odor. Can you blame me for tossing the plant onto the compost pile?

Vine Peach. Any plant that has too many aliases is suspect. The vine peach is also known as the mango melon, the garden melon, the orange melon, the melon apple, and the vegetable orange. One catalog says that the vine peach has the same size, color, and food value as the tree peach. Perhaps so, but there is no mention of taste. In fact, the vine peach is a dull-flavored melon. The fruit is fit only for pickling. This is one of the few "lemons" that I have managed to avoid growing. Perhaps the pickles are good.

'Pixwell' Gooseberry. I love gooseberries. However, 'Pixwell' fruits are too small, too tough, too leathery, and too tart. The claim to fame of 'Pixwell' is that it is less thorny than other gooseberry varieties: it "picks well." 'Pixwell' is the variety most commonly offered by nurseries, but with a little sleuthing, varieties with sweet, tender, aromatic berries — 'Achilles', 'Jumbo', and 'Hinnonmakis Yellow', for example — can be found.

Manchurian Bush Apricot. This plant is a native of Manchuria, so is undaunted by howling, bitterly cold winds. However, warm weather does not linger in Manchuria, so when spring comes, the Manchurian bush apricot is genetically programmed to awaken quickly. The plant wastes no time in blooming, and these early blossoms succumb to late spring frosts. The result — no fruit — is not all that bad, since the fruit does not taste very good anyway. On the positive side, the dainty pink blossoms on the leafless red stems are a welcome sign of life in the barren landscape of early spring.

Stuffing Tomato. Here is a tomato that looks very much like a pepper — solid walls and hollow, except for a few seeds around the core. You can stuff it, slice it in rings, or use it in any other way that you would a pepper. Why not grow peppers instead?

Garden Huckleberry. This is my favorite "least favorite" plant not to grow. The catalog description claims that the clusters of plump fruits look like large, dark blueberries. True. The description continues: ". . . cooked with some lemon and sugar, the berries will rival blueberries for pie." False! Garden huckleberries are tasteless. The pie will taste like a lemon-and-sugar pie. As if that were not enough, there is some question as to whether garden huckleberries are poisonous. I am sure the plant would not sell well under its other name — black nightshade!

April 16

Spring Radishes — For a few seasons, spring radishes were a flop in my garden. Yields were meager, and too many radishes were sharp flavored, pithy, or riddled with brown trails of the cabbage-root maggot (yecchhh!). This admission of failure does not come easily, especially because there is a sentence in nearly every gardening book about how easy radishes are to grow. Because of this, and because they grow quickly, radishes are often touted as an ideal vegetable for children's gardens. Perhaps this knowledge lulled me into neglecting the few basic needs for growing a good radish. Well, that's not going to happen this spring.

To grow good radishes, the seeds must be sown early. This means now. If sowing is delayed too long, radishes mature during hot weather and develop an acrid flavor. Such roots often are puny and have hollow centers because as days lengthen, energy is channeled into seed stalk rather than root formation. If I go out to the garden and sow seeds today, however, in a month or less I will harvest radishes that are juicy, crunchy, and piquant.

Radishes must grow quickly in order to be tender and to mature before the onset of hot weather. The three- or four-week sowing-to-harvest period stated on the seed packet is realized only with good growing conditions. This means a rich soil (my annual two-inch dressing of compost should be adequate) and adequate water (rarely a problem in early spring).

Given good growing conditions, each radish root needs elbow room. I sprinkle the seeds along the furrow, and when the seedlings come up I will thin them to one or two per inch. To ensure a good stand, I make sure to use viable seed, which is seed that either is fresh seed or has been stored properly — cool and dry — for no more than four years.

Insects are the next bugaboo in this radish saga. The only two worth troubling about are cabbage-root maggots and flea beetles. Flies of the cabbage-root maggot lay eggs that hatch into maggots that tunnel through radish roots. A sprinkling of wood ashes, renewed after rains, should convince this pest to desist in its tunneling. Early plantings need no help to escape this maggot, because the roots mature before the maggot fly becomes active. Flea beetles riddle radish leaves with small holes, and this slows growth of the plants. A rapidly growing plant usually outgrows the beast. Either cabbage-root maggots or flea beetles can be deterred by covering radishes with an insect-proof barrier like cheesecloth or floating row cover. Past experience has taught me, though, that if I give the plants good growing conditions, they are little troubled by either insect.

Radishes demand little garden space because they are planted so early and grow so quickly. I sow a few between slower-growing plants, like cabbages or lettuces, and scatter them thinly with carrot seeds, which germinate slowly. For a continuous supply of fresh radishes, I sow a batch of seeds every week or two from now until mid-May. The peak of perfection of radishes passes quickly, especially with later sowings, so harvest must keep pace with ripening or else all this effort at early sowing and quick growth is wasted.

I think good growing conditions are more important for flavor than is choice of variety. I have grown 'Scarlet Globe', 'French Breakfast', 'Comet', 'Sparkler', and 'Cherry Belle', and when any of these are good, they are very good. Perhaps I cannot distinguish between varieties because I am not a radish connoisseur, but I do know that a radish-and-butter sandwich on a slice of French bread demands a well-grown radish.

April 23

Perennials — A friend of mine who is a very good gardener gets a laugh from the current vogue for perennial flowers. "Sure, perennials are some of our most beautiful flowers, but a lot of people are attracted to the *perennial* in perennials — you plant once, then just sit back thereafter to enjoy flowers. Well, 'tain't so." He goes on to contend that annual, not perennial, flowers are easiest to grow. Each year, you can rototill or hand-dig a bed of annual flowers and begin with a clean slate. Weeding a perennial bed, on the other hand, must be done carefully and with a hoe. And if the bed has been neglected for even one season, the job requires getting down on all fours and digging out weeds with a trowel. Clumps of perennials also need to be divided periodically, when they become old and woody.

I take issue with my friend's contention that annuals are less work than perennials. It really is a matter of what each of us considers "work." Because I regularly weed my perennials, the weeds never get a strong foothold; I find the short, undemanding sessions I spend weeding pleasurable. And because I do not till any part of my garden, digging up and dividing a clump of tansy satisfies what seems to be a primal urge I have to dig in the soil this time of year. Is this any less fun than transplanting annuals?

I now am keeping my eyes on emerging leaves of delphinium, chrysanthemum, coneflower, tansy, and other perennial plants. During that window of time when these plants just begin growth but before they have grown so much as to be unduly shocked by digging, I must decide whether division is in order.

To divide an aging clump, I first work around its edge with a shovel or spading fork, thrusting the tool into the ground at an angle to get under the clump. As I work(?), I push up and down on the handle to lever the clump up on top of the ground, and to shake dirt loose from the roots. Next I take my knife (if the clump is small) or my shovel (if the clump is large and woody) and separate the clump into pieces, each piece with emerging leaves and some roots. I selectively save vigorous, young pieces from the outside edge of the clump and keep them fresh with a covering of moist burlap.

Before I replant is the one opportunity I have to improve the soil beneath the plant. If the soil seems poor, I mix in some compost and perhaps some phosphorous (in the form of bone meal), since phosphorous applied on top of the ground moves only slowly downward.

To plant, I build a mound of soil in the planting hole on which to set the crown, adjusting the height of the mound so that when the soil is firmed the crown will be at ground level. With the new crown in place, I sift soil in among the roots, finally topping the soil with a layer of sawdust or compost. A gallon of water, poured slowly, settles the plant in its new home.

To look their best, perennials such as asters and hardy chrysanthemums need to be divided every spring. I also divide invasive perennials such as bee balm, tansy, and artemesia every year, not to spruce them up, but to keep them from wandering out of bounds. Division every three or four years is sufficient for phlox, coral bells, Canterbury bells, cerastium, Siberian and Japanese irises, veronica, and Shasta daisy.

Although dividing perennials satisfies my need to get my hands in the dirt this time of year, I must exercise restraint. Perennials such as oriental poppy, bleeding heart, and bearded iris go dormant in midsummer, and that is when they like to be divided. I also have to think twice before dividing perennials like Christmas rose, peony, monkshood, butterfly weed, lupine, and baby's breath. Such flowers need division perhaps once a decade, and they often express their resentment to the treatment by not blooming for a year or more thereafter.

April 28

Color in the Garden — I would not consider painting a room in my house without thinking about color, or buy a pair of shoes in randomly mixed colors. I try to apply the same philosophy when choosing flowering annuals for the garden. Too often, seeds or seedlings are sold in color mixtures: 'Ruffles Hybrid' Zinnia, Mixed Colors; 'Springtime' Verbena, Mixed Colors; 'Glitters' Impatiens, Mixed Colors; 'Dwarf Beauty' Phlox, Mixed Colors. But single colors of many flowers — bachelor's button, morning glory, ageratum, alyssum, and petunia — are easy to find, and flowers such as marigold exist only in shades of one basic color.

Randomly mixed colors appear busy in the garden, which blurs the offensiveness of some combinations and the pulchritude of others. With single colors, I do have to pay closer attention to the "seating arrangement" of flowers. But this attention rewards my creative impulses and eyes more than does a mixed bag of colors.

Here are five general rules I follow when using color in my garden:

Rule 1. I mass like colors together. For that matter, I also mass together the same types of flowers of a single color. One yellow snapdragon standing alone, or even a single file of yellow snapdragons does not make much of a show. A solid two-foot by two-foot patch of snaps makes a bold statement. Contiguous masses of color should flow together harmoniously (see rule 3).

Rule 2. I keep in mind that flowers are not the only source of color in the garden. Leaves are various shades of green, yellow, and red; bricks are red; stones are gray and brown; and soil is brown. The subdued colors of walls, fences, and leaves contrast, harmonize, and highlight the colors of nearby flowers. For instance, although midday sun washes brilliance from the most fiery poppy, a dark yew livens even a plain white daisy in such light.

Rule 3. I consider harmony and contrast in colors, using plenty of the former and not too much of the latter. Contrast should be used as spice is in cooking, to break monotony. A good way to predict how a color will feel about its neighbor is to visualize a color wheel. Start at the top with red, then progress clockwise through purple to blue, down to green at the bottom, up to yellow, and then back to red. Primary colors (red, blue, and yellow) and colors across from each other on the wheel clash because they share no common hues. The most harmonious combinations are those that are close to each other, such as red and purple, or purple and blue. White combines easily with all colors.

Rule 4. I consider the vantage point from which flowers will be viewed — from the chair by the window, from the patio, or perhaps from the garden bench. Red has a tendency to draw a flower close, which is perturbing if that flower is, in fact, distant. Red geraniums look just right spilling out of planters and window boxes right against the house. Blues are a better choice for distant viewing.

Rule 5. I consider season of bloom. Summer blossoms of blue cornflowers will not be around in autumn to clash with the ruddy red of a chrysanthemum.

These rules do seem somewhat strict for a bucolic activity like planting flowers. Convention and an innate sense of beauty make these rules. But I do not hesitate to stretch and break them, for I use them as guides, not tethers. Who is to say what visual pleasures the flower garden might offer with adventurous new combinations?

In any case, when planning what the garden will look like in the months ahead, I visualize the scene in terms of reds, violets, oranges, mauves, and pinks, not just in terms of marigolds, petunias, lobelias, and zinnias.

MAY

Whan that the month of May
Is comen, and that I here the foules synge,
And that the flaires gynnen for to sprynge,
Farewel my bok, and my devocioun!

Geoffrey Chaucer, "The Legend of Good Women"

MAY IS A MONTH of action, one of the busiest in my garden. In the flurry of activity, I can barely force myself to pick up a pencil to record what I have planted where, and what I am doing when. There is a continuing succession of planting out of transplants and of sowing seeds, indoors and out, all orchestrated according to the dictates of the season. I move trees and shrubs around, and set new ones in the ground — even these usually permanent features, the bones of the garden, are not exempt from the whims of spring.

The garden needs close attention now, with more than just an admiring eye. Plants may need protection from frost, still a possibility, and from pests such as slugs, flea beetles, and plum curculios that are awakening from their winter slumber. Lawn and garden edges need care, and I swing my scythe through the tall grasses and weeds of the hayfield next door, for the first cutting of the season. Once essential tasks are completed, I fill up spare space and time planting some oddball plants: this year I will grow, for the first time, sea kale (*Crambe maritima*) and sweet Annie (*Artemisia annua*).

Enthusiasm for May's activities is fueled by successive bursts of color, the month beginning with corpulent purple and white peonies, and the month ending as the first rosebuds of the season unfold.

May 7

Growing Up — Right now, the most prominent things "growing" in my garden are wire fences, bamboo tepees, and tomato stakes. Soon they will be covered with plants. I train my plants upward to economize on space. Getting plants up off the ground also allows leaves to be bathed in sunlight and air, and out of reach of slugs, sow bugs, and other ground-dwelling critters. Upward-trained vines also are a way to hide an unsightly wall, or to create a screen to give privacy from a neighbor or the street.

How do vines grow upward? Some need coaxing. Tomato plants' natural inclination is to sprawl. The long, blue spires of delphinium really do want to point skyward, but they are too easily toppled by rain and wind. The same holds true for "dinnerplate" dahlias, which make their best show high above the ground in full view.

For dahlias, tomatoes, and other plants that need help growing upward, I put a stake in the ground as I plant. Driving a stake into the ground next to an established plant will damage its roots. (In the case of delphiniums, which are perennials, I pull out the stake as I clean up the garden each autumn, then carefully put it back in place each spring.) Bamboo stakes or long, straight saplings are sturdy enough for flowers, but tomato vines laden with fruits will topple any wooden stake less than an inch thick. Sometimes I use old iron pipe, one inch in diameter, for the tomatoes — not very attractive, but easy to pound into the ground and surely sturdy. As the plants grow, I tie them to the stakes with thick string or strips of rag, which will not cut into the plant stems. To avoid strangling the plants, and to keep them from sliding down their supports, I first tie a tight loop around the stake, then tie the free ends of the string or rag piece loosely around the stem.

Pole beans and morning glories are vines that climb by means of twining stems. Three bamboo poles tied together tepee-style provide support for beans. Poles need to be less than one inch in diameter or the bean vines cannot reach around them with each revolution. I have trained 'Heavenly Blue' morning glories up a wall along strings stretched between metal eyelets screwed near the base and roof of my house. Moonflowers, whose fragrant and ghostly white flowers open only at night, or 'Scarlet Runner' beans, with scarlet blossoms and edible beans, could be grown in similar situations. A few years ago, I "liberated" from a neighbor's garbage some ten-foot-long by half-inch-diameter hollow iron rods. I now use these rods — they are more permanent and, rusted dark brown, even more unobtrusive than bamboo or string — as supports for pole beans, morning glories, and moonflowers.

Vines that climb by means of tendrils actually reach out and grasp onto their support. Wire fences provide support for the groping tendrils of cucumber, pea, and melon plants in my garden. To keep melon fruits from falling from their own weight, I nestle each one in a mesh bag that I pin to the fence with a clothespin.

Virginia creeper and English ivy are vines that cling to flat surfaces such as tree bark and brick or wooden walls by means of aerial roots or holdfasts. (Holdfasts look and function like miniature suction cups.) Such plants are ideal for softening the lines of buildings and houses, and bringing them into visual harmony with natural surroundings. With time, these plants can soften the appearance of a structure too much, as they pull out paint or work their way under shingles, eventually removing them. English ivy is creeping all over the concrete front stoop of my house, and each year I hack it back as it creeps toward the brick of the house proper, seeking loftier heights.

Invasive Plants — Keep out of my garden!

This admonition is directed at horseradish, mint, and garlic chives — three incorrigible plants that have disrupted my garden. Once again, it's time to look around at new growth poking up through the ground, and make sure these plants are gone for good. I now know that the place for such plants is a patch kept in bounds with a lawn mower, or a semiwild back corner where their unruly manners can be used to advantage or at least ignored.

By far the worst offender, the most unruly plant in my experience, has been horseradish. Three years ago I wisely decided to get rid of some horseradish I foolishly had planted among some berry plants. Ha! Try digging it up. The most thorough digging does not remove every bit of root, and even the smallest bits of root resprout leaves and start growing again. I tried starving the roots by repeatedly cutting off the leaves, and new leaves just kept pushing out. Finally, after three years of diligent digging and leaf removal, I have rid my garden of horseradish — I hope.

Horseradish is one of the few plants I am afraid to put into my compost pile. The traditional method for disposing of quackgrass should be equally effective for horseradish: pull it up, burn it, then spread the ashes where you are sure you'll never want it to grow.

Garlic chives, a clump of which I once planted just inside my garden gate, is another plant that frightens me. That one plant self-seeded, and the following year was surrounded by a score of plants. I usually have no aversion to weeding, but trying to weed out garlic chives is an unsatisfying task. The seedlings cling tenaciously to the soil, the straplike leaves are slippery, and when I finally get hold of them, they snap off, leaving the roots intact to resprout. I suppose I could snip off the flower heads so seeds do not form in the first place, but if I did grow this plant, I would want to see the starlike balls of white flowers at least as much as I would want to taste the garlicky flavor of the leaves.

Mint is almost as bad as horseradish. Wherever I see a sprig of mint poke up through the ground, I know that there is an underground stem pushing a foot or more distant, from which will sprout new sprigs, ad infinitum. I once read that mint would deter cabbageworms, so I stuck sprigs (they root easily) between cabbage plants. The next spring, I found a mesh of mint stems radiating just beneath the surface of the ground. I spent a month tracing the courses of these stems, combing them out of the soil, and finally ridding my garden of mint.

Although I consider horseradish, garlic chives, and mint the most unruly plants, there are others. I am especially wary of any plant that spreads where I can't see — underground. Or any plant whose stems arch to the ground and root. Tansy and yarrow spread both these ways. I do grow both these plants in my garden proper, but I annually hack back their tops and chop back their roots to within bounds. Certain gooseberry varieties have a similar wanderlust. 'Lepaa Red', a vigorous variety from Finland, must be the horseradish of gooseberries; I keep finding plants a couple of feet or more from the mother bush. It needs the same treatment as do tansy and yarrow.

I also am wary of plants that, like garlic chives and horseradish, either self-seed too readily or repeatedly sprout from root pieces. Self-seeded dill and borage are welcome in my garden, in moderation. I annually weed out excess. These seedlings, unlike those of garlic chives, are easy to uproot, so with a little diligence they never get out of hand. Jerusalem artichoke plants repeatedly sprout from even the smallest tubers left in the soil, but they don't really spread, so the weed status of Jerusalem artichoke is far eclipsed by that of horseradish.

I am not advising against planting any of these potentially unruly plants. All have assets to offset their bad behavior — the yellow, buttonlike flowers and pungent aroma of tansy; the garlicky flavor and white-flowered umbels of garlic chives; the pungent, sinus-clearing flavor of horseradish; and so on.

Such plants dramatically demonstrate that a weed is merely a plant in the wrong place.

May 10

Manure — Using manure is one way to fertilize the garden, but hauling it hardly seems to make sense these days, considering that lugging five hundred pounds of horse manure gives plants about the same amount of food as a fifty-pound bag of 10-10-10. And the latter for only a few dollars! But whereas 10-10-10 supplies only food (and often only three of the sixteen needed nutrients, at that), manure has other benefits: it aerates the soil, helps soil capture and cling to water, and renders nutrients already in the soil more available to plants. Nutrients from synthetic fertilizers are used up or washed out of the soil by the end of a season, yet benefits from each application of manure continue for years.

Manure is a traditional way of feeding plants, to the extent that applying synthetic fertilizers once was referred to as a form of "manuring," and certain plants grown specifically to improve the soil are called "green manures." When we talk of manure, though, we really mean animal excrement plus bedding. The bedding itself — usually hay, straw, or wood shavings — is responsible for some of the benefits of manure. The amount of nourishment manure supplies to a plant the first season depends on the ratio of bedding to excrement. Higher ratios result in less nourishment to plants the first season, but greater residual effect for subsequent seasons. Unfortunately, bedding also can be a source of weed seeds.

"Hot manures" are so called because they readily heat up when stacked in a pile. The heat comes from the burst of microbial activity stimulated by these manures' relatively high concentrations of nitrogen and low concentrations of water. Horse and poultry manures are "hot"; cow and pig manures are "cold." (Caution: never use dog or cat manure, because they can transmit diseases.) I am not particular about what kind of manure I use. The horse manure I haul from the stable up the road is just fine. The only manure I will not use is pig manure — the smell offends me.

With manure in hand, or rather in pitchfork (a five-tined pitchfork is my preference for manure handling), what next? Most gardeners dig manure into the soil immediately. If the manure is well rotted — meaning bits of hay and the like are no longer recognizable — planting can proceed as soon as the soil is smoothed. If the manure is relatively raw, at least two weeks must elapse before planting for things to settle down, microbially speaking. In lieu of digging, manure can be laid on top of the ground as mulch. This is fine if the manure is rotted, but nitrogen volatilizes from fresh manure exposed to sun and wind. The nitrogen loss is wasteful, but may be worth the sacrifice considering the benefits of the mulch.

The amount of manure to add to soil depends on whether the manure is rotted or fresh, and what kind of animal provided the manure. You can add too much — I once had a neighbor with a chicken farm who killed his asparagus bed by laying down too thick a mulch of chicken manure (very hot stuff!). Twenty-five to fifty pounds per hundred square feet is about the right amount.

I compost most of the manure I haul before putting it on the soil. This means moving it twice, but the heat and the variety of ingredients within the compost pile (vegetable trimmings, orange peels, tree leaves, and so on) create a product that is well balanced nutritionally and almost free of weed seeds.

The word *manure* comes from the old French word *manoevrer*, meaning to cultivate by hand (in turn from the Latin words for hand and work). Manure handling is a lot of physical work, but is not exercise another benefit of gardening?

May 17

Pink Seeds — Hot pink! Now there's an eye-catching color for seeds. And the color is supposed to be eye-catching, because the seeds are dyed to show that they have been coated with a poisonous pesticide. Somewhere on the seed packet is a statement to the effect that the seed has been treated and should not be used for "food, feed, or oil."

More important to me — I'm not planning to eat the seeds — is to exercise caution when handling pesticide-coated seeds. I *never* let children handle pesticide-treated seeds. As I pick up the seeds while planting, my fingers turn pink, which is enough of a hint not to touch my hands to my eyes, my mouth, food, or anywhere else where I do not want pesticide. I wash my hands thoroughly as soon as I finish planting. I could wear gloves, but even large seeds would then be difficult to sow; small seeds, perhaps impossible.

Seed treatment goes back to the Middle Ages, when wheat seed was shoveled back and forth over the heat of a fire to rid it of smut, a disease that affects the mature plant. In the early nineteenth century, it was found that seed soaked in water in a copper bucket picked up enough copper to protect against smut.

The pink seeds you see when you peel open a packet of peas, beans, or corn are treated not to protect growing plants, but to protect those seeds from rotting in the soil. All seeds, especially large ones, contain stored food to give the tiny plant a boost until it reaches sunlight and is big enough to manufacture its own food. If a seed does not germinate quickly, soil microorganisms queue up for the stored food, rotting the seed. Pesticide on treated seed kills microorganisms near the seed, providing relatively cheap insurance to increase the chances of germination. Treating seeds to prevent them from rotting is a relatively recent practice, dating only from the early part of this century.

In spite of the benefits of treated seed, I plant *untreated* seeds whenever they are available. Some of the fun of gardening is drained if I cannot reach over to grab a bite of lettuce as I plant corn, or if I cannot let my young daughter help me plant.

I take a few extra precautions when using untreated seeds, to make sure they germinate quickly. This means using viable seeds, planting in soil that is well drained, and taking care not to overwater. For me, the most difficult precaution to abide by with untreated seeds is waiting to plant until the soil has warmed sufficiently. Pea seeds just sit — and possibly rot — if the soil is below 40 degrees Fahrenheit, as do bean and corn seeds below about 60 degrees Fahrenheit. When trying to get a jump on the season, I plant seeds a bit on the shallow side and more thickly than recommended, thinning diligently later, if necessary.

Note that all these "special" precautions for handling untreated seeds (except perhaps shallow or thick sowing) are earmarks of good gardening anyway.

May 23

Transplants — Today's telephone call to my sister caught her (with her cordless telephone) setting zucchini transplants in her garden. "Transplanting zucchini?" I queried. "Have some faith in nature." Transplants for sale this time of year entice my sister and other beginning gardeners too often to set plants rather than seeds in their gardens.

I pointed out that not every plant likes to be transplanted. Tomato plants yanked out of the soil will resume growth if their roots or even just their stems are covered in due time with moist dirt. But the roots of plants like corn, poppies, melons, cucumbers, and squashes (zucchini included) resent disturbance. Carrots, parsnips, and other root crops also transplant poorly. Their taproots become the harvested roots, and if bent or broken while young, forked rather than straight carrots and parsnips result.

This is not to say that to successfully transplant squash, poppies, beets, and the like is impossible. Any plant can be transplanted if enough care is taken not to damage the roots. A plant does not even know it has been moved when a large enough ball of soil is carried along with the roots. (To paraphrase Archimedes, "Give me a big enough shovel and I can transplant any plant.") My sister told me that her zucchini plants were growing in plastic cell packs. If the roots were not yet crowding each other against the plastic, and if the plants were gently slid out of their containers, the transplants will survive. I have heard of gardeners transplanting even carrots — very carefully, no doubt.

Many plants do transplant easily, yet are not worth the effort. A friend transplanted peas one year. Granted, his peas were a foot high indoors when mine were just breaking through the ground out in the garden. But how many pea transplants can one care for? I grow about sixty feet of double rows of peas in my garden, from which I expect about twelve pounds of peas. Each pea plant, though, yields only about a quarter of an ounce of peas. Who has enough space and time to sow, water, then transplant even two dozen pea plants for the paltry six ounces of peas those plants would yield?

Generally, plants whose seeds are sown closely spaced in the garden are not worth transplanting. In the flower garden, this would include alyssum, portulaca, and pot marigolds (although I admit to starting a few alyssum plants indoors so they would spread and flower sooner). In addition to peas, some other vegetables not worth growing as transplants include spinach, mustard, and beans. Leaf lettuce should be sown directly in the ground, although heading lettuces like iceberg, bibb, and romaine should be transplanted, because each plant needs space in order to head up well. (Alternatively, heading lettuce could be sown directly in the garden, then thinned to the appropriate spacing.)

"Trust nature," I told my sister. "Sow seeds on the correct planting date in good garden soil, and they will germinate. Save transplanting efforts for vegetables like tomatoes and peppers, which need to be started early indoors in order to ripen their fruits in a reasonable amount of time. Or broccoli and cabbage, because individual plants yield a substantial amount to eat. Tomato, broccoli, and cabbage plants do not object to being transplanted, and not too many transplants are required since they are set a couple of feet or more apart in the garden."

Seeds that are particularly finicky or valuable (due either to scarcity or cost) also are worth growing initially in pots.

There, seedlings can be watched and nurtured individually. I am again trying to grow blue poppy (*Meconopsis* sp.) this year. Because the seeds are very small, and germination is very slow and erratic, I am sowing them in a seed flat rather than in the ground outdoors.

And sure, it may be worthwhile to start a few corn plants indoors, because fresh sweet corn is one of the ultimate gustatory pleasures of the vegetable garden. But is zucchini that toothsome?

May 24

Asparagus — With most vegetables, by the time you taste them fresh-picked somewhere, it is too late in the season to plant them in your garden. Not so with asparagus. Borrow a taste from a neighbor's asparagus bed, or from a wild clump along a fence row, and you are likely to want some growing

outside your own back door. Minutes-old asparagus tastes different from (and better than) any asparagus that reaches the markets. Now is the time to plant.

Asparagus is a perennial, and now that my bed is established, I spend more time picking than anything else. My asparagus bed is a double row only ten feet long, but when the days are warm I go out every single day and pick a few stalks to eat. With a little care, I can expect tender green spears from this bed for half a century or more. My asparagus is set off to one side of the garden, out of the way of annual vegetables and flowers.

Frugal or patient gardeners sow seeds; others buy roots and begin harvest a year earlier. I must be both, because I have begun asparagus beds both ways. Seed sowing is straightforward, but germination is slow. Soak the seeds in water for a few hours before sowing to shorten germination time. One-year-old roots are the best to purchase. Any older, and they reputedly never recover from the shock of transplanting (although a friend told me that she has successfully transplanted old asparagus roots). The fleshy roots radiate out from the central crown, on which small buds — future spears — are evident. The crown is planted with these buds pointing upward.

Asparagus grows best in soil with a near-neutral pH in full sun, with eighteen inches between plants in the row and four feet between rows. With so many other plants in my garden, I could not afford to let asparagus luxuriate in all that space, so I put my rows only two feet apart, at no great sacrifice of yield. The traditional method for planting an asparagus bed entailed digging a trench a foot or more deep, setting the roots in the bottom with a covering of a shovelful of soil, then filling in the trench gradually as the stalks grew. Whew! I planted my asparagus with the roots just deep enough to cover the crowns, and the plants do just fine. The main reasons for the traditional deep planting were to protect the crowns from overzealous hoes during tillage, and from knives during harvest. But I do not cultivate my asparagus bed, I just pile on some mulch every year. And I harvest by snapping the stalks off with my fingers, rather than cutting into the soil with a knife.

Although asparagus roots stay alive year after year, the

feathery tops turn brown and die back to the ground every fall. Then, when the spring sun warms the soil, energy stored in the roots fuels growth of the spears. As the spears grow higher and higher, feathery green branches unfold. Photosynthesis within these green branches pumps energy to the root system, energy that keeps the roots alive through the winter and fuels early growth of spears the following spring, thus completing the plant's annual cycle.

When you or I harvest asparagus, we steal some of the energy that has been stored in the roots. The plant must build adequate reserves before tender stalks can be spared for our plates, so no asparagus should be harvested the season it is planted. If good growth was made the first season, some can be harvested the second season. The plants are ready for a full harvest by the third season. Full harvest means cutting the stalks from the time they first emerge until early July, then leaving all new green stems untouched until they brown in autumn, to nourish the roots in preparation for winter.

The steaming dish of asparagus on my table today is virtually identical to the asparagus enjoyed by ancient Greeks and Romans over two thousand years ago. Even our word for the vegetable is nearly identical to, and derived from, the Greek word *asparagos*. Asparagus was native to the shores of the Mediterranean before plants were transplanted to Greek and Roman gardens. The Elder Cato gave directions for the culture of asparagus in 200 B.C. Asparagus was brought to America with the early colonists and has been cultivated extensively here since then. The red berries borne on female plants attract birds that spread the seed, so asparagus now pops up as an escape from cultivation along fence rows and roadsides.

May 25

Knot Gardens — Walls that surrounded the medieval monastic garden imposed their geometry on planted beds within. These beds usually were rectangular, and areas within the beds were further subdivided into more rectangles or other geometric shapes, according to the plants. Soon, people began to notice that all these lines and curves within the beds were quite ornamental in and of themselves, and thus originated the knot garden.

A knot garden is a two-dimensional garden where neat, compact plants draw lines on the ground. Areas defined by these lines are filled with plants of casual growth habit, or with materials such as sand, gravel, or wood chips. In Elizabethan England, the design drawn by the knot garden began to take such prominence over the plants themselves that not only were plants omitted between the lines — these spaces were filled with variously colored earths — but the lines themselves were "drawn" with wooden boards, lead strips, or sheeps' shank bones. Sir Francis Bacon was among those who protested this "making of Knots and Figures with divers Colored Earths . . . they be but toys, you may see as good sight many times in Tarts."

Although the knot garden now is rarely seen, except in historic gardens, why should it not today decorate a part of a vegetable garden or a brick patio, or form a bed in a lawn with a sundial or a birdbath? The knot garden is a good home for herb plants and is well suited to the small garden.

The first step in making a knot garden is to draw the design on paper. Make the design symmetric and the pattern either of interwoven (closed knot) or separate (open knot) shapes. Begin with rough sketches, then plot the garden out to scale, allowing for a foot or so of plant width for the lines (assuming you are going to use plants rather than sheep shanks). Then indicate on the design the colors, shades, and textures of plants and inert materials that you want for each part of the design. Finally, on the basis of your notes, hone in on specifically what plants to use.

Compact evergreen plants, at least for the lines, carry the design through the year. Unfortunately, there is not a wide selection of such plants hardy where I live. Four possibilities, given some shelter from the full brunt of winter cold, are Korean boxwood, germander, cowberry, and heather. Sage and lavender are other possibilities. They are semievergreen, but even when they are killed back during winter their presence still is evident by the glaucous green leaves frozen onto the stems. Farther south, English boxwood is a good choice. The scope of plants is widened if winter effect can be forgone: chives, basil ('Spicy Globe' is very compact and fine textured), even parsley or lettuce (use leaf lettuce, so you can harvest just the outer leaves, leaving plants — and design — intact).

Spaces enclosed by the lines could be filled with annual bedding plants such as petunias or marigolds, although I prefer more subdued effects created by shades of green and occasional, quiet flowers. (Bedding plants bring a knot garden up to Victorian times, when "bedding out" was the rage — a rage from which we have yet to recover.) Suggestions to fill these spaces include pachysandra, vinca, thyme, and viola, perhaps dotted with a few small, early season bulbs such as snowdrop or crocus.

A knot garden is not a low-maintenance garden, but, then again, a knot garden need not be large. Maintain the beauty of a knot garden by religiously keeping out weeds and maintaining crisp lines. And then, to quote Gervase Markham in *The English Husbandman* (1613), ". . . (oh happy gardener!) if you stand a little remote from the knot . . . you shall see it appear like a knot made of divers coloured ribans, most pleasing and most rare."

May 26

Foundation Planting — The very phrase "foundation planting" makes me cringe, conjuring up images of thin rows of evergreen meatballs backed up against houses.

There are some rationales for pressing trees and shrubs right up against a dwelling. A foundation planting visually softens the abrupt transition between the vertical wall of the house and the horizontal surface of the ground. Foundation plantings also are useful in guiding eyes and feet toward the front door of a house. The most obvious reason for a foundation planting, though, is to hide the foundation. But stone houses and many newer houses lack unsightly or visible foundations, yet still commonly are adorned with globs of green.

Spring is a time of temptation, with even grocery stores selling potted junipers and yews, the bread and butter of foundation plantings. A few years ago I succumbed to the offerings spread on the sidewalk in front of a discount store, and proceeded to buy, then plant, upright junipers around the front-door landing of my house. My head reminded me that preplanning, rather than impulse buying, is the only way to make an attractive planting, but my heart said, "Plant."

A foundation planting should strike a pleasing balance between harmony and accent. Harmony is achieved by repetition of one type of plant, or different types of plants sharing similarity in form, texture, or color. Accent is achieved by contrasts in form, texture, or color. A planting should not have too much harmony or accent, though, because excess of the former is boring and excess of the latter is unsettling.

When designing a foundation planting, think of the plants last. Visualize the planting first in terms of pleasing combinations of abstract forms, such as tall and low rectangles, circles, and squares. Then translate these abstract forms into plant forms — columnar, low spreading, round, and squarish. The next step, still keeping in mind that elusive balance of harmony and accent, is to decide what texture each of the shapes should be — small leaves or thin twigs make a plant fine textured, larger leaves and more robust branches make a plant increasingly coarse textured. Finally, the shapes need color, primarily shades of green, perhaps enlivened for a few fleeting weeks with splashes of other colors from flowers or fruits.

Once form, texture, and color have been decided, it is time to go out and find a plant that meets those requirements. A deciduous plant with a round shape and coarse texture might be a tree peony or one of the viburnums. An evergreen that is low and spreading, and fine textured, is creeping juniper. This also is the time to become enticed by details, such as the winged bark of burning bush euonymous, the red bark of redosier dogwood, or the spicy aroma of the clove currant. Of course, a plant must be suited to the exposure: junipers and spruces in full sun, rhododendrons and Oregon grape holly in part shade, and so on.

The corners of a house, where the contrast between wall and ground is most severe, generally warrant the tallest plants. Since the purpose of the planting is to smooth that transition, plant height needs to be less than eave height to carry the eye groundward in a smooth, flowing arc. The next tallest foundation plants generally are placed around, and draw attention to, the front entrance of a home.

There is no reason to shove all foundation plants right up against the house. A planting is easier to maintain and is more attractive if the plants are grouped into deep beds. Taller plants should be closest to the house (but not too close — a common mistake), and the taller the plants in the bed, the deeper the bed should be.

I expanded my juniper planting of past years with an adjacent bed of rhododendrons surrounding a cornelian cherry tree. The row of junipers and the bed of rhododendrons each are expansive enough to achieve harmony, yet the planting is lively because of contrasts between the fine, glaucous juniper leaves, the coarse, dark-green rhododendron leaves, and the strong upright accent of the single tree.

No law of garden design mandates that all the outside walls of a home require a foundation planting. But wherever trees and shrubs dress up a foundation, that planting should be exuberant, billowing out from the wall in waves, yet never engulfing windows and doors.

May 28

Caring for New Trees — Planting of trees that began in early April finally has drawn to a halt; the last of my new trees are in the ground. I planted carefully: I protected the roots from the sun as I dug each hole; I fanned out, then firmed the soil against the roots in each hole; I made sure that each tree was planted at the same depth as it stood in the nursery, indicated by the trace of the old soil line on its trunk; and I did *not* put fertilizer or manure in the planting hole (it would burn tender new roots).

I cannot just walk away now and forget about the trees. This first year is critical to their future well-being.

Water can be one of the most important factors determining whether growth is luxuriant or feeble. A good rule of (green) thumb is to apply the equivalent of one inch of rainfall once a week, unless, of course, it rains. This translates to two gallons of water per week for every square foot of spread of a tree's roots. I never just heave a bucketful of water around each tree all at once. Besides washing away the soil, and ruining its surface texture, most of the water would run across the soil surface out of reach of my trees' roots. Soils can absorb just so much water within a given time. Around each new plant, I build up a catch basin of soil to contain the water — from the sky or my watering can — until it is absorbed.

Luxuriant growth that results from following this prescription needs to be throttled toward fall, so trees can toughen up to face winter's cold. I turn down the throttle by gradually withholding water at the end of August.

Weeds growing too close to my young trees would rob water and nutrients. A tall, aggressive weed like pigweed can shade out a small, young tree. I maintain a weed-free area three feet across around every new tree. Even lawn grass is

out of place nuzzled up against the stem of a newly planted tree. Only as the tree ages do I permit grass or some other ground cover to grow right up to the tree trunk.

I could keep this area weed-free by hoeing, but I prefer to use a mulch of any organic material — usually straw or grass clippings — that I have on hand. Mulch has the added benefit of preventing the evaporation of water from the soil. Also, water percolates more quickly into soil covered by mulch than into bare soil, which has a tendency to form a surface crust. Mulch should not be piled right up against a plant's stem or the stem is liable to rot. Weeds like quackgrass and ground ivy always make repeated attempts to push into the mulched area, so I have to periodically pull out their underground runners and trailing stems.

Mechanical damage from any one of a number of garden tools is a third potential problem in the life of young trees, and even older trees for that matter. Thin bark of young trees can be injured by "weed whips." Bumping from the lawn mower is another common cause of trauma to young trees. (One otherwise dry book on plant pests calls this problem "lawn-mower blight.") The weed-free area around each tree helps avert mechanical damage. This buffer zone will ensure that all but the most negligent lawn mower or weed whipper keeps its distance.

My newly planted trees still look like sticks poked into the soil. But I am confident that if I water and keep weeds and lawn mowers at bay, each swelling bud on these sticks will push out two feet, or more, of new growth by season's end.

JUNE

Tell you what I like best —
'Long about knee deep in June,
'Bout the time strawberries melts
On the vine — some afternoon
Like to jes' git out and rest,
And not work at nothin' else.

James Whitcomb Riley, "Knee Deep in June"

THE FEVERISH PITCH of spring planting relaxes by June. Now that frost is reliably past, I can finally put away flower-pots, cloches, and pieces of cloth I had readied to protect transplants. Bare ground is psychologically unsettling to me, and not good for the soil, so I already have planted a transplant or a seed to cover almost every bit of dirt. Roots of transplants have begun to push out into the surrounding soil, so these plants require little further care from me.

Amid the flurry of planting, I did reserve some space for successive plantings of corn and beans for late summer harvest, and for seedlings of perennial and biennial flowers that I will plant out in late summer. June sowings of cucumber and summer squash will begin bearing just as earlier plant-ings inevitably succumb to bacterial wilt and vine borers, respectively.

There is a lull in the garden. Although flower, vegetable,

and fruit plants are beginning to grow strongly, my senses still easily take in the bounty they yield, and hunger for more. This strong growth is building like a wave, soon to sweep over the garden and transform it into a cornucopia overflowing with colors, smells, and flavors.

June 5

Strawberries — I just picked the first ruby jewel of a strawberry from the garden, and in a week I should have enough for a meal a day. That first berry of the season is never the best because I yield to temptation and pick it slightly under-ripe. But once strawberries start ripening faster than I can eat them, all are delectable. Even a small backyard patch of strawberries yields a respectable amount of fruit, about a quart for every square foot.

The garden strawberry is of relatively recent origin. Up to two centuries ago, the strawberry was a delicacy harvested almost exclusively from the wild. Here in eastern North America, the small, aromatic fruits of the Virginia strawberry (*Fragaria virginiana*) were plucked from among the grasses of

open meadows. On the other side of our continent, the large fruited, mild-flavored Chilean strawberry (*F. chiloensis*) blankets sand dunes and coastal mountains from Alaska down to Patagonia. Throughout the Northern Hemisphere grows yet another wild strawberry, the wood strawberry (*F. vesca*), with small, yet tasty, fruits. And finally, from northern Europe comes one of the most flavorful strawberry species: the musk strawberry (*F. moschata*), with soft, pale-pink fruits, utterly delicious with hints of pineapple and raspberry flavors.

I still grow white alpine and musk strawberries, but as delicacies. Fruits of the former species are too small, and fruits of the latter species are too few, to fill the larder. The common garden strawberry is what gives me sheer bulk of berries — and good flavor.

But what is the common garden strawberry? This strawberry has the botanical name *F.* × *ananassa*, which signifies that it is an artificial hybrid. It first appeared by accident in a European garden in the eighteenth century. One parent was the Virginia strawberry, which had been transplanted into a few European gardens in the early seventeenth century. The other parent was the Chilean strawberry, five plants of which were carefully nursed in the early eighteenth century on a long boat voyage from Concepción, Chile, to France by a French army captain, Amedée François Frezier. These two strawberry species, one from either side of the North American continent, happened to meet in a garden near Brest, France, where they naturally hybridized. The merits of the offspring were quickly realized, and by the early nineteenth century, breeders were deliberately hybridizing the two species.

Encroachments of civilization have not yet taken their toll on wild strawberries. As I walk along the abandoned railroad bed behind my property, the edges of woods, and rarely mown fields, I find some small, albeit luscious, wild strawberries ripening now. *Uncultivated* would perhaps be a better term than *wild*, for among wildings are pure native species, hybrids of the natives with cultivated forms, and escapees of the cultivated forms.

Although these wild plants take care of themselves, strawberries respond to coddling. My cultivated plants are in fertile soil and in full sun. Once a bed is established, each spring I remove old plants and thin out young ones to eight inches apart. The reward for my efforts? My cultivated berries are four times larger and much sweeter than those wild berries.

Some experts contend that the name *strawberry* is derived from the plant's habit of strewing itself all over the place; others claim the traditional mulch — straw — is the source of the name. At any rate, mulching is an especially good practice for strawberries. Mulch keeps the shallow roots cool and supplied with water, quells weeds, and provides a soft, clean cushion for the ripening gems.

June 7

Columbines — My columbine flowers, now in bloom, seem destined for flight. They hover above the plants' leaves, tethered to the ground by slender stalks. Even the form of the blossoms — petals flaring forward, then tapering to the rear in long-pointed spurs — resembles shooting stars or fireworks. Perhaps it was this volant quality that induced women of colonial America two centuries ago to dangle the freshly picked flowers, attached to thin hoops of gold, from their ears as earrings.

Our native Canadian columbine (*Aquilegia canadensis*) is among the daintiest of columbines. Its flowers, small and bright with yellow petals shading to orange at the spurs, would make delightful earrings. I have admired this flower for years, yet I have never gotten around to planting it, perhaps because it blossoms so profusely in the woods behind my property. Yet another columbine with dainty flowers, but one that I have never seen, is the Alpine columbine (*A. alpina*). This species usually has blue flowers, although sometimes they are so pale as to be almost white.

Gardeners inclined to tawdriness might choose to grow a hybrid variety like 'McKana's Giants', for enormous flowers, or 'Nora Barlow', for double flowers. I grow 'McKana's Giants', mostly, I like to believe, because these are the columbines most commonly offered for sale as seeds or plants.

But I draw the tawdriness line right there. The double flowers of 'Nora Barlow' would be just too much, and they would obscure the quintessential shape I associate with columbine flowers. Similarly, I do not care for columbines with small spurs (the Granny's Bonnet, *A. vulgaris*) or no spurs (the fan columbine, *A. flabellata*).

If spurs characterize a columbine flower, then the Rocky Mountain columbine (*A. caerulea*) and *A. longissima* (sorry, no common name) are the most columbine-ic. Spurs of *A. longissima* trail backward four to six inches. Flowers of *A. longissima* are pale yellow, while those of the Rocky Mountain columbine usually are blue and white.

I could go on, for there are about sixty-five species of columbines. Because all these species interbreed promiscuously, there are many hybrid forms — some natural hybrids and others the result of intentional breeding. With the exception of the somewhat stocky fan columbine, all columbines have light, airy foliage. Each leaf is composed of three fanlike leaflets that resemble those of the maidenhair fern.

The soft mounds of columbine foliage not only enhance the grace and airiness of the flowers hovering overhead, but are attractive in the garden in their own right. My columbines are grouped under a dwarf cherry tree, with other flowers, where the columbine leaves soon are obscured among other vegetation as summer progresses. But then, about mid-autumn, when subfreezing weather has killed most other herbaceous plants down to the ground, there stand columbine leaves, still soft and airy, perhaps a little bluish from the cold, but welcome all the same.

Columbines are easy to grow. They are not choosy as to soil and thrive in full sun or partial shade. Although classified as perennials, they often die out after a few years, but new plants are easily propagated by division of old plants in late summer or by sowing seed. The seeds may need special treatment before they will germinate, for they lapse into dormancy with age. Dormancy can be broken by a cold treatment, which is a good idea unless you are sure the seed is fresh. To treat, sow the seed in a flat, water, then put the flat in a plastic bag in the refrigerator. Take the flat out of the refrigerator in a month or so, and the seeds then should germinate within a couple of weeks.

Do not be intimidated by the extra step needed in sowing columbine seeds. The numerous columbine seedlings now stealing into my vegetable garden, a few feet from the cherry tree, are testimony to the ease with which columbines grow from seeds, especially fresh seeds.

Since my original plants are hybrids, the seedlings they produce are not. After a few generations, seedlings of seedlings of hybrids should revert back to their wild parents, which is fine with me, especially if my hybrids have some Canadian columbine in their blood.

June 9

Yellow Flag — Gardeners with boggy soils must become disconcerted, constantly reading that such and such plants (which are *most* cultivated plants) need "well-drained soils." One plant that thrives in the boggiest ground — even in ten inches of water — is yellow flag (*Iris pseudocorus*).

Today I spotted some yellow flag blossoms. The yellow petals — flopping sideways against a background of straplike, vertical leaves — always catch my eye even from a distance. Unlike most garden irises, whose petals are iridescent with colors, the yellow of yellow flag is clear and rich, untainted by other tints. Petals of yellow flag also lack the frills and even the beards of common garden irises. And unlike bearded irises, whose leaves have a bluish cast, leaves of yellow flag are emerald green.

From my car window, I have admired clumps of yellow flag growing in what appear to be a wild, or at least semiwild, state. In fact, the plant is native to Europe, but was brought here and spread naturally. The plant reputedly seeds readily and becomes weedy, so anyone who plants yellow flag usually is admonished to remove seedpods from spent flowers. All the clumps I see are apparently untended, yet well behaved. (Who wants to wade into the muck to deadhead the plants, anyway?)

Various clones of yellow flag possess special qualities. My preference is for the pure, rich yellow of most wildings, but 'Bastardii' has creamy yellow flowers, 'Alba' has white flowers, and 'Sulphurea' has sulfur-yellow flowers. Leaves of 'Variegata' have pale-yellow stripes, although the stripes fade as the leaves mature. The only clone that might appeal to me more than the semiwild plants is 'Immaculata', whose flowers are so pure as even to lack the pencil-line throat markings.

With its reputation for becoming weedy, yellow flag seeds should germinate readily. Mine germinated after a cold treatment similar to that recommended for columbine seeds. Dividing clumps is an even easier method of propagation, and more rapidly makes blooming size plants. Divide a clump just after blossoming is finished, when the plants take a breather before growing new roots. To divide, first dig up a clump, then cut the leaves back to about six inches. Next cut the thick rhizomes (swollen roots) into short pieces, each with a fan of leaves and some fine roots attached. Now for the words "boggy gardeners" have been longing to hear: plant the pieces twelve to eighteen inches apart in *poorly* drained soil.

Most of my property consists of well-drained soil, but near the road I have a small stream flanked by boggy land — perfect for yellow flag. What about gardeners so unfortunate as to have only well-drained soils? Must such gardeners relegate themselves to growing marigolds, tomatoes, peaches, and roses? No. Yellow flag will grow in less than standing water if plants are watered occasionally and planted in humusy soil with a bit of shade. A more noble gesture would be to create a bog for yellow flag by excavating an eighteen-inch depth of soil, lining the hole with a sheet of plastic, then backfilling the soil. (If I was going to go expend all this effort, I also would include in my bog some other bog plants, such as arrowhead, cattail, sweet flag, and pickerel rush.)

When grown in the boggy soil it so enjoys, yellow flag

gives the best show of bloom in full sun. Now what about plants for boggy soils in the shade?

June 13

Gardener's Vocabulary — My sister telephoned today and soon our conversation turned to gardening. She had a question: "What do the instructions on the seed packet mean by 'thinning out'?" As one who has pointed an accusing finger at computer jockeys for assuming that everyone understands their terminology, I now realize that we gardeners are guilty of the same transgression. Just as bytes have nothing to do with eating in the world of computing, thinning out, as I explained to my sister, has nothing to do with losing weight in the world of gardening. I went on to give her a brief explanation of some basic gardening terms.

Thinning out is the removal of excess plants. When I sprinkle carrot seeds along a furrow in the garden, or press three cucumber seeds into the soil in one pot, I am taking out insurance. I really want only one carrot every inch and one cucumber plant in each pot — each plant needs a certain amount of space. Corn farmers traditionally planted four corn seeds wherever they wanted just one corn plant — one to just sit, one for the crow, one to rot, and one to grow.

Once my insurance policy has paid off and many more seedlings come up than should mature, I start thinning out, or removing superfluous plants. The skill in thinning out comes from, on the one hand, being sufficiently ruthless with excess plants, and, on the other hand, being sufficiently gentle to the plants that are to remain. Ideally, thinning out should be done late in the day and just before watering or rainfall, so that plants that remain have time to recover from root damage that might occur as their neighbors were wrenched from the soil.

Deadheading, not nearly as gruesome as it sounds, is merely the removal of spent flowers. As soon as flowers of annuals fade, the plants funnel their energy into making seeds rather than new flowers. I have no qualms about picking marigolds, zinnias, and asters for bouquets, because picking coaxes these plants to keep making new flowers rather than seeds. I shear back allysum and low-growing annuals when they begin to look shabby. Even perennials respond to dead-heading, although less so than annuals. Delphiniums are more likely to bloom again at the end of the season if their flowering spikes are cut away after the flowers fade. Other perennials, such as columbine, respond by extending their period of bloom.

When I read directions to plant cucumbers in *hills*, no excavation of the soil is implied — not even the smallest mound a fraction of an inch high! A hill in gardening terminology is a grouping of plants, a station, a cluster. Certain vegetables (cucumbers and squash are examples) are easier to manage in hills from which trailing vines can radiate. I have never read the origin of this particular use of the word, but a friend recently told me that it was named after a Mr. Hill who first planted in these groupings. (I don't believe it.)

A *stand* is a group of plants in an area, which might be a row or a hill. If all my seeds sprouted, and the seedlings look sturdy, I brag about my good stand. Poor soil, poor weather, or poor seeds results in poor stands.

At this time of year, most plants have been removed from their *flats* and planted in the garden. A flat is a shallow box, with holes for drainage, in which seedlings are started before they are planted outdoors. *Flat* seems like a reasonable term, since a flat is flatter than it is tall. The traditional flat is made of wood, about twelve inches wide by eighteen inches long by two or three inches high. Nowadays, flats usually are plastic and are divided into cells to house individual plants.

Pinching is a term that means what it says, almost. The dictionary says that to pinch is "to squeeze between the finger and thumb." The objective in horticultural pinching is to remove the tips of plant shoots, so *nipping* might be a more accurate term. Fingernails come in handy here. The uppermost buds on plants are most dominant, and they suppress growth of lower buds. When the tips of shoots are pinched off, lower buds on a stem are released from inhibition and push forth into shoots. Pinching is a way to make plants bushy. On the other hand, pinching off side buds, and leaving only the top bud, directs a plant's energy into the main stem — this is the route to mammoth tomatoes and dinnerplate dahlias.

Seedlings raised in flats in sunny windows and greenhouses are too coddled to face the real world outside all of a sudden; they must be *hardened off*. In a literal sense, the soft succulent plant tissues are toughened, accomplished by gradually exposing the seedlings to sun, wind, cool temperatures, and even a *little* drying. After a week or two of treatment, the once-tender seedlings are tough enough for a permanent home out in the garden, exposed to the whims of nature.

Cultivate has more than one meaning in gardening. In a general sense it means to care for plants. A flower garden is a cultivated piece of ground. A wildflower meadow is not cultivated; it pretty much takes care of itself. However, a seed packet's instruction to "cultivate weekly" is directing me to get out there with a hoe or rototiller and rough up the top inch or so of soil. English gardening books commonly phrase this in a way that I like: they direct one to "stir the soil." Loosening the surface uproots small weeds before they gain a foothold in the garden and breaks any surface crust so rainfall penetrates easily.

To sum up: By now, seedlings in *flats* have been *hardened off* and planted in the garden, perhaps in *hills*. As delicate seedlings from seeds sown directly in the garden prove themselves sturdy, I *thin out* the *stand* to the correct spacing, as per directions on seed packets. I am ready to *deadhead* flowers. Good times to cultivate are mornings and following rains. Such are the joys of a person called a *gardener*.

June 14

Planting by the Moon — For no apparent reason, seedlings sometimes take longer than usual to come up through the soil. Or one day's transplants get off to a rousing start right after planting, whereas another day's transplants sulk for a while before they grow. Fickle plants, or perhaps the problem is with the moon?

Some gardeners believe that the phases of the moon dictate the best times for gardening. No one has told me that my garden will be a flop if I ignore the moon, but paying attention to it as I go about my gardening activities will "take advantage of the impetus provided by nature" (as one moon gardener has stated). Old-time gardeners used to say, "Plant potatoes by the dark of the moon." Nowadays, instructions are more refined, taking into consideration the sign of the zodiac along with phase of the moon. Planting is not the only activity covered; there are ideal days for fertilizing (with different days for organic or synthetic fertilizers), for mowing the lawn (depending on whether I want to hasten or retard growth), for harvesting, and even for making pickles. One year, to get the most beauty from my flowers, I was supposed to set transplants out on June 6.

Detailed instructions can be simplified for those who merely want to dabble in moon gardening. The period from two days before to seven days after the new moon is the best time to sow seeds whose germination times are either very short (broccoli, for example) or very long (parsley, for example). In the month or so that the latter seeds require to germinate, they will start to grow just as the moon has gone full cycle and is ready to enhance growth. Between the time of the full moon and seven days thereafter is the time to trans-plant seedlings and sow seeds such as peppers and eggplants that require a long (but not *very* long) time to germinate.

The basis for these instructions allegedly resides in influ-ences of the moon's gravity, light, and magnetism. Lunar gravity, for example, is said to promote leaf growth and inhibit root growth. Hence seedlings should establish well if trans-planted during the third quarter, when decreasing moonlight and tidal pull slow leaf growth and stimulate root growth.

Is there any scientific basis for reckoning with moon phases when gardening? No and yes. The theory has some fundamental weak points. For instance, ocean tides occur be-cause gravitational attraction is a function of distance, result-ing in a differential pull of lunar (and solar) gravity between the side of the earth closest to, and the side farthest from, the moon. But the two sides of a seed are only a fraction of an inch different in distance from the moon, so tidal effects in seeds are negligible.

On the other hand, there is no question that the moon has an effect on such phenomena as barometric pressure, tem-perature, and cosmic radiation flux. And carefully controlled experiments have detected periodicities in plants — water uptake by seeds, shoot growth, nutrient uptake, and respira-tion — coincidental with the lunar day of 24.8 hours and the synodic month of 29.5 days.

The periodicity of these responses is rarely in simple harmony with only lunar cycles. There seem to be other cosmic influences at work. The zodiac, perhaps? Scientists concede that influences from the heavens affect plant growth, and these "pervasive geophysical factors" (to quote from one scientific journal) probably are mediated via radiation to the earth and/or water in the plant or the environment.

I perceive a large gulf between an experiment showing water uptake by beans varying over the course of a month and instructions that tell me that the best day to sow bean seeds is on May 17. The whole area of moon gardening seems worthy of further investigation, and perhaps backyard experimentation. It's a good thing our planet has but one moon.

June 16

Potentilla — From now until fall, the cheery flowers of potentilla (*Potentilla fruticosa*) will brighten the border of my terrace. As the five buttercup-yellow petals of each flower open wide, they seem to smile back at the sun. The quantity of bloom will taper off after this month, but even a few of these two-inch blooms, set above the dainty foliage, are enough to liven each of the foot-high plants.

Potentilla is an ideal plant for my terrace border. Most of the plants are unshaded, where they happily bask in summer sun, even though the sun's heat is intensified as it beats down on adjacent terrace bricks. Come winter, the plants are undaunted by icy cold. And the cold hand of winter reaches especially deep beneath my bushes, because the planted border is raised above ground level. Because the border is raised, this soil also tends to get dry in summer. Did I say soil? Actually, I filled the bed with whatever I could find in the way of sand, soil, and organic materials. But no matter, potentilla tolerates soils that are acid or alkaline, and wet or dry.

The plant is at its best now; in winter the row of potentillas looks like a roll of tumbleweed bordering the terrace. But the tangle of brown stems is somewhat attractive poking up through and catching snow, definitely preferable to bare soil. The bushes are scraggly (potentilla has been described as a "shrubby shrub"), but, because of their small size and tight growth habit, never overly so. With age, plants do get ragged enough to require some pruning. Pruning low every few years removes old wood and stimulates tidy, new growth originating near the ground.

I took some liberty in assigning the species name *fruticosa* to my plants, because most cultivated potentillas are hybrids that can include other species. Among the many hybrid potentillas exist plants with flowers ranging from white

('Abbotswood'), to pale yellow ('Moonlight' and 'Primrose Beauty'), to pure yellow ('Goldfinger'), yellow-red ('Tangerine'), and vermilion ('Red Ace').

Aside from these cultivated potentillas, there also are numerous wild and weedy potentillas. These wild plants are the source of the common and scientific name *potentilla*. *Potens* is Latin for potent, which refers to medicinal uses of this plant. In old herbals, potentilla was recommended as an astringent and to bring down fevers. *P. reptans* was used as a sedative for hysteria and epilepsy, and as a gargle for sore throats or swollen tonsils. Tormentil (*P. tormentilla*) infused into hot teas or enemas was used for epilepsy.

Potentilla was a favorite herb of witches and sorcerers, perhaps because of its pentagram, or hand-shaped leaves. (Another common name for potentilla is cinquefoil, meaning five-leafed.) It is odd that potentilla should have such sinister associations, especially since the seventeenth-century herbalist Culpeper wrote that potentilla is ruled by the planet Jupiter, and therefore considered soothing, cheering, benevolent, and otherwise jovial. Jupiter aside, Culpeper's observations tally with my perception of the plants along my terrace.

June 22

Edible Landscaping — Edible landscaping is in vogue, and for good reason. Too many plants have been pigeonholed as being either ornamental or edible. But why shouldn't I plant a row of celery right against my terrace, in front of the rosebush? And thyme need not be confined to an herb garden. How about red cabbage planted among marigolds in the flower garden? After all, cabbage's cousin, flowering kale, has long been planted as an ornamental rather than as a vegetable, although its flowers are, in fact, curly leaves in shades of pinks and bluish greens. A few hundred years ago, when tomatoes were thought to be poisonous, they were planted in European and American gardens solely as ornamentals. And visitors to old estates stroll through arbors overgrown with the bower actinidia, unaware of the delectable kiwilike fruits hidden behind the leaves.

A whole slew of plants is waiting to be taken out of the vegetable garden, where they can be enjoyed for their beauty. And similarly, many ornamentals await the opportunity to be appreciated for their gustatory qualities. Let's take a walk around the garden and see what plants have escaped their traditional roles. We'll begin at ground level and work our way upward.

In full sun, two nice choices for plants to blanket the ground are chamomile and thyme. Dainty white, daisylike blossoms cover chamomile plants throughout the summer. Chamomile is one of the easiest plants to grow: the seeds germinate almost as soon as they hit the ground, and the seedlings grow quickly and are almost immune to disease. The plant spreads by runners and by self-sown seeds, so needs to be planted where its exuberance is appreciated rather than scorned. Thyme is more sedate, easily kept in tow with occasional shearing. There are many varieties from which to choose, from those that creep a mere half-inch above the ground to those that rise to a half-foot. Both chamomile and thyme emit delicious aromas when brushed against so are ideal for planting along walkways. Or even right in walkways, because "chamomile, the more it is trodden on, the faster it grows" (William Shakespeare, *Henry IV*).

A ground cover for partial shade is the lingonberry, a relative of our native cranberry. The dwarf form has tiny, hollylike leaves that creep along the ground. Red "cranberries" appear at summer's end. Like cranberry, lingonberry needs a moist, acid soil, with plenty of organic matter. My plants are very slow growing, in good years growing only an inch.

I like to combine colorful vegetables with flowers. In many cases, it is the fruits (botanically speaking) that are ornamental: picture a pepper plant covered with bright yellow or red fruits, or an eggplant plant covered with purple or white fruits. (Yes, there are white eggplants — how do you think it got its name?) 'Ruby' Swiss chard has bright-red leaf stalks, making it a nice companion interplanted with marigolds or planted in front of my dark-green yew hedge. Rather than color, a vegetable plant might bring order or harmony to the flower bed. The neat row of celery plants along my terrace adds order to that bed of roses and thyme. I also once had a backdrop of asparagus to a flower bed; the asparagus provided a neutral, fine-textured foil for the flowers.

No garden is complete with only annual plants; woody shrubs anchor the design of a garden and carry its beauty through the winter. My blueberry bushes are as pretty — year-round — as any bona fide ornamentals I have planted. Blueberry starts the season with flowers like those of lily of the valley, ends the season with leaves almost as fiery red as burning bush euonymous, and even goes through winter with red stems that almost rival those of red twig dogwood. Other ornamental shrubs producing edible fruits include elderberry, highbush cranberry, beach plum, and nannyberry viburnum. Another of my favorites is Nanking bush cherry, which is festooned with pinkish white flowers in very early spring, then small scarlet cherries in summer.

Walking around to the front yard, where shade would hinder growth of most flowers and vegetables, we come to three fruit trees that have merit for their beauty: the pawpaw, whose large green leaves and bananalike fruits are reminiscent of the tropics; the juneberry, a small woodland tree whose blueberrylike fruits follow its cloud of white blossoms in spring; and the cornelian cherry, a relative of flowering dogwood, with pale-yellow blossoms in very early spring, followed by beautiful and edible scarlet-red "cherries" in summer. An added plus is that these three trees require little care from me, surely not the rigorous spraying and pruning my apples and peaches demand.

Finally, we look around for some ornamental-edible vines. The grape, clambering up, then over, the arbor on the terrace, comes into view. Sunlight making its way between the leaves casts a dappled shade onto the terrace, and this same light filtering through the leaves gives those leaves a pleasing glow. Other vines include the previously mentioned bower actinidia, and the akebia vine, which produces somewhat odd, perhaps ornamental, fruits that burst open at maturity to reveal a jellylike interior embedded with seeds. Edible, but ominous.

One caution with edible landscaping: Pesticides used for ornamental plants are not necessarily suitable (or even legal) to use on edibles. Systemic pesticides especially should not be used on edibles, for these pesticides are taken into and translocated throughout the plants. I am very careful about using pesticides in a mixed planting of ornamentals and edibles: forgo spraying your rose if you grow cabbages at its feet.

June 25

Edible Flowers — Am I carrying edible landscaping too far? First I moved pepper plants out of the vegetable garden and into the flower garden. Then I replaced the traditional privet with a hedge of espalier-trained apple trees. And now — well, I am eating flowers, flowers whose traditional place has always been in the flower garden.

Obviously, not all flowers are edible; some are not palatable, and others are poisonous. The latter includes such familiar garden denizens as delphinium, monkshood, lily of the valley, *and others*. Never eat a flower unless you know it is edible. Or any flower suspected or known to have been sprayed with a pesticide.

Beyond this caution there are many other flowers that are tasty and wholesome. And they can be consumed in various ways. As beverages, for instance. This morning I drank a cup of chamomile tea. Dandelion and elderberry flowers are used to flavor wines, and hop flowers add richness to beers and ales. A handful of clove pink flowers, a type of carnation (*Dianthus caryophyllus*) with a spicy fragrance, livens a white wine (strain the wine before you drink it, though).

Many flowers — whole flowers, petals, or unopened buds

— are used in condiments to whet the appetite, or as sweets to end a meal. I came across a recipe in *The Flower Cookbook* (1973), by Adrienne Crowhurst, for pickling unopened dandelion flower buds. (Use one quart of buds to one cup of white vinegar, a quarter-cup of brown sugar, one cup of water, one teaspoon of salt, two tablespoons of dill seed, one crushed clove of garlic, and a pinch of cloves. Cover the buds with water and boil for five minutes. Boil the other ingredients for ten minutes, then pour them over the buds. Seal in jars and store one month before using.) The stamens within the flowers of the saffron crocus (*Crocus sativus*) yield the well-known and expensive spice of that name. Vinegar can be flavored with elderberry flowers by covering the blossoms with plain vinegar, letting the mixture steep for a week, and then straining out the flowers.

Lavender flowers lend a nice flavor to apple jelly if added when the apples are boiling. Once again, strain out the flowers before packing the jelly into jars. Make a rose petal flavored jelly by boiling together a couple of quarts of rose petals to every quart of water and sugar each, with a dash of lemon added.

Flower petals, especially those of rose or violet, can be candied by boiling them briefly in a sugar syrup, then used to garnish cakes or as after-dinner sweets. Or dip the petals in beaten egg white, then sugar, and let them dry on wax paper. Candied mint flowers make a genuine after-dinner mint.

Okay, you may be snickering by now and saying to yourself that almost any nonpoisonous flower can be made palatable by doctoring it up with alcohol, vinegar, or sugar. Well, some flowers are good raw, or cooked into main-course dishes. I often pluck daylily or violet flowers from my garden to pop right into my mouth. Admittedly, they're no match for a fresh-picked tomato, but they're good nonetheless. Incidentally, daylily flowers can be eaten before they open, when fully open, or after the petals have wilted. Nasturtium also tastes good raw. A few such flowers add a peppery taste to a sandwich.

Traditional flowers for cooking into omelettes are squash, marigold, or calendula blossoms. I wonder if the fact that all are shades of yellow have anything to do with this use? Squash flowers even taste sort of like eggs. Making soup? Blend in some dandelion or daylily flowers. Blooms of elderberry, lilac, daylily, or squash can be fried in a batter of eggs, milk, butter, and flour. Even sunflower buds reputedly can be boiled and eaten like globe artichokes, although I could not sacrifice such a dramatic flower for just one meal.

Edible flowers can be used to decorate a food just as flowers are used to decorate the garden. A nasturtium flower floating in a bowl of soup not only adds pungency but makes a picture. A few violet or rose petals similarly ornament and flavor a salad.

Eating flowers is not so odd. After all, no one thinks it particularly strange to eat broccoli, cauliflower, or artichoke flowers.

June 29

Weekly Tasks — By the end of June, the garden pretty much takes care of itself. Frost is past, transplants are established, and seeds are sown. A periodic oiling of the garden machinery is in order to keep things chugging along. I set aside one day a week for attending to those repetitive gardening tasks necessary for the remainder of the season. By assigning them to a specific day, I am less apt to forget them. What can be done in and around the garden on a strict once-a-week schedule?

Plants in pots are growing luxuriantly this time of year, so need weekly fertilization. I meticulously follow directions on the label for the type of fertilizer I am using. More fertilizer than is recommended does not make plants grow better, and too much fertilizer can burn a plant. Also, I must not forget about watering potted plants — probably more than once a week.

I make it a point to take a weekly stroll around the yard to deadhead spent flowers. In my weekly round, I also pinch off runners from strawberry plants, only allowing a daughter plant to set root where there is a vacant spot in the strawberry bed. I also religiously attend to any trees or shrubs I planted this spring or last fall, giving them a weekly pablum of water with fertilizer dissolved in it.

One of my least favorite tasks, unfortunately necessary, is spraying apple, peach, and plum trees. I will not continue this drudgery all summer, though. First, spraying must be discontinued a certain number of days before harvest (specified on the pesticide label). And second, I have some biological controls up my sleeve for use later in the season. For now, I have to spray to keep plum curculios off the fruits. But in a few weeks, as apple maggots, for example, are stretching their wings and looking around for juicy apples in which to lay eggs, I will hang sticky red spheres in the trees — ersatz apples — to dupe those insects.

I saved the most important weekly job for last. Weeding, of course. Whether weeding is done with a hoe or on all fours, or if weeds are smothered under mulch, diligently keeping weeds out of the garden now ensures an attractive and productive garden in the fall. And not allowing weeds to set seeds or establish perennial root systems in the garden abates next year's weed problems.

I spend a pleasant few minutes each week pulling the few small weeds that poke through mulch. Most of my garden is mulched with compost, but one section is in long, straight rows of bare earth. I cultivate this latter section with a "Lightning" scuffle, a hoe with a V-shaped head, sharpened front and back, that lies parallel to the ground as I hold the hoe's handle. I use it walking backward, moving my arms with the same smooth motion that it takes to sponge-mop the kitchen floor. The thin slice of cut earth flows over the blade, then drops back in place with each push and pull of the handle. Once again, just a few pleasant minutes at this activity each week leaves the soil surface loose and weed-free. The minutes are few and pleasant *only* if the job is done regularly, before weeds grow large.

> *Now 'tis spring, and weeds are shallow-rooted;*
> *Suffer them now and they'll o'ergrow the garden.*

> William Shakespeare, Henry IV

JULY

Then came hot July, boyling like to fire,
That all his garments he had cast away:
Upon a Lyon raging yet with ire
He boldly rode, and made him to obay;
Behind his back a sithe, and by his side
Under his belt he wore a sickle circling wide.

Edmund Spenser, The Faerie Queene

JULY IS THE MONTH I would choose in which to show off my garden. Annual flowers finally fill in the beds, and peas, lettuce, and other spring-sown, cool weather vegetables linger even as I sample the first tomato and cucumber of the season. The garden offers a succession of summer berries: strawberries yielded to red currants, which are followed by black currants, then gooseberries, blueberries, raspberries, and blackberries.

Weeding and watering continue, as does planting of perennial and biennial flowers, and vegetables for late harvest. But timing is not critical, as it was in spring, and these are pleasant activities if they are not ignored for too long. The same is true for keeping strawberry runners in check. Left alone, the strawberry bed becomes a tangled, wiry mass by summer's end. But the runners are easily pinched off with my thumbnail when they are young.

July reaches out to touch both the beginning and the end of the gardening season. Early in the month, the garden and I retain the exuberance of spring; leaves are still lush and fresh. Yet before the end of the month, I am pulling out pea vines, digging spent foxgloves, and ridding the garden of other plants whose glory is past, all the while making plans for autumn.

July 10

Blueberries — Only eighty years ago, blueberries were a rare item on grocery shelves, and you could not even have bought a blueberry bush to plant in your yard. Most blueberries were picked from wild bushes. Only at the beginning of this century did Dr. Frank Coville, a scientist from the U.S. Department of Agriculture, begin selecting and hybridizing superior high-bush blueberries (*Vaccinium corymbosum*) from wild stands, and studying how they could be grown under cultivated conditions.

Wild blueberries still grow in abundance in the mountains behind my property, and grocery store shelves now are well stocked with the fruit. But neither source of blueberries can match the plump, juicy, flavorful berries I pick from cultivated bushes in my backyard. The berries in the mountains usually are small, and the birds take many before they are ripe. Commercial growers harvest blueberries as soon as they turn blue, but it takes another few days for the best flavor to develop. I harvest my blueberries by tickling them when they turn blue; only those that are dead-ripe drop off into my hand.

Highbush blueberries have much to commend them as a backyard fruit. Insects and diseases are rarely a problem. Pruning consists simply of shortening lanky branches and removing branches that droop, crowd the center of the bush, or have grown too old. No pruning at all is needed until the bushes are five years old. Blueberry bushes are tidy, without thorns, and there is no need to crawl around on all fours to harvest the fruits. What's more, a bush begins bearing in its second or third season and continues to do so for decades.

Blueberries are finicky about their soil, and attention to the soil before planting can spell the difference between a productive and a sickly plant. (My graduate research focused on blueberries' soil needs, so I would be embarrassed if my backyard plants sickened because of improper soil conditions.)

Blueberries' first requirement is for a very acidic soil, with a pH between 4 and 5. (Acidity is expressed on the pH scale, which goes from most acidic at pH 1, to least acidic at pH 14.) Soil pH can be determined with a soil test or by noting what other plants are thriving at the proposed planting site. Acidify soils that are too alkaline with sulfur or aluminum sulfate. Thriving red maples, sweet ferns, white cedars, mountain laurels, rhododendrons, or azaleas indicate soil already suitable for blueberries.

Blueberries also demand a soil that holds moisture yet is well drained. I selected a well-drained spot for my plants, then mixed a bucketful of peat moss with the soil in the planting hole. I also religiously watered my plants their first season.

Blueberries also need a soil rich in organic matter. The bucketful of peat moss in the planting holes got each of my plants off to a good start, but I ensured that organic matter was continually being added to the soil by blanketing the ground around each plant with a layer of sawdust six inches deep. Each year I replenish the mulch as necessary, using sawdust, leaves, or straw, whatever is most available at the time. These organic mulches buffer soil acidity (which means that I no longer need to pay attention to it), conserve soil water, and keep the roots cool. After all, the roots of blueberries growing in the wild are naturally blanketed beneath leaves that fall from nearby trees.

Although fourteen highbush blueberry plants provide ample berries for eating and freezing from now through the end of August, I decided one year to plant some lowbush blueberries (*V. angustifolium*) as well. Lowbush blueberries grow only two feet high or less, so would make a nice ground cover for the beds on the east and south sides of my house. The plants' crimson foliage in autumn, and bare, red twigs in winter, also would visually complement the brick of the house. Lowbush blueberry fruits usually are powdery blue and are sweeter, but less aromatic, than those of the highbush blueberry. There is great variation from plant to plant. Although one of Dr. Coville's first selections was a lowbush blueberry, this species is still rarely grown in backyards, and even commercial plantations are of wild plants rather than selected varieties.

Soil requirements for the lowbush blueberry match those for the highbush blueberry, but the plants differ in growth habit. Lowbush blueberries spread by underground runners, which is just what I needed to fill solidly those two planting beds. The way to prune lowbush blueberries is to cut the plants completely to the ground every second or third year. Plants do not bear the season following pruning, so I prune alternate halves of my bed each year to ensure an annual supply of berries.

The only problem in growing blueberries, high or low, comes at harvest time. In my experience, birds are more fond of blueberries than any other cultivated fruit (except perhaps juneberries, which look just like blueberries). I have outwitted these feathery berry lovers with a temporary walk-in cage I set up around the highbush planting each July. I push metal poles into the ground around the periphery and up the center of the planting, wire crosspieces between the poles around the periphery, cover the tops of the center poles with jars, and then drape a large net over the whole thing.

Birds seem somewhat less fond of the lowbush blueberries (perhaps because of the plants' proximity to the house), so, thus far at least, I have been willing to share these fruits and leave the plants unnetted.

July 11

Lawns — Lawn lovers, prepare for battle! By July, your defenses surely have been dulled by the weekly mowing ritual.

Ecologically, the ideal lawn is not much better than an asphalt parking lot. A study in 1977 estimated that 200 million gallons of gasoline were used each year to power lawn-mowing equipment. Three million tons of fertilizer, whose manufacture also is based on petrochemicals, are used each year to keep grass green. Much of this fertilizer is carried away by rain as a nutrient-rich solution that eventually trickles into lakes and streams, causing them to become choked by excessive weed growth. Too often, lawns are drenched with insecticides to kill such insect pests as chinch bugs and grubs; with fungicides to knock out leaf spots, brownpatch, and snow mold; and with herbicides to stop crabgrass and dandelions. In fact, more pesticide per acre is added to lawns than to any other land.

And what about noise? I still remember the musical clickety click sound of the push mower on weekend mornings when I was a child. Now the angry roar of gasoline-powered mowers and the high-pitched whine of power trimmers fill the air.

The lawn of today is a relatively recent phenomenon. Prior to the middle of the last century, the lawn was not the close-cropped, homogeneous expanse that it is today. Rather, the lawn of yore consisted of wild grasses and wildflowers, maintained with the swing of a scythe four or five times a year, or with grazing sheep.

Once the lawn mower was invented, you no longer needed to own a flock of sheep or have hired gardeners to maintain a greensward. A recent survey by the Lawn Institute shows that there are over fifty million households with lawns in America, and, taken together, these lawns encompass over six million acres — an area ten times the size of Rhode Island! To keep this acreage green, weed-free, and no more than a couple of inches tall cost us over $4 billion per year, with another $2 billion or so for professional lawn-care services.

Having gotten that off my chest, I can admit to loving the fresh scent and the neat appearance of a freshly mown lawn. And what a nice surface a lawn is for children to tumble on. Lawn Institute research found that people feel "green is clean": a beer can is less likely to be tossed onto a lawn than onto an unkempt field. The quintessential use of a large expanse of flat lawn is, in my opinion, that social institution familiar to many towns of the Northeast, the town common. Here the lawn is at its best, providing a place at which to eat, read, meet friends, and stroll.

How can the good be balanced with the bad when it comes to lawns?

First, treat a lawn correctly. Grow a grass adapted to your site's soil and light conditions. Mow regularly to a height of about two inches (high mowing inhibits crabgrass). Unless the clippings are longer than an inch, leave them where the mower blows them. Less fertilizer is needed if the clippings are not harvested. Do not apply chemicals routinely. And, if you must water, water deeply and infrequently.

Second, consider alternatives to a lawn. A ground cover such as euonymous (*E. fortuneii*) or sedum grows well in the sun; for the shade, try English ivy, creeping myrtle, or pachysandra. The bed around my house in which I planted lowbush blueberries was once a grassy bank, difficult to mow and less attractive than the present blueberries.

Third, change your ideal for a perfect lawn. Let some

clover and ground ivy mingle with your grass. A perfect lawn can be boring. My lawn has received compliments (in wet seasons), yet the only care I give it is correct mowing.

And fourth, convert a part of the lawn into a meadow. A meadow consists of grasses with a healthy dose of annual and perennial flowers. The grasses for a meadow are bunch grasses (such as sheep fescue or chewings fescue), which stabilize the soil but do not spread, as do lawn grasses. Annual flowers such as plains coreopsis, cornflower, icelandic poppy, and corn poppy splash color in the meadow their first season, then resow themselves for subsequent years' blooms. Biennial and perennial flowers — yarrow, chicory, perennial gaillardia, purple coneflower, butterfly weed, evening primrose, and even such commonplace beauties as Queen Anne's lace and goldenrod — remain year after year. The meadow need not be large, for even a backyard can be brightened by a small patchwork of wildflowers. The only care demanded by a meadow is once-a-year mowing (with a hand scythe — a mower would get bogged down) and occasional weeding by hand.

Planting a wildflower meadow is not like planting a vegetable or flower garden. You cannot just till up an area, sow seeds, then keep weeds down between the plants with a hoe or rototiller. A wildflower meadow is . . . well, somewhat wild, and there are no neat rows of plants flanked by tillable soil.

Nonetheless, weeds, especially aggressive grasses, must be kept in tow from the very start. All vegetation could be initially wiped out with a chemical herbicide, but I prefer to till the soil, then smother weeds through the summer with a cover crop such as buckwheat, a rapidly growing plant with broad leaves. Because buckwheat matures in a couple of months, it should be resown a couple of times during the summer to keep the ground covered the whole season. Each time, mow the old plants down, then scratch the soil surface just enough to sow buckwheat seeds again.

A wildflower meadow is the obvious choice for large fields. On a backyard scale, use a small meadow as a transition between, for instance, mowed lawn and tall trees, a stream, or a property line. And if your meadow has any size to it, occasional swaths cut through it beckon a stroll.

I am fortunate to have a meadow adjacent to my property. Like many pieces of reasonably fertile, well-drained land in the Northeast, this field became a meadow not because it was deliberately planted as such, but because annual mowing prevented the encroachment of forest. My neighbor's field provides me with wildflowers and mulch. Right on my property, I am progessively replacing my wall-to-wall lawn with more bushes and fruit trees, and mounds of flowers that will spill over onto a remaining, intimate pocket handkerchief of a lawn.

July 18

Midsummer Sowings — Sometime this month I will retrieve my canning jars full of seed packets from the back of the refrigerator and sow another batch of seeds. Planting seeds in midsummer, the second-to-last sowing of the season, is relaxed compared with the feverishness of spring sowings.

The average date of the first autumn frost determines which vegetables to sow now. Frost usually hits my garden in early October, but whether it occurs on "the average date of the last killing frost" is a moot point. Plants must be wellnigh ready for picking by summer's end, because plant growth just lumbers along slowly with the cool temperatures and short days of late summer and early autumn. Almost any vegetable that matures in about sixty days can be sown now, including carrots, beets, heading lettuces, and any of the many types of Chinese cabbage. Peas, however, are one vegetable with which I have inconsistent success as a fall crop. Too often, they languish in midsummer's heat; then, when the weather turns cool, they grow too slowly or are killed by hard frost.

I also am sowing perennial and biennial flower seeds. Perennial seedlings will not bloom this season, but, sown now, will have a good start on next season. Biennials are plants that complete their life cycle, from seed to flowering (and seed again), in two seasons, growing leaves their first season, then flowering their second season. After blossoming, the dying plants are relegated to the compost heap. Caring for a plant that needs two seasons to flower and then is tossed out may seem more trouble than it's worth, and no garden center is going to sell a plant with such a habit. Yet biennials such as hollyhock, foxglove, and wallflower have an old-fashioned charm that warrants them a place in my garden. And the spaces left in midsummer by spent biennials can be filled with clumps of chrysanthemums.

I sow vegetable and flower seeds either in flats or in a small nursery bed. The advantage of flats is that the plants can be more carefully tended. I can watch each seedling, I can move the flat out of the wind, and I can water less or more according to the needs of each plant. But flats need constant attention. Even one sunny, windy day without water can leave plants desiccated beyond revival.

The main problem with midsummer sowings of flower and vegetable seeds in a nursery bed or out in the garden is dry soil. My technique for ensuring quick seed germination in midsummer is as follows: I open a furrow and sprinkle it with water, then sow seeds and cover them with soil. Next I firm the soil over the seeds with the back of a rake; this snugs the seeds against the wet soil and establishes capillary channels to bring water to the seeds. Then I sprinkle the row again with water. Finally, I lay a temporary covering over the row. This cover can be burlap, straw, or even wooden boards — anything that can be taken off as soon as the seedlings poke through the ground.

When I was of elementary school age, midsummer displays of school supplies and back-to-school clothes made me a little nervous that summer's end was not far off. Now, as a gardener, I get a similar twinge as I realize that summer will end, and I must plan now which perennial and biennial flowers to sow before winter closes the door on the season. As soon as the present sowing is complete, I will forget about autumn and enjoy summer.

July 19

Plant Pests — Two of my gardening friends — both fond of growing fruit plants — are at opposite ends of the spectrum when it comes to dealing with plant pests. The first friend keeps a keen eye on his own plants, so when he recently visited my garden, he quickly alerted me to a few apple leaves curling inward because of aphids, a gypsy moth sauntering down the trunk of a plum tree, and the frothy evidence of a spittle bug on a strawberry plant. To this friend, insect trespass is intolerable, and he diligently sprays his plants with the goal of making every leaf, stem, and fruit perfect.

My other friend takes a laissez-faire attitude toward plant pests. He gives his plants the minimum amount of care, perhaps a bucketful of water sloshed onto the soil, perhaps an occasional handful of fertilizer. Then again, this friend does not expect his plants to produce what most of us would consider an acceptable harvest.

Both friends' gardens have problems. The first friend's garden gets doused with too much pesticide. This is unhealthy for both him and the environment, and sets the stage for outbreaks of chemical-resistant pest species. In this garden, there is little opportunity for plants to mobilize their natural defenses against plant pests, or for "good bugs" to help out. On the other hand, in the second friend's garden, too many plants look sick. There, the edible harvest is low in quality and minimal or nonexistent in quantity.

I suggest steering a middle course in one's attitude toward pests. Sometimes pest problems disappear on their own. For example, eggplants are predictably riddled with flea beetle holes in my garden (and most other gardens in spring), but just as predictably, the problem abates as summer comes rolling in. Similarly, aphid populations often soar, then plummet equally fast.

At some point, of course, pest damage may become intolerable. Then something must be done. But even when caterpillars threaten to gobble up a whole plant, there may be alternatives to getting out the measuring spoons and mixing up a toxic spray. Many pests can be controlled by trapping (jar lids filled with beer trap slugs), by mechanical means (a toothpick poked into the soil next to the stem of each of my vegetable transplants thwarts cutworms), by genetics (butternut squashes are less susceptible to squash vine borers than are buttercup squashes), and by timing (I plant carrots in late spring so they emerge after carrot flies have laid their eggs).

When all else fails and sprays are needed, the ideal pesticide is one which can be directed only against the pest causing the problem. When cabbageworms start to eat more cabbage leaves than I deem healthy for the plants, I spray with *Bacillus thurengiensis*, a commercially available bacterial insecticide that is toxic to cabbageworms and nontoxic to just about everything else, including me. For aphids on my apple tree, I mix up some insecticidal soap in a hand sprayer. Insecticidal soap is toxic to many insects, good and bad, so I spot-spray only the few infested branch tips. Spraying always should be a last resort in order to give potential predators and parasites of the pest a chance to rally. Never discount the importance of "good bugs."

Also, there is no need to strive for 100 percent pest-free plants in a backyard garden. Just as it takes a lot more effort to go from a grade of B to an A than from a C to a B in school, it takes a lot more spraying to go from almost pest-free to the 100 percent pest-free demanded of commercial growers. Is it worth it? I try to tolerate a bit of pest damage on my plants. After all, plants themselves tolerate some pest damage without ill effect. Experiments show that when apple trees lose part of their leaves, those that remain compensate for the loss with increased efficiency.

Cultivating a healthy degree of tolerance for plant pests demands continual, close attention to the garden. This practice should be applied with no less diligence than fertilizer. As the saying goes: The best fertilizer is the gardener's shadow.

Portulaca — The genus *Portulaca* is a vegetable, a weed, and a flower in my garden. All flourish undaunted by heat or drought — a comforting thought as I drag the hose around to keep broccolis and zinnias alive.

Let's start with the flower, *P. grandiflora*, which goes by the common name portulaca or moss rose. In truth, the plant is neither a moss nor a rose. But the tufts of lance-shaped leaves do bear some resemblance to a large moss. And portuclaca's bright flowers — an inch across, with single or double rows of petals in colors from white to yellow to rose, scarlet, and deep red — are definitely roselike. The plant grows to a half-foot-wide mound, with stems that are just barely able to pull themselves up off the ground under the weight of their fleshy leaves.

Moss rose is native to the sunny, dry foothills that rise up along the western boundary of the pampas. As might be inferred from its native habitat, moss rose not only tolerates, but absolutely requires, full sun and well-drained soil. Such

requirements, and low stature, make the plant ideal for dry rock gardens.

Moss rose is easily grown from seed sown in situ, or started in flats for transplanting. I mix the extremely fine seed with dry sand before sowing to ensure uniform distribution.

Once blossoming begins, it continues nonstop until plants are cut down by frost. Moss rose is an annual, but sometimes it self-sows, in which case forms with double petals revert to volunteers with single rows of petals.

The vegetable and the weedy *Portulaca* can be dealt with together, for they are the same plant, *P. oleracea*. The succulent, reddish stems and succulent, spoon-shaped leaves hug the ground and creep outward in an ever-enlarging circle. The common name is purslane, although it has many aliases, including pussley, Indian cress, and the descriptive Malawi moniker, "the buttocks of the wife of a chief."

Tenacity to life and fecundity accord purslane weed status. Pull out a plant and toss it on the ground, and the plant stays turgid long enough to reroot. Chop the stems with a hoe, and each piece will take root. Even without roots, the inconspicuous flowers stay alive long enough to make and spread seeds.

What about purslane, the vegetable? Take a bite of this weed. The young stems and leaves are tender and juicy, with a slight, yet refreshing, tartness. Purslane, delicious raw or

cooked, is appreciated in many places around the world besides its native India.

There are cultivated varieties of purslane for planting in the vegetable garden. These varieties have yellowish leaves and a more upright growth habit than the wild forms. Wild or cultivated, the plants can be grown from seed or, of course, by rooting cuttings from established plants. As far as actually planting purslane in my garden, I must agree with Helen Morganthau Fox, who wrote, in *Gardening for Good Eating* (1943), that "it is a reckless gardener who would plant purslane." That does not mean that I do not grow purslane, though, for plenty appears wherever I am remiss with my weeding. I leave a few of these plants to grow in odd corners of the garden, where they do not cause trouble yet can be harvested periodically.

Any "reckless gardener" who opts to plant purslane must do so yearly. Like the moss rose, purslane is an annual plant. Once established in the spring, both purslane and moss rose need no further care.

July 24

Daisies — I plan to confirm this someday with a survey of children I know, but I would wager that if you gave a child a box of crayons and a piece of paper, and asked for a picture of a flower, you most likely would get a picture of a daisy. Daisies also hold attraction for poets. Chaucer wrote, ". . . of all the floures in the mede, Thanne love I most thise floures white and rede, Swiche as men callen dayses in our toune." Daisies are my favorite, too. For me, a daisy is the essence of flowerness.

What makes a flower a daisy? The child's daisy is a circle surrounded by straplike petals, their bases attached to the circle. To the botanist and gardener, the meaning of daisy is not so simple. The botanist explains that the daisy is a composite flower made up of many small, individual florets. Florets that make up the eye of the daisy have inconspicuous petals. Different types of florets — ray florets, each with one large, outward-pointing petal — skirt the daisy's eye. The petals that you actually see on a daisy flower are made up of the single large petal of the ray florets.

Taxonomically, all daisies are in the Compositae, or daisy, family. But the daisy family also includes a host of other plants not called daisies. For example, would you call lettuce or zinnia, which also are members of the daisy family, daisies? (The daisy family actually has two subdivisions, one of which is exemplified by the child's flower drawing, sunflowers, coneflowers, and other daisies with "eyes." For examples of the other subdivision, look closely at a dandelion or chicory flower; all their florets are ray florets, each with a single, large, straplike petal. There is no eye to these flowers.)

The original daisy, the one of poetry and literature, is the English daisy, *Bellis perennis*. These squat, cheerful flowers, with yellow discs surrounded by petals in shades from deep rose to white, originated in the grassy fields of England and now are widespread in America. Some cultivated forms have so many rows of petals that their yellow eyes are hidden. These plants self-sow readily to give seedlings that revert to the wild form with a single row of petals, in which case they sometimes are considered weeds as they invade lawns and gardens. I grew English daisies once, but they unfortuately never reappeared on their own.

Nowadays, gardeners use the appellation "daisy" for many different flowers representing various genera within the daisy family. *Chrysanthemum* is one such genus with many members called daisy: the oxeye daisy (*C. leucanthemum*), the Nippon daisy (*C. nipponicum*), the painted daisy (*C. coccineum*), the high, or giant, daisy (*C. uliginosum*), and the crown, or garland, daisy (*C. coronarium*).

Plants in the genera *Erigeron* and *Aster* also include some daisies. Those in the former genus sometimes are called fleabanes (they are supposed to drive away fleas), and those in the latter sometimes are called Michaelmas daisies. Fleabanes generally bloom in spring and early summer; asters bloom from late summer on into autumn. Two representatives of *Erigeron* — the orange-petaled orange daisy (*E. aurantiacus*) and the seaside, or double-orange, daisy (*E. glaucus*) — are good garden daisies.

The list goes on . . . the globe daisy (*Globularia trichosantha*), the Swan River daisy (*Brachycome iberidifolia*), and the blue daisy (*Agatheae coelestris*). Next spring I will paint a pastel landscape with a broad sweep of African daisies (*Arctotis grandis*), whose petals, white skyward over lavender undersides, surround steel-blue centers. In contrast, individual attention is demanded from each flower of the Transvaal daisies (*Gerbera jamesonii)* blossoming in shades of salmon, pink, and apricot in clay pots on my terrace.

A green thumb is not required to enjoy daisies. Most are hardy, free of pests, and able to tolerate poor, dry soils. Daisies are adaptable plants and bring a sunny face to the formal garden, the cottage garden, the meadow, or the abandoned lot. After all, the name daisy comes from reference to the sun — "day's eye."

July 25

Lilies — Another person might have been down on his haunches, chawing a piece of straw. But I stood flicking bulbils out of the leaf axils of my neighbor's lily one late June afternoon as he and I chatted. By conversation's end, my hand was filled with shiny, black, pea-size balls. I decided to plant them in my garden, and dropped them a couple of inches apart into a furrow at the end of a garden row. This was a few years ago, and the next season small rosettes of leaves sprouted from the ground. The season after that, elongating stems were capped by a flower or two. By the third season, a half-dozen mauve-tinged, white trumpets, each five inches long, nodded from the tops of the regal, six-foot stems, and this is how the plants look today.

Lilies have a reputation for being difficult to grow. This might be true of some lily species, but the basic requirements of most are easily met. The plants I have — probably *Lilium sargentiae*, as evidenced by the yellow throat, brown-red stamens, and wonderful fragrance of each flower — must be of the easy-to-grow group. I believe it almost could become a weed in my garden!

Of course, not all lilies grow six feet high and have white

flowers. The American Turk's Cap lily (*L. superbum*) grows from four to eight feet high, with orange-red flowers bobbing downward. The candlestick lily (*L. dauricum*) holds its cup-shaped flowers upward, atop three-foot stalks. The tiger lily (*L. tigrinum*) has maculate tepals (botanically, lily petals are not "petals," but "tepals") rolled backward at their ends. There are eighty species of lilies, including numerous hybrids, with a range of flower types and colors. Daylilies, incidentally, are a completely different genus, *Hemerocallis*.

Not all lilies make the bulbils — the small bulbs that form in leaf axils on the stems — that I used for propagation. Lilies also can be propagated by bulblets, bulb scales, or seeds. Bulblets are small bulbs that form along the stem below the ground. Bulb scales are fleshy scales, arranged like shingles

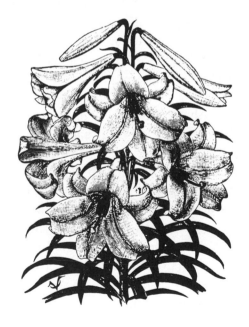

on a roof, which can be peeled off the large mother bulb of a plant. This is different from tulip and many other fall bulbs, which have concentric scales encircling the bulb. Lilies also differ from tulips in that the lily bulbs, scales, and bulblets die if they dry out. Thus they must be dug for replanting right after flowering ceases, when the plants take a brief rest, then replanted immediately.

Whereas all the plants grown from bulbils, bulblets, and bulb scales are genetically identical to each other and to the mother plant from which they came, seed-grown plants are at least a little different from each other. Sow seeds as soon as they are ripe. Depending on species, germination may take from a few weeks to more than a year. Patience is needed, because sometimes seed will germinate but not show any aboveground growth for a few weeks. Count on about four years to flowering.

Most lilies need proper soil conditions to thrive. This means a well-drained soil, although some lilies, such as meadow lily (*L. canadense*) and American Turk's Cap lily, will tolerate sodden soil. Lilies also like a soil rich in organic matter. Peat moss, well-rotted manure, or compost should be added to the planting hole. An organic mulch such as leaves or straw protects the underground bulbs from winter cold and summer heat.

Lilies flourish in either full sun or partial shade. The flowers last longer in partial shade, and the dimmer light also highlights the pale color of the flowers. An ideal lily site is shielded from wind so the plants do not need staking.

Tall stems look gawky floundering alone, so plant tall-growing lilies next to a fence, a wall, or a tall, dark-green shrub. Another good spot is among low shrubs, where the flowers rise just above the shrub's foliage. I eventually moved the plants from my garden to the base of a sixty-foot willow, where they enjoy partial shade and are aesthetically anchored to the massive willow's trunk.

July 27

Pure Blues — The flower garden needs some cooling colors to thwart, at least psychologically, summer's heat. The reds and yellows of spring and early summer were welcome after a winter of gray and brown, but it's time to calm things down.

Blue is cool, and the purer it is, the cooler it is. Not many flowers, though, have a color as pure a blue as that of the bluebird or the sky on a crisp, cloudless morning. Many bluish flowers, among them delphinium, cornflower, campanula, and veronica, come close, but the red lurking in these blues heats them up a bit.

The ultimate in pure blue flower color is found in the blue poppy (*Meconopsis betonicifolia*, also known as *M. baileyi*). I have this information on good authority, although I have never seen or grown the plant. It's not that I haven't tried to grow it! The seed is very slow to germinate, and once up, the plants require cool, moist summers and mild winters — not exactly what we have here in the Northeast. My two attempts at germinating the seeds failed, although on one of those occasions some weed (I think) germinated, then lan-

guished through the summer. I am trying again to grow this plant, for by every account the six-foot-high plants, capped with sky-blue, three-inch flowers, would be well worth the effort.

Some of the purest blues also are found on gentians, specifically *Gentiana angustifolia*, *G. verna*, *G. septemfida*, and *G. oregana*. Like blue poppies, gentians generally are a challenge to grow. Besides the extra-special soil conditions demanded by some species (some like alkaline soil, others like acidic soil), virtually all resent blistery summer heat and require a soil with perfect drainage. Seeds are small and slow to germinate, and seedlings do not bloom until their third year. But just imagine the feeling of accomplishment of flowering one of these after three years of nurturing.

So much for the difficult blues. One blue flower is not only fairly pure in color but also easy to grow. Morning glory, of course. Morning glory does come in colors other than blue, but the one to grow for blue is the appropriately named 'Heavenly Blue'. My best morning glory planting was near the east edge of a north-facing wall of my house. There the flowers unfurled as soon as the first rays of morning sun shot through the trees to warm the waiting buds. As the sun rose in the sky, the wall shielded the blooms enough to keep them lingering on into the day.

A bit of shade from midday sun is good, aesthetically, for any blue flower. Blue flowers, especially pure blue flowers, pale in bright sunlight, but radiate a cool glow in slight shade or morning and evening light.

No need to fill the whole flower garden with blue flowers. Bright reds and yellows still are needed to liven the scene. And I must reserve some room for the tawny red and yellow flowers of autumn, for these warm colors will be welcome when winter is just around the corner.

AUGUST

Fairest of months! ripe Summer's Queen
The hey-day of the year
With robes that gleam with sunny sheen,
Sweet August doth appear.

R. Crambe Miller

AUGUST IS FAT AND JUICY. Apple leaves show signs of age and scars from scab, and mildewed cucumber leaves are beginning to brown at their edges. But dry soil and signs of decline in the garden are offset by an abundance of plump fruits — tomatoes, cucumbers, peaches — almost bursting (sometimes actually bursting) out of their skins with juice. Summer flowers now spill out of their beds, prodded on by the hot sun. What the garden lacks in lushness it makes up for with juice and color.

Planning for the autumn garden now begins with greater resolve. As in spring, timing is important. I want my turnips to swell to size just as crisp weather arrives, not before. I want to move perennial and biennial flower seedlings to their permanent positions soon enough so that their roots take hold before the soil freezes, but not so soon that summer heat and dryness cause the transplants to languish.

I seize these final opportunities for the season, and then quench my thirst as I sink my teeth into a ripe tomato.

Onions — One by one the tops of my onions are flopping over, wilting, and turning yellow. I am happy, for this indicates that the onions are ripening. Gradual drying and cooling of the bulbs will put them in a condition fit for storage until April.

The ripe onion is a storage bulb, much like a tulip, which allows the plant to survive a period of adverse growing conditions, such as heat or cold, in a dormant state. In the first part of the onion's growth cycle, the young seedling develops leaf after leaf through which the sun's energy feeds the growing plant. Sometime during the past month, the number of hours of daylight reached a critical length, and a reaction was triggered inside the onion plant, which directed it: "Stop making leaves, and start storing food for your dormant, leafless period." Each variety has its own critical daylength — this is why the few leaves left on my 'Vidalia' onions are floppy and shriveled, whereas those on my 'Sweet Spanish' onions are still turgid and pointing skyward. As the leaves on each variety cease growth, energy in the form of sugars is pumped into the developing bulb. This makes onions taste good.

As the bulbs become stocked with food reserves, the leaves wilt, no longer needed. The bulbs ripen best with their shoulders exposed to the sun. Hot, dry August weather is conducive to onion ripening. Even for a single variety, not all the tops flop down at the same time, so I coax along hesitant onions into ripening by gently pushing over their green tops. If I wait too long for these stragglers to ripen, those that are dormant might be stimulated out of their dormancy with untimely rains.

As ripening continues, the bulbs grow upward, lifting themselves out of the soil. Because the onset of dormancy also stops root growth, the bulbs practically roll out of the soil. At this stage, I harvest any onions still in the soil, then spread all of them in a single layer on top of the ground.

After a week of basking in the hot, dry sun, the onions, with their tops shriveled and necks thin, are ready for storage.

Now the fun begins, as I create neat ropes of braided onions. (I put aside any onions with thick necks, for these will not keep and should be refrigerated for quick use.) One at a time, I brush the dirt off each good bulb, leaving its gold, parchment covering intact, and add the onion to the growing braid hanging from the nail on my garage rafter. Each time a braid grows to a foot-and-a-half onions long, I start a new one. When the job is completed, I get satisfaction from admiring the row of onion braids hanging from the rafter, created from onions which had their start as seeds sown on a cold winter day.

For long-term storage, onions need to be kept dry and gradually cooled to just above freezing temperature. I leave the braids hanging in my garage into autumn, where they are conveniently cooled by decreasing ambient temperatures, and then I move them to my partially heated basement for storage through the winter.

Even under the best storage conditions, onions eventually sprout as stored food is mobilized and the onions enter the next phase of their growth cycle. (Commercially, onions may be sprayed with sprouting inhibitors.) American-type onions

reputedly keep better than the European-type onions. 'Ebenezer', 'Danvers', and 'Globe' onions, representative of the American types, are hard and pungent. Onion sets are usually of American-type onions. I mostly grow European types, such as 'Sweet Spanish', because these onions are milder and sweeter than the American types. European-type onions are supposed to keep only a couple of months, but I always have them at least until March. I like to think it is because I braid them.

Tomato Troubles — Finally I settle back to enjoy the fruits of my labor. Tomato plants, nurtured as tender seedlings through early spring, now are robust and yielding their juicy, red bounty.

But wait! I now recall that towards the end of this month, tomato plants in many gardens will lose their vigor and fruit production will slow. By September the plants might even peter out, well before temperatures dip anywhere near freezing. And I am not alone with my tomato troubles. Last August a friend reported that her tomatoes were struck with verticillium — is this a catchall term for tomato malaise? As I remember, tomato plants in just about every garden begin to lose their steam by this month's end.

A little investigation has uncovered two facts: first, the same few problems are responsible for tomatoes' running out of steam in gardens almost everywhere; and second, it need not be so.

As it turns out, a major malady of tomatoes usually is not verticillium, but leaf-spot disease. The symptoms are all too familiar — brown spots first appear on tomato leaves closest to the soil, and by mid- to late summer the plants have lost a good part of their leaves. Staked tomato plants take on the appearance of trees, with bushy heads of young foliage capping bare stems. This leaf loss is serious, for fewer leaves mean fewer tomatoes.

Three fungal diseases cause leaf spots: early blight, septoria leaf spot, and late blight. Although the individual names are enough to conjure up fear of plague, all three can be lumped together when it comes to controlling them.

My first line of defense against any of the leaf-spot diseases is keeping disease spores away from tomato plants. Spores spend the winter in old plant debris, then are awakened and splashed onto new tomato leaves by rain during the growing season. Early blight and septoria winter in old tomato refuse on the ground. Late blight spores winter in infected potatoes left in the soil. Come spring, shoots growing from these potato pieces bring spores above the ground. I literally take the spores out of my garden — as many as I can "find," at least — with a thorough garden cleanup. I cart away to the compost pile old tomato and potato stems, leaves, and fruits, and potato tubers.

During the growing season, mulch keeps raindrops from splashing spores up onto plant leaves. Also during the growing season, I occasionally remove infected leaves from growing plants, although I doubt the efficacy of this measure.

Crop rotation each year moves tomato plants away from any spores left from the previous season's crop. I plant tomatoes in a new location in the garden each year, returning them to the same spot only after four years have elapsed. (There is an unavoidable source of late blight infection. With cool, moist weather — which favors late blight — and cooperating air currents, late blight spores can hitchhike north from infected fields in the south.)

I also do what I can to create an inhospitable environment for the fungi. Fungi thrive where the air is dank and leaves remain moist for long periods of time, so I plant my tomatoes in full sun and where weeds, fences, or other obstructions do not block breezes from drying tomato leaves following rain or morning dew. I give each tomato plant adequate elbow room, and stake them or grow them in cages to expose each plant to the air — hanging the leaves out to dry, you might say — and put as much distance as possible between the leaves and spores on the soil.

Note that I have said nothing about preventing leaf spots by growing one of the new hybrid tomato varieties. That's because most of the highly touted, new "disease-resistant hybrids" are resistant to verticillium, fusarium, and/or nematodes (designated by V, F, or N after the variety name) but not to leaf spots. So I'll keep growing my old favorite varieties of tomatoes and rely on good husbandry — cleanliness, selection of a good site, and crop rotation — to ensure a yearly prodigious "love apple" harvest until that first frost blackens the vines.

August 11

Water — If the garden is going to need watering any month, it is in August. I consulted a weather chart and was surprised to learn that there is *not* usually less precipitation around here in August than in other months. It's just that by this time of year, the combination of heat and lush plant growth quickly dries the soil.

Standing with hose in hand, showering the tomatoes or the marigolds, is not, in my opinion, the way to water. This is another one of those tasks that seems to satisfy some gardeners but usually does nothing for the garden. Even gardeners who find such a pose relaxing on a hot summer evening rarely have the patience to stand in one place long enough to do any good. I challenge anyone who does not believe me to probe into the soil with a finger after watering in this manner. I will bet only the surface is wet.

The average garden plant drinks about an inch depth of water per week from as great an area as its roots spread (this inch equals about two gallons per square foot). So, to quench a plant's thirst, the soil either can be flooded with an inch of water once a week or dosed with water in smaller increments more frequently, such as one-seventh of an inch every day.

Up to a few years ago, almost every morning (after at least a week without rain, that is), I would drag my hose and sprinkler around and water a different quarter of the garden for an hour. I previously had determined that it would take my sprinkler an hour to put an inch depth of water in a coffee can. I was finished watering after four days, but three days later, I had to begin the process again.

There is a popular misconception that midday sprinkling is harmful to plants — that beads of water on the leaves will act as magnifying glasses and burn the leaves. Not true! (How many plants die after a sunshower?) Midday is not the best time to water because evaporation and wind will carry much of the water off target. Nighttime also is not a good time to water because the leaves stay wet too long and then are prone to disease. Early morning and late afternoon, when the air is usually cool and calm, and leaves will dry reasonably fast, are the best times to water with a sprinkler.

Eventually I installed a "drip irrigation" system in the main part of my garden. Drip irrigation, which feeds plants water in small, frequent doses, is simplicity itself, in theory at least: thin-walled, black polyethylene pipes, on or in the ground and with specially designed emitters at intervals, slowly drip water right along the garden rows. Dripping takes longer but is more efficient than sprinkling (it was developed for farming the desert by Israeli agricultural scientists), for the water can be applied slowly to just offset plant transpiration. Also, water dripped near the roots of a crop plant does not spur weed growth in paths or between rows, is not subject to evaporation, and does not promote disease by wetting leaves.

Working my way back to my hose spigot, I have, in this sequence, a 150 mesh filter (small emitters might otherwise clog) and a pressure regulator (low pressure is needed for even flow, and to prevent blowing out the emitters). I calculated, from the flow rate and ground area to be covered by each emitter, that my system should turn on for one hour each day. Turning the water on six times a day, ten minutes each time, would come close to replacing water at the rate at which plants drink it up, but I am not about to be tethered to the garden to the extent of running out to turn on the spigot that often. And so enters the final component of my drip irrigation system — the water "computer." This technological marvel is threaded right onto the spigot, is powered by one battery, and can be programmed to turn the water on and off up to six times a day for the amount of time, for the times of day, and for the days of the week that I designate.

I still have to water parts of the garden by dragging the hose and sprinkler around by hand, and it always seems to rain just as I finish that process. I know that the rain and my watering are concomitant events, not cause and effect, but one time it was hard to resist the feeling that I had fooled some higher power. I watered a little one day, then had to leave town for a couple of days without finishing my job. Sure enough, there was a torrential downpour in my absence — just about when I would have finished watering. Ha!

August 13

Glads — On schedule, salmon-red flowers from my one clump of gladioluses are unfurling sequentially from the bottoms to the tops of their stalks. The flowers appear reliably every year, with no help from me.

Besides being care-free — demanding only full sun and average soil — gladioluses are inexpensive to purchase and easy to propagate, and they come in a spectrum of colors. They can be, and are, grown in chilly Canadian gardens as well as those in sultry Florida. Gladioluses are excellent cut flowers. (Yawn.) The flowers keep for over a week if the stalks are cut in the cool air of morning and when the lowest flower buds are just beginning to open.

Gladiolus corms are supposed to be dug when the leaves finally senesce and turn yellow, or are nipped by frost. The leaves then are cut to within two inches of the corms and the corms are put away in a cool cellar for planting the following spring. Digging and storing the corms for winter is little trouble; the plants really are care-free. (Yawn.)

This humdrum attitude in my brief synopsis of gladiolus culture reflects my dislike of gladioluses. A few years back, I had quite a few plants. At the end of each season, I would dig the corms for storage, collecting the small cormels that formed around each large corm. In the spring, I would plant the cormels in a nursery row, and after a season or two of such care, the cormels would reach blooming size. It did not take long to amass a large collection of glads, especially since they form a prodigious number of cormels in the light soil of my garden.

I did an about-face, and began to dislike glads after I was told that the bulk of cut gladioluses are grown commercially for funeral arrangements. Since then, glads have seemed out of place to me except in a room with powder-blue draperies on the walls and ceiling. Even gardeners who like these flowers often relegate the plants, dryly described as "unattractive in form, habit, appearance, and general mode of growth" in one text, to a cutting garden out of view.

So why do I have any gladioluses in my garden? I do not really grow them. The one clump that keeps coming back to haunt me grows from corms that successfully overwinter in the garden — a legacy from when I was fond of them. For a while I tried to weed out the clump, but it kept returning each year, so I let it remain. I snicker when I read that you are supposed to dig gladioluses for winter storage, and that you should delay planting in the spring until the soil has warmed. Would any gladiolus-lover dare grow gladioluses the way I do, I wonder?

Perhaps a historical perspective of the development of the gladiolus would at least increase my appreciation for them. Opening my garden encyclopedia to the heading "gladiolus," I learn that, although the ancient Greeks and Romans used native gladioluses, and "corne flags" were grown in sixteenth-century Britain, the development of hybrids is what really caused a surge in glads' popularity. The first hybrid was introduced in 1823, but "a furor in the gladiolus world" was created in 1841, when the gardener to the Duke of Aremberg developed a hybrid that was a majestic vermilion flower, with chrome, amaranth, and brown on the lower petals. Even Napoleon III's gardener sought to procure this flower (and was successful). Breeding continued into the twentieth century on both sides of the Atlantic, with amateurs and professionals seeking flowers with "fluted, ruffled, and crimped" forms, flowers with large petals, and flowers of brilliant color.

Over time, likes and dislikes can change. I once disliked hostas, but I recently caught myself admiring a planting of a variegated sort against a white clapboard house. Someday I may wander by the persistent clump of gladioluses in my garden and cast a fond glance on it once again.

August 20

Basil — There's always something new to learn about gardening. Take basil, for instance. I have grown basil for years and have always been satisfied with good harvests, enough for chopping over tomato salads in summer, and for preserving — dried, or frozen as pesto — for the winter. But basil growing became more involved this season after a seed company sent me sample packets of various types of basil, and then I spoke with some commercial herb growers.

In spring I planted short rows of all the basil varieties I had, with a wooden marker at the head of each row. The markers were unnecessary, for no two varieties looked alike

and I could have deduced the variety names by the catalog descriptions.

Flavor has always been my reason for growing basil, and I wondered just how different each variety would taste from its neighbor one row over. So I picked leaves of each variety and nibbled at them. I rubbed the leaves between my palms, then inhaled deeply the aroma. I invited visitors to sample each variety, and as they sampled I badgered them with questions and jotted down notes. A pasta dinner was needed so we could evaluate each type of basil made into a pesto sauce. What sweet work!

There actually were differences in taste among the basils. The variety called 'Sweet' lived up to its name with a mild flavor. The similarly mild flavor of 'Napolitano' had the slightest hint of licorice; that of 'Spicy Globe', the slightest suggestion of mint. Progressively stronger in flavor were 'Lettuce Leaf', then 'Fino Verde'. The taste of 'Genova' was strong, bordering on acrid. 'Syracusa' was one of the best — strongly aromatic, yet smooth to the palate.

But mind you, these differences in taste were not dramatic; they were subtle nuances of the familiar basil flavor. And after tasting a few varieties, I must admit that objectivity is on shaky ground. Maybe even the order of tasting is important.

So which is the best variety of basil? This brings me back to the striking difference in appearance among the varieties. Since the differences in taste were not that great, next year I will probably choose a basil variety on the basis of plant size, and the size, color, shape, and texture of its leaves. If I want a basil with a very large leaf — perhaps large enough to stuff with rice — I will grow the variety 'Mammoth'. For drying or pesto, I like a plant with a lot of leaf and a minimum of stem (the dried stems are useless; they are basil-flavored twigs), so any variety except small-leaved 'Fino Verde' or 'Spicy Globe' would be suitable. For eating fresh in salads, even the small-leaved varieties are okay, because the fresh, young stems are tender. I will grow one of the purple-leaved varieties to use fresh for a splash of color in salads.

I might grow some basils just for decoration, even if they had no culinary use. 'Spicy Globe' basil, planted close together, makes soft, green mounds resembling a miniature boxwood hedge — a nice border for my terrace or flower garden. The deep-purple color of 'Dark Opal' would contrast nicely with bright yellow and orange zinnias in a sunny flower border. 'Purple Ruffles' could be used for a more frilly effect. The large-leaved, green basils make an island of lime green if massed together, with a texture dictated by the leaves of the variety chosen: smooth and shiny, wrinkled, or ruffled.

And who knows, maybe I will grow certain basil varieties just for the musical sounds of their names. When someone innocently asks, "What kind of basil is that?" I might gesticulate and sing 'Genova Profumatissima', 'Syracusa', or 'Fino Verde Compatto'.

August 21

Evening Scents — By day, evening stocks and nicotiana are almost eyesores in my garden, but as the cloak of darkness drops on summer evenings, the petals of each of these flowers unfurl to release delicous, heavy scents. The long, white nicotiana trumpets begin to glow in the moonlight, and evening stocks shine like little bright stars.

There are a few species of nicotiana (pronounced *nee-kó-shee-ay-na*), but for scented evenings, the one I chose is *N. alata*, with the appropriate common name Jasmine Tobacco. (The word *nicotiana* looks like the word *nicotine* because smoking tobacco also is a *Nicotiana* species — *N. tabacum*.) Nicotiana is an annual that forms a rosette of leaves at ground level and a flowering spike a couple of feet, or more, high. New varieties that have a bushy growth habit have been bred. Some of the newer varieties also flower in the daylight, hopefully with no sacrifice of scent.

Nicotiana is in the nightshade family and, like its other relatives — tomatoes, eggplants, and peppers — demands a rich, warm soil in the sun. For earliest blooms, I sow the seeds indoors a few weeks before the last spring frost. If I am not over fastidious in my weeding, the plant self-sows, with later flowers.

Evening stock is one of two types of garden stocks. One

is grown mostly for its showy flowers. The other, which I am growing — evening, or night-scented, stock (*Matthiola bicornis*) — is the one for scented nights. Evening stock is an annual that will bloom from July through September. In contrast to nicotiana, evening stock is a low-growing, straggly plant, a ball of wiry stems with small leaves and flowers. Wilted remains of the previous night's flowers and unopened buds of flowers for nights to follow make the plant not much to look at by day.

Because nicotiana and evening stock are attractive and heavily aromatic once darkness falls, they should be grown where they can be enjoyed on summer nights. Outside my back door, on the terrace, I have a small, semicircular flower bed that includes both these night-scented plants. Because they are so homely by day, attention to their floral companions is needed. A nice companion for evening stock is gazania. Like stock, gazania is low growing with thin petals; but gazania's flowers are large, solitary, sunny yellow daisies. Gazania and stock are near the front of the sunny bed, where they are not shaded or hidden by taller plants.

Tall, spiky nicotiana is near the back of the bed. The spaces that nicotiana flowers leave bare by day are filled in with other tall flowers such as large zinnias and asters, which recede into darkness as night falls.

On nights when atmospheric conditions are just right, the heady aromas of stock and nicotiana gather beneath the window just above the flower bed and waft indoors with the slightest breeze. I am not sure what, exactly, characterizes atmospheric conditions that are "just right," but the typical summer night seems to fit the bill.

August 22

Magic Lily — An eerie-looking plant blooms about mid-August each year in a neighbor's garden. The flowers, ghostly pink and lilylike, appear atop yard-high, naked stalks. What's more, the flower stalks appear all of a sudden, without any leaves! The plant is known as the magic lily or hardy amaryllis

(*Lycoris squamigera*). (In northern California the dramatic effect is heightened as this plant pops up as the only actively growing, let alone colorful, bit of plant life in the otherwise parched late summer landscape of that area.)

If the sudden appearance of the pink flowers does not raise an eyebrow, how about the fact that the plant was given the generic name *Lycoris* after the mistress of Mark Antony, a woman famed for her intrigues? Or better still, a related species, *L. radiata*, has sometimes been thought in Japan to be possessed by the soul of a dead person (and is not cultivated there, presumably for that reason).

In the right setting, the magic lily is more than just eerie; it can be quite beautiful. Since the plant's leaves appear in early spring, then disappear in June, you need a plant to fill in the bare spot that remains. Companion plants should be low growing, to keep out of the way of the magic lily blossoms when they appear. A companion plant's colors should not clash with the pink of magic lily blossoms. No orange or yellow flowers, please! Low-growing foliage plants such as creeping junipers, hostas, low-growing ferns, and artemesias also make nice companions for magic lily. Cerastium has two qualities that ensure a happy marriage to magic lily: low stature and gray foliage, which harmonize well with the pink magic lily flowers.

Given the magic lily's growth cycle, this plant also might be good for a meadow that is mowed once a year, in early summer. Mowing would not interfere with either the early spring leaf growth or the late summer flowers of the magic lily.

With the site chosen, magic lily bulbs should be planted four inches deep and a half-foot apart. The plants grow best in full sun or just a small amount of shade, in a soil that is well drained and rich in humus.

As a planting ages, offsets, or small bulbs, grow on the sides of large established bulbs. When a planting becomes too dense due to these offsets, the bulbs should be lifted, separated, then replanted. This operation is best done right after the foliage dies down in late spring.

Other species of *Lycoris* besides *L. squamigera* are occasionally cultivated. *L. sanguinea*, also cold-hardy outdoors here, has small orange-red flowers atop foot-and-a-half to two-foot stalks. *L. aurea* and the red spider lily (*L. radiata*) probably are not hardy here. *L. aurea* has bright orange or yellow flowers. The red spider lily is evergreen and usually is grown as a potted plant. The petals are bright red and short, with the stamens protruding. Not a bad plant to grow if you do not mind the deceased souls reputedly in possession of the flowers.

My own magic lilies look fine coming up through clumps of alpine strawberries. But my plants are especially eerie, because they appeared for the first time this August, yet I cannot remember ever planting them!

August 23

Rose Hips — I had just about given up for lost my hedge of rugosa rose (*Rosa rugosa*), planted as an ornamental and edible barrier in the narrow strip of land 'twixt the street and the stream in front of my house. Rugosa rose seemed an ideal choice for that location. The plant is extremely cold hardy (to minus 50 degrees Fahrenheit!) and tolerates salt, whether from ocean spray or road de-icing trucks. The plants, set two feet apart, sprawl outward to grow as a continuous hedge.

The hedge has grown well, but unfortunately not as well as the grasses, goldenrod, jewelweed, even loosestrife that have visually engulfed it. The beautiful and fragrant carmine flowers peek through the vegetation here and there, but they surely do not steal the show.

Then, a couple of weeks ago, I did a double take as I walked past the hedge — a profusion of fruits were prominently staring out at me. The hips (or heps), as the fruits are called, festoon the plants even as flowering continues. They are beautiful: cherry tomato–size, orange red, shiny with a few bristles. The hips would last well into winter, except that I plan to harvest some of them.

I occasionally eat a few fresh hips, and they have a refreshing, brisk flavor. Their main defect is that they are too seedy. The hips can be halved and spread out to dry in the sun or a warm oven, for later use in tea. A cup of fresh hips simmered fifteen minutes in a cup and a half of water, then allowed to stand for twenty-four hours before straining, makes a tasty juice to add to fruit cobblers, fruit drinks, and fruit soups (the latter a Scandinavian delicacy). The juice and the dried hips are also nutritious — fresh rose hips have about fifty times the concentration of vitamin C as fresh oranges!

The whole rugosa rosebush is quite attractive, forming a mound about six feet high and wide, with leaves that are bright green and crinkled ("rugose"). The leaves reputedly turn clear yellow or orange in autumn, but I never have been impressed by this aspect of my plants. The stems are completely covered with prickles and bristles.

Rugosa rose is no sissy of a rose. Unfazed by winter cold, this rose is equally tolerant of summer heat and even the poorest of soils. The plant is native to the Far East, but now is naturalized along our Atlantic seacoast, thriving in almost pure sand. You will not find black spot, mildew, or other maladies that afflict hybrid tea roses on rugosa roses.

Rosa rugosa even gets on well year after year without pruning. Eventually, older stems lose vigor and plants become leggy, and occasional winter pruning of the oldest stems down to the ground induces new, vigorous shoots. And as long as I am pruning, I shorten any younger stems that have grown too lanky. The one sin that can be committed against the rugosa rose — an aesthetic sin, harmless to the plant — is to hedge the plant with shears.

My plants are seedlings, which I find satisfactory, even with occasional white-flowered plants. Rugosa rose has been hybridized with other rose species. 'Sarah van Fleet', 'Sir Thomas Lipton', and 'Mme. Georges Bruant' (the latter two with double white flowers) are among such hybrids.

Notable plants also have been selected from within the species *Rosa rugosa*: the variety 'Frau Dágmar Hastrup' has hips that are extremely high in vitamin C; varieties such as 'Belle Poitevine' and 'Scabrosa' have very large hips; and 'Topaz' has yellow flowers. Varieties such as 'Agnes', 'Blanc de Coubert', and 'F. J. Grootendorst' have double flowers, but I prefer the more uncivilized look of a single row of petals. Besides, double flowers rarely produce hips.

August 31

Preparing for Autumn — One morning in the next two months, I will look out on my garden and see tomato plants hanging limply on their poles, knocked back suddenly by frost or finally yielding to extended cool weather. Will this mark the end of my garden for the season? No! Lush green leaves of kale, lettuce, and cabbage, and the autumn yellows and oranges of chrysanthemums, will then dominate the garden scene. A good fall garden separates the men from the boys, just as it separates the hardy from the tender plants. A garden in autumn can be a weedy remembrance of summer activity or a carpet of productivity and beauty.

I do two things in August to ensure a lush garden in the autumn — plant and weed.

I now sow seeds of vegetables that mature in thirty to forty days or less and that enjoy the cool, crisp weather of fall. Seed-stalk formation and the resulting woody radish roots and bitter lettuce leaves, inevitable during long summer days, will not occur during the short days of fall. Short rows of radish seeds, sown every week, supply crisp radishes for salads through October, maybe into November. So-called winter radishes grow to enormous sizes and can be stored in the ground under a thick mulch for eating throughout the winter. The advantage of sowing winter radishes now is that the roots will not get too big. Catalogs tout the potential for thirty-pound winter radishes, but I have no idea what I would do with a 'China Rose' radish the size of a beach ball. Turnips grown in the fall are a delicacy — sweet and crisp. I also sow quick-maturing leafy vegetables: lettuces such as 'Black-Seeded Simpson', 'Salad Bowl', and red-leaved 'Ruby'; and other fall greens such as spinach, arugola (also called rocket or rucola), leaf mustard, and *mâche* (also called corn salad, fetticus, and lamb's lettuce, but delicious under any name).

Now let's turn to the weeds. Lazy days of summer give weeds the opportunity to inch their way into the garden. These weeds compete with fall vegetables for nourishment and water from the soil, even for light. Every weed that ripens and spreads its seeds will mean more trouble in the garden next year. It does not take long to give the garden a thorough weeding now to set the stage for the fall garden.

As I write, the weather in the river valley where I live is not unlike that along the Amazon River — hot and steamy. It's hard to believe that in only a month it will be cool. In this case, the calender and notes from last year's garden are better guides for planting than is intuition.

SEPTEMBER

Next him, September marched eeke on foote;
Yet he was heauy laden with the spoyle
Of haruests riches, which he made his boot,
And him enricht with bounty of the soyle.

Edmund Spenser, The Faerie Queene

SUMMER IS FADING from the garden. Even lingering heat fails to convince the low, slanting sun and tawny colors that the end of the outdoor gardening season is not approaching. One part of the garden is spared late summer's decline. The cool weather greens — ornamental kale, cabbage, lettuce, mustard, and turnips — all thrive in the chilly, moist weather of September and suddenly stand out in the garden as pockets of lush, springlike greenery.

Ripening fruits awaken my senses even before I bite into them. Overlooked grapes ferment on the vines or on the ground, infusing the air with a vinegary aroma. September weather puts the blush on apples. I watch the apples closely so that I can successively harvest each variety at its peak of perfection.

Houseplants, most of which have unassumingly spent the summer outdoors, recapture my attention. I move them indoors well before nights become frosty, pulling weeds from their pots and pruning off wayward branches and diseased leaves, in anticipation of the cold months ahead.

Preserving the Harvest — Just a little more than a month ago I stood impatiently tapping my foot next to a tomato plant, waiting for the first fruit to ripen. Those plants now bear more tomatoes than I can eat. How can I deal with the garden's surplus? I could orphan zucchinis on my unsuspecting neighbor's doorsteps. Or I could preserve some of the harvest for times of dearth. I do not know the economics of home food preservation versus buying from a supermarket, but I do know the rewards of pulling a package of homegrown peas out of the freezer on a cold winter day.

The only vegetables I preserve by canning are tomatoes, because tomatoes are acidic enough that there is little threat of food poisoning, and because other vegetables become too limp for my taste when canned. When I first read about peeling tomatoes as the first step for canning, I knew the process could stand some modification. I simply squeeze each tomato over a big cooking pot to break the skin and get the juices flowing, then plunk the squished tomato into the pot. I cook down the mass by about half to thicken it, let it cool, blend it, and pack it into jars for canning.

Besides freezing and canning, I also use traditional storage methods for some of the harvest. A hundred years ago, rafters of farmhouse kitchens were festooned this time of year with strings of drying produce. One autumn I emulated my forebears by running strings through the holes of cored apple slices and pulling a threaded needle through whole green beans, then hanging the strings of apples and beans across my kitchen ceiling. The apples were delicious, but the beans were no match for frozen ones. I also have prepared sweet corn in the traditional manner of steaming the whole cob, then slicing off the kernels and drying them on a screen. Packed into airtight canning jars, the shriveled kernels kept the whole winter. When soaked or cooked in a little water, they were as sweet as the day I picked the corn.

Leeks, carrots, turnips, and beets could remain in good condition the whole winter out in the garden if covered with a thick mulch of leaves to prevent wide swings in temperature. Alternate freezing and thawing, not just freezing, is what ruins them. One year I even kept cabbage and celery out in the garden by pulling the plants up by their roots, setting the roots in the bottom of a trench eighteen inches deep, then covering the trench with boards and a pile of leaves. Alas, trudging out in midwinter to dig under a foot of snow and leaves does not appeal to me, so I no longer leave any vegetables in the garden through the winter.

Some vegetables ripening now need no preparation, only the right environment, and they keep for months. Common storage, as it has been called since the invention of modern refrigerated storage, in my house means finding the right microclimates in and around the house to suit the needs of each vegetable I want to store — thus, the onion and garlic braids hanging from garage rafters, the squashes on a shelf behind the still-cool wood stove, and the tomatoes in various stages of ripening in bushel baskets on the foyer floor.

I will start moving bushel baskets loaded with produce to cozier quarters as soon as subfreezing weather settles on the garden in earnest. Most fruits and vegetables keep best at temperatures just above freezing. Before the days of refrigerators, freezers, and central heating, unfinished cellars beneath homes were ideal for storing fruits and vegetables. My basement is rustic enough that the temperature in some spots drops to near 40 degrees Fahrenheit by winter — not the ideal temperature, but sufficiently cold to store carrots and onions through February.

Carrots and other root crops need high humidity in cold storage. I twist off their green tops, then layer the roots in a box with slightly moist sawdust (not from pressure-treated wood), peat moss, or leaves. Or I just toss them into plastic buckets with loose-fitting lids. Onions and garlic keep best with dry air, so when the weather gets cold I move the braids from the rafters in my garage to the exposed joists of my basement ceiling.

One vegetable I have not been able to keep reliably in common storage is cabbage. I once tried the traditional method of hanging the heads upside down from basement joists, but the cabbages dried out. Another year I tried the traditional method of laying them outdoors on a bed of straw, then covering them with more straw, then with dirt and leaves. The cabbages rotted. My cabbages did keep fairly well the year I bedded them in slatted wooden boxes among almost-dry leaves, although an occasional head rotted — not a pleasant sight or smell!

I pick winter squashes when their rinds harden and stems dry. These squashes ideally are cured for a couple of weeks at warm temperatures before being stored cool (about 55 degrees Fahrenheit) and dry. I put the squashes on a shelf behind my wood stove, then move them next month to a cooler room where they provide hearty, warm fare until Christmas.

After Christmas, I will be slicing the last of this season's onions into a salad, then digging deep into the freezer for peas just as I am sowing seeds for next spring's garden.

September 13

Pressed Flowers — I almost envy my brother and sister, living in Florida and basking in year-round summer. I enjoy seasonal changes in the North, but the first brisk night causes in me a nervous urge to scurry around quickly and preserve bits of summer to tide me through the frigid months ahead. Hence those jars of tomatoes lined up on shelves in the basement, the braids of onions hanging in the garage, and the strawflowers hanging from the kitchen rafters. Even photographs of the summer garden help. Yet another way I carry the torch of summer through winter is by pressing flowers.

One season's pressed flowers actually will carry the torch of summer through many winters. Pressed plants have been used for years by botanists as herbarium specimens. The Bodleian Library of Oxford University, England, still houses pressed specimens of plants that were collected in Virginia in the seventeenth century first for King Charles I and then for King Charles II.

The tools needed to press flowers are simple: a few heavy books, such as encyclopedias or dictionaries, and some tissue paper. For a fancier press, and one that is portable, sandwich folded newspaper and sheets of corrugated cardboard between two pieces of quarter-inch plywood (about eighteen-by-eighteen inches). Squeeze this press together with four bolts passed through holes drilled in each corner of the plywood and held firmly with wing nuts, or with a piece of rope crisscrossed around the bundle the way you gift-wrap a package with ribbon. The enemy of pressed flowers is moisture, so keep the press or books with flowers in a warm, dry room.

Collect flowers for pressing about midday on a dry day. Pressing them immediately after cutting, before they wilt, will preserve as much of their natural form as possible. I flatten the centers of thick flowers between my thumb and index finger before putting them in the press, or take off only the petals for pressing.

If I am using a book as a press, I open the book, lay a sheet of tissue paper down on the page, then arrange a flower on the tissue paper. I lay another sheet of tissue paper on top of the flower before closing the book. Books filled with many or thick flowers need to be weighted down with more books or with bricks, rocks, or the like. One book can house more than one flower as long as each flower is separated by about ten pages.

To use the fancier press, arrange flowers between two sheets of newspaper held in turn between two sheets of corrugated cardboard, then cinch up the plywood. One press can hold many flowers in various stages of drying as long as each flower is sandwiched between newspaper, then corrugated cardboard.

Virtually any flower can be preserved by pressing (they all are for herbarium specimens), but some are more attractive than others. Earlier this summer, bleeding hearts, poppies, even blackberries would have made nice pressed flowers, but at that time I did not have that nervous urge to preserve summer. Now, mums, clematis, dahlias, violas (including pansies), purple coneflowers, pot marigolds, and daisies are especially good for pressing.

A pressed flower dries in two or three weeks and, once dry, can be mounted in a picture frame with a backing of cloth, as is, or used with other flowers and flower petals to "paint" colorful designs or pictures. For a card or bookmark, lay dried flowers on heavy paper, then cover them with a sheet of plastic coated with clear adhesive.

Left in the book in which it was dried, a pressed flower provides a pleasant surprise. Every time I open my dictionary to the page beginning with the word *pteryla,* I am greeted by the smiling blue and yellow face of a dried pansy I forgot to remove years ago.

September 18

Cardoon — Is it a type of derby, a tropical rodent, or a Scottish sweater? No, it is a vegetable (*Cynara cardunculus*) that is closely related to globe artichoke. Whereas the flower bud is the edible part of the artichoke, the leaf stalks are the edible part of cardoon (similar to celery). And whereas the artichoke is difficult to grow in cold climates, cardoon is easy.

Last night I harvested my one cardoon plant. Cutting down such an imposing plant was a big event. Picture a giant thistle, whose gray-green leaves form a prickly vase towering to four feet high, with a similar spread. I cut the plant off at its base, then lopped off the upper leafy portion. I pulled a few stalks off this giant "celery" and boiled them up after removing any last traces of leaves along the edges of the stalks. (The leaves are bitter.)

I should have known cardoon would taste good, for Apicius recommended it in the first century A.D. in his *Cooking and Dining in Imperial Rome.* Cardoon tastes just like artichoke. To this day, cardoon is popular with the French and the Italians, who eat it fried, or boiled and drizzled with a vinaigrette sauce.

This was my first success with cardoon. In previous attempts, the plants grew well but the stalks were disagreeably woody. I attribute this season's success to blanching, a procedure that makes the leaf stalks succulent and tender by keeping them in the dark — not an easy task with a four-foot spiny monster. Blanching began early this month, when, with gloved hands and some assistance, I tied the tops of the plant together with string. I then swaddled the base of the plant in a cylinder of tar paper eighteen inches high, giving the whole affair the look of a giant, green shaving brush with a black handle. Straw, soil, or collars made of wood or cardboard

could have been used in lieu of tar paper. Two to four weeks are needed to blanch cardoon.

In the southern Mediterranean region, where cardoon is native, it grows as a perennial. Here in the Northeast, its winter-hardiness is questionable. If cardoon does not survive winters here, I can continue to grow it as an annual, just the way I did this year. The seeds, sown indoors in May, germinate readily. I transplanted the seedlings outdoors after danger of frost was past to rich soil in full sun.

Cardoon is quite beautiful for its foliage, but if it survives as a perennial here, it should become even more dramatic in its second and subsequent seasons in the garden. With age, it will tower as high as six feet and send up flower stalks capped with bristly purple flowers.

Next year I intend to grow a few cardoon plants. Additional plants can be propagated by seed, or by pulling off and replanting in spring the small suckers that grow around the base of the plant (assuming winter survival). Each cardoon plant needs at least a couple of feet of elbow room all around, but carrots or lettuce can be interplanted and harvested before the cardoons reach full size.

I have read that cardoon can become weedy in some places where it grows as a perennial. It invaded the pampas soon after its introduction to Argentina. Darwin said that "no plant has run wild on so extensive a scale as cardoon." Uh-oh.

September 20

Fox Grapes — The word *foxy* has not been complimentary to grapes. It refers to the dominant flavor in one of our native species, the fox grape (*Vitis labrusca*). Although the Indians ate this grape, early white settlers were not impressed by it. In 1672, John Josselyn wrote that fox grapes had "a taste of gunpowder." Two Dutchmen visiting New York in 1679 recounted how they "went along the shore to Coney Island . . . and discovered on the roads several kinds of grapes still on the vines, called *speck* (fox) grapes, which are not always good, and these were not; although they were sweet in the mouth at first, they made it disagreeable and stinking." Around 1880, the botanist William Bartram went so far as to suggest that the epithet *foxy* was applied to this grape because of the "strong, rancid smell of its ripe fruit, very like the effluvia from the body of a fox." (Others suggested the epithet came about because foxes ate the grapes, or because the leaves resembled fox tracks.)

Wherever white settlers landed in America, they attempted to establish plantings of the grape with which they were familiar, the European wine or vinifera grape (*V. vinifera*), which was the grape cultivated in the Old World since biblical times. In America, vinifera culture began as long ago as 1619, when the best vines and skilled growers were brought from France to establish a vineyard in Virginia. That planting, and virtually all subsequent plantings in the East, failed because the vinifera grape cannot tolerate our cold winters or the insects and diseases to which our native grapes are accustomed. (An Indian massacre also contributed to the failure of that first planting in 1619.)

In spite of repeated futile attempts at growing vinifera grapes in the East, few people considered growing our

tougher, native grapes before the nineteenth century.. Only then were superior varieties developed, beginning about 1820 with 'Catawba'. One reason for the delayed interest in fox grapes was that vinifera is the better fruit for wine, and not until the nineteenth century were fruits generally appreciated for fresh eating. (Wine recalls another possible source for the epithet *foxy*; horticulturalist Liberty Hyde Bailey suggested in 1898 that the name arose due to "the lively foxing or intoxicating quality of the poor wine which was made from the wild grape.")

As you might imagine, fruits of the vinifera and the fox grape are quite different. You can pick out the difference from the grocer's shelf today. The fox grape is represented by 'Concord': bite into a berry and the thick skin slips off the jellylike meat, releasing a strong, aromatic, although not excessively sweet, flavor. The vinifera grape is represented by 'Thompson Seedless': eat the whole berry, tender skin and all; the fruit is sweet, with a neutral flavor. Vinifera berries are less apt to shake off the bunches, so ship better. This is one reason you may not even find 'Concord' at the grocer's.

The above is not an academic exercise in grape history. Because I grow grapes, survival of the vines and taste of the fruits is topical. Although I have heard rumors of vinifera grapes being successfully grown in the Northeast, three hundred years of failure teaches me something. For those gardeners who strive for a grape akin to vinifera, there are hybrids between vinifera and fox grapes. These hybrids exhibit the full spectrum in flavor, hardiness, and pest tolerance, depending on which varieties were used as their parents. For gardeners interested in growing grapes closer in flavor (or lack thereof) to 'Thompson Seedless', hybrids such as 'Himrod' and 'Lakemont' are fairly cold hardy and can be grown at favorable sites, preferably south-facing slopes in full sun. A bit more foxy, and unfortunately also only fairly cold hardy, is 'Vanessa', a delectable small berry which is pale red, crisp, sweet, and flavorful.

Notwithstanding the previous testimony against foxiness in grapes, I happen to like my grapes foxy. I am not alone: Ulysses P. Hedrick, who wrote *The Grapes of New York* early in this century, conceded that many vinifera grapes "are without character of flavor" compared to American grapes, which are "more refreshing . . . do not cloy the appetite," and make a better juice. My taste preference is fortunate, because in my garden (the bottom of the bottom of a frost pocket) grapes are particularly prone to both cold injury and disease.

This month, I have Elmer Swenson, a dairy farmer and grape breeder living near the Wisconsin-Minnesota border, to thank for the grapes I am eating. 'Swenson Red' berries are medium sized, sweet, fairly foxy, and just slightly slipskin. By month's end, 'Edelweiss' (thanks again, Elmer) will be ripening. The only defect of 'Edelweiss' is its vigor; canes commonly grow twenty feet in a season in my garden. But the vine has proven very cold hardy and disease resistant at my admittedly poor site for grapes. And best of all is the flavor of 'Edelweiss': sweet and *very* foxy.

September 22

Mexican Bamboo — A weed has been defined as "any plant out of place." One plant that is horrendous in the wrong place, yet worthwhile in the right place, is an herbaceous perennial known variously as Mexican bamboo, Japanese knotweed, *Polygonum cuspidatum*, or, in its weedy guise, stronger names.

Although Mexican bamboo dies to the ground each winter, the plant remains attractive throughout the year. The show begins as clumps of bronze shoots poke straight up through the ground in spring. As the season progresses, the shoots quickly telescope out into jointed canes that arch to the ground like a fountain of water. (These "joints" are the source of the generic epithet *Polygonum*, meaning "many knees" in Greek.) The four- to eight-foot-high canes are clothed in heart-shaped, soft green leaves. Mexican bamboo becomes particularly attractive this time of year, as the arching stems froth with greenish white flowers along the upper parts of the stems.

After the leaves fall in autumn, the hollow, dead stems persist through the winter and really do resemble bamboo. Mexican bamboo stems are thin-walled, so have none of the utilitarian value of true bamboo for plant stakes and fishing poles. Mexican bamboo is not even related to the true bamboos, but is kin to smartweed, buckwheat, dock, and rhubarb.

Now for the darker side of Mexican bamboo: This is the most aggressive plant I ever have encountered. It is similar to true bamboo in the vigor with which it spreads outward by underground rhizomes, and the speed with which the shoots grow upward. Last year I had a standoff in my yard between real bamboo and Mexican bamboo. You see, the back corner of my property seemed an ideal spot to start a grove of real bamboo. But the Mexican bamboo, backed against the edge of the woods in that corner, crept forward into the ground I prepared for the true bamboo and choked it out. (Admittedly, the Mexican bamboo was fighting with the aid of an already established root system.)

Mexican bamboo should be allowed to grow only where it can be contained, surely never in a garden. The only plants that can successfully compete with Mexican bamboo are established trees and lawn, the latter only because Mexican bamboo cannot tolerate persistent mowing.

There is a dwarf selection of the plant (*P. c. compactum*) that also is attractive, yet not so aggressive. Of course, *compactum* never can become the bold clump of greenery that the larger sort can. For decorative value, the foliage of yet another form, *P. c. spectabile*, is marbled green, white, and red.

If you look up *Polygonum cuspidatum* in most gardening books, the discussion usually concerns methods of killing, rather than growing, the plants. The way to eradicate them is with persistent hand-digging to remove every bit of root, or with an herbicide labeled for use against the plant, sprayed while the plants are in bloom. By persistent digging, I finally have driven my Mexican bamboo back to the margin of the woods, where I still can enjoy its beauty. Now I hope to keep the plants in place with a fiberglass barrier sunk two feet into the ground (a technique used by gardeners farther south to keep real bamboo from spreading).

Since growing Mexican bamboo seems to be mostly a

question of keeping the plant in bounds, even mentioning how to grow it is perhaps foolhardy. If one were to go so far as to actually plant Mexican bamboo, I suggest dropping a piece of root on the ground, covering the root with some soil, then jumping out of the way.

September 27

Autumn Bulbs In — Every time I walk past those bins of spring-flowering bulbs now on display in garden centers, hardware stores, and food markets, I can hear the bulbs crying out, "Plant me, plant me." I can't resist. For a few dollars, I will be rewarded this spring with dainty white snowdrops blooming before snow has gone, crocuses and daffodils popping up where I won't even remember planting them, and tulips, finally baring their beauty only after warmish weather has settled in.

Bulbs are prepackaged flowers, with the blossoms for next spring already locked inside. The beauty of next year's spring blossoms is more dependent on bulb quality than on a green thumb. Therefore, as I sift through those bins full of bulbs, I select those that are large, plump, and free of mold. I want solid bulbs and toss back into the bin anything flabby. And I want bulbs that are not shriveled from having been stored too long.

I have found that mail-order bargain mixtures are no bargain but usually provide an opportunity for inferior nurseries to unload inferior bulbs of inferior varieties. Now, when I do buy bulbs through the mail, I buy only from firms I know are reliable.

With bulbs in hand, it is time to plant — the sooner the better, except for tulips, planting of which can be delayed even until next month. In deciding where to plant what, I consider microclimates around my yard. A sunny nook near the house is where snow will melt first; it is also where I can expect to see the first blossoms of dainty purple and yellow crocuses. Formal areas are for tulips and hyacinths. Tulips can maintain their erect dignity only if planted where they can enjoy some protection from wind and full sun. Large Dutch hyacinths in formal clumps need to be planted within nose distance so their fragrance can be enjoyed.

Many gardeners, when devoting a whole bed to a formal planting — of tulips, for example — excavate all the soil to the required planting depth, line up the bulbs soldierlike, then backfill the soil. Because I do not like to disturb the soil, and perhaps because I never plant a whole bed only to bulbs, I prefer to plant bulbs individually with a trowel. Using a trowel, I easily nestled species tulips in some creeping thyme beneath a clove currant bush, hardly disturbing the plants. When the soil is mellow, just a few seconds is needed to plant each bulb.

The way to avoid any hint of order in a naturalized planting of daffodils is just to scatter a bucketful of them on the ground, then plant each bulb wherever it falls. This is also a good way to create a drift of naturalized squills, bluebells, or grape hyacinths. To plant each bulb, lift a flap of grass, make a hole deep enough so the bulb can be planted at a depth about three times its height, set the bulb in the hole flat end down, then cover the bulb with soil and the flap of grass. This may seem somewhat tedious for a whole drift of bulbs, but planting is a nice activity for these cool days and the results will be enjoyed for years.

One year I made the mistake of creating a drift of naturalized daffodils in the lawn. It was a cheery brush stroke of yellow in early spring. But leaves are what feed a bulb for the following season's flowers, so I was unable to mow the lawn until late spring, after the daffodil's leaves had finished their season's work and died down. A better setting would have been a meadow, where the grass and flowers are mowed to the ground in autumn. Or in a woodland setting, where there is no grass to be mown, and clumps of yellow daffodils would stand out against the drab gray and brown of the woodland floor in early spring.

Summer Bulbs Out — While wandering about planting hardy bulbs, I make mental notes of where tender bulbs such as cannas, dahlias, and begonias are growing. It is time to start digging them, so they can be tucked away for the six months of cold weather that is about to descend on the garden.

These bulbs are not really bulbs; they represent, in fact, a few different types of botanical structures. They all have multiplied, in their own unique manners, during the preceding warm months. One dahlia planted this past spring becomes four or five plants for next summer. What better excuse to enlarge the garden than to accommodate the multiplying plants?

Some general rules for digging and storing any of the cold-tender bulbs: First, dig carefully. Bruises might become blue mold in a couple of months. I slide a garden fork into the ground about a foot from the plants and then gently lever up the clod of soil. Second, store bulbs where they can breathe. I use wooden boxes, with the bulbs nested in dry sawdust. The moisture given off by the bulbs themselves suffices to maintain a slight, even moisture. Plastic bags would cause the bulbs to sweat, mold, or grow. Even the last is undesirable in early winter. Finally, store boxes of bulbs where they cannot become food for hungry rodents.

Before frost has struck is the time to dig begonias. After digging, I spread them in an airy room or in the sun to dry, cut off the tops after they wilt, then continue drying them for a couple of weeks more. Technically, a begonia's bulb is known as a *tuberous stem*. More and more sprouts arise from this tuberous stem as it enlarges, so that eventually it can be cut up and the individual pieces planted.

The other tender bulbs can remain in the ground until the first frost blackens their tops. Once this happens, I dig up cannas and caladiums, brush off the soil, and let them air dry. I cut dahlia stems to within a half-foot of the ground, then dig them up. The stems hold water, which might cause rotting, so I turn them upside to dry before packing them away for the winter.

All the bulbs — with the exception of caladiums, which like room temperature storage — go down in the basement where they will keep cool, but not cold, until I am ready to plant them again next spring. Once the bulbs are tucked away is a good time to begin pondering what to do with their ever-increasing numbers.

September 30

Acidanthera — September is not a month only for deferred gratification, spent packing away vegetables for the winter and summer bulbs for next spring's planting. All the fanfare about fall bulbs (more deferred gratification) is not so loud that I cannot turn some of my attention to a summer bulb that is flowering, or at least trying to flower, right now. The plant is acidanthera (*Acidanthera bicolor*), which was introduced into Europe from Ethiopia in the fourteenth century but remains uncommon in America.

Acidanthera is sometimes called fragrant gladiolus and is, in fact, closely related to gladiolus. (Although commonly referred to as bulbs, both gladiolus and acidanthera are not true bulbs, but thickened, bulblike stems, called corms.) Like gladiolus, acidanthera has swordlike leaves, which are the source of another common name, the Abyssinian sword lily. Both plants enjoy a rich soil in full, or almost full, sun.

Although my gladiolus bulbs come up every year without my digging and storing them for the winter, acidanthera, unfortunately, has never shown such hardiness. As soon as hard frost blackens acidanthera leaves, I dig up the corms and store them as recommended for gladiolus: in a cardboard box in my cool basement. I also save some of the small cormels that form around the mother corm. These cormels reach flowering size after a couple of seasons' growth.

I much prefer acidanthera to gladiolus. Whereas gladiolus flowers — ruffles of colors such as fire-engine red and lime green — are gaudy in both form and color, acidanthera is delicate and restrained in its beauty. A typical acidanthera plant has three or four flowers open at a time. Each flower is a white star three inches across, gracefully bowing toward the earth from the end of its slender stalk. Inside the throat of each flower is a chocolaty purple blotch.

Best of all is the intoxicating fragrance of acidanthera — sweet and tropical, reminiscent of ylang-ylang. Acidanthera is an excellent cut flower, and as I write I am enjoying the fragrance of a half-dozen cut flowers sitting in a vase on the table in front of me.

I do not mind digging the corms each season, but acidanthera does have the more serious shortcoming of wanting to blossom late, often so late that freezing weather cuts short its career. Right now the clumps of leaves look healthy enough

scattered at various locations around the garden, but there just are not enough flowers to please me.

What am I to do? In the next few days I will dig up a few plants, salvaging as many of each plant's roots as is feasible, then pot the plants up and bring them inside to flower.

I never have tried this, but the roots do not seem extensive, so the plants may not be so shocked as to be dissuaded from flowering.

Next year my tack will be different. In early spring I will pot up some corms in pots just big enough to get growth started. Once warm weather settles in, I will tip the growing corms out of their pots and plant them in the garden, whence they will have plenty of time to flower. I also might pot up some corms in large pots in late spring. These I will water and fertilize through the season, then bring them indoors — their roots undisturbed by digging — to carry at least one of the fragrances and flowers of summer well into autumn.

OCTOBER

Season of mists and yellow fruitfulness!
Close bosom-friend of the maturing sun;
Conspiring with him how to load and bless
With fruit the vines that thatch-eaves run;
To bend with apples the moss'd cottage-trees,
And fill all fruit with ripeness to the core;
To swell the gourd and plump the hazel shells
With a sweet kernel, to set budding more,
And still more, later flowers for the bees,
Until they think warm days will never cease
For summer has o'erbrimmed their clammy cells.

John Keats, "To Autumn"

LATE SUMMER WEEDING has paid off — the garden is swathed in cultivated greenery. The bright green of mustard and lettuce leaves, the glaucous green of leek and cabbage leaves, and the crimson-hued green of blueberry and clove currant leaves stand out against the brown earth.

I capitalize on any lingering warmth of the season. The compost pile grows weekly, as I heap on and chop with a machete garden remains such as brittle, old zinnia plants, succulent ropes of squash vines, and large, flat discs of sun-flower heads, already pecked free of their seeds by birds. Until the weather turns cold enough to slow down microbial activity, the compost pile will snort steam into the calm, morning air. The soil also is still warm enough for some root growth, so I plant new trees and shrubs and move old ones around. Autumn and spring rains will settle these plants in place and give them a jump on spring. A thick mulch is needed, though, to prevent widely fluctuating soil temperatures in the coming months from heaving these plants out of the soil before they are well rooted.

The first indoor blossoms appear this month, on a cactus. But after a summer and early autumn overflowing with color, I have to keep reminding myself to look at the carmine flowers.

October 5

First Frost — The first frost of autumn traditionally descends on my garden in early October, although sometimes it shows up at the end of September. If severe, it brings the season of summer vegetables and flowers to a dramatic end. Tomato, eggplant, and cucumber plants suddenly darken and turn limp, bowing out to the succulent green cabbages, broccolis, and lettuces of autumn; the bright, summery colors of marigolds and zinnias are replaced by the subdued autumn colors of chrysanthemums.

The date for the arrival of the first fall frost is unpredictable. Even in the county where I live, the frost date for the year varies by a week or more. Mountaintop gardens are always colder, but on those still, clear nights when cold air settles to the ground and then flows downhill, my low-lying garden is struck first.

I prepare for the first frost *before* it occurs. There is no need to attend to perennial plants: trees, shrubs, and vines; flowers such as daisies and daylilies; and vegetables such as asparagus and rhubarb. They all are hardy. The same is true for certain annual flowers, such as snapdragons and pansies, and vegetables such as lettuce, cabbage, and root crops. It is the tender plants that succumb to that first frost — vegetables such as tomatoes, peppers, eggplants, squashes, and beans, and flowers such as marigolds, zinnias, and dahlias.

If the first frost arrives at the garden gate earlier than usual, I throw a blanket or plastic sheet over the tender plants for protection. Plants are better protected if the covering is held off the foliage by stakes. (This is an advantage of staked tomato plants; the stakes are already in place.) Some years, an early, light frost is followed by a long, balmy Indian summer, and if I can keep that first frost from nipping tender plants, I can eke out a few extra vine-ripe tomatoes and bush-ripe peppers in autumn.

If the temperature is going to plummet fast and low, I start picking. I remember one such crisp autumn evening — I raced the setting sun and frantically filled baskets with tomatoes and peppers, and jars of water with the last marigolds of the season . . . a last-ditch effort to hang onto summer. Tomatoes lined the kitchen windowsills for over a month. (Incidently, kitchen windowsills may be a convenient place to ripen tomatoes, but tomatoes do not need light to ripen.)

Some years, that first hard frost postpones its visit to my garden until late October. This has been one such year. Tender plants have remained alive, although waning, through the month as temperatures gradually cooled and days shortened. Even before hard frost finally arrives, I pick tomatoes to ripen indoors where their flavor develops better than those ripened in the chilly outdoors. When late frost in a year like this finally arrives, it lacks the drama of an early frost.

October 9

Choice Apples — In a couple of Octobers hence, I hope to harvest bushels of apples from my young trees. One of these trees is called 'Esopus Spitzenburg'. What a name! Now why would I plant such a tree, especially when this variety is known to bear only moderate crops and be susceptible to apple scab? I planted this tree strictly for its flavor.

In the more than two thousand years that apples have been cultivated, thousands of chance seedlings have been selected for some meritorious quality; they were named, and then clonally propagated (by grafting). Yesterday, I harvested some 'Lady' apples (one of my more precocious trees). This small apple, occasionally seen in markets around Christmas-time, is the same variety that was cultivated in France at least four hundred years ago.

At one time, each apple-growing region in this country had its own local favorites — 'Newtown Pippin' on northern Long Island, 'Fameuse' along the Saint Lawrence River, 'Willow' and 'Gilpin' from West Virginia, 'York Imperial' from Pennsylvania. Commercial growers now must choose varieties that grow, ship, and store well. Red apples must be all red, and green apples must be all green. Flavors need to appeal equally to consumers from New York to Nebraska to New Mexico.

In my garden, though, I can plant any one of the more than five thousand(!) apple varieties that strikes my fancy. I can choose varieties without regard to their appearance, shelf life, or any other commercial attribute. Here's a list of some of the apples I have planted, all chosen on the basis of one quality — flavor. They may have other shortcomings, but they all taste great!

'Esopus Spitzenburg' heads my list. This old American apple does not have the appearance needed for today's commercial markets but, as pomologist William Coxe said in 1817, Spitz "possesses great beauty, and exquisite flavour." The crisp fruit has a skin that is rich yellow and covered with a commingling of bright and dark red. Thomas Jefferson, as skillful a plantsman as he was a statesman, preferred 'Spitzenburg' to all other apples.

Many good-tasting apples come from England. Two hundred years ago, a seedling apple tree that had sprung up in a cottage garden in Cornwall bore a crop of ugly fruit, russeted brownish red over an olive base. But the tree was preserved because the flavor of the apples, now known as 'Cornish Gilliflower', is supreme — a rich sweetness, with a hint of clove. 'Ashmead's Kernel', another delectable, old variety, originated more than two hundred years ago in Dr. Ashmead's garden in Gloucester. The fruit is russeted golden brown with a reddish bronze cheek where struck by sunlight. Inside: a delicious, crisp, yellow flesh. 'Cox's Orange Pippin' is still popular in England. The fruit is small, and some years it cracks just before harvest. The color, orange and red, washed with carmine over a yellow background, might look good to some, but this apple is not for markets that demand pure red, shiny apples. 'Cox' is an apple prized for its flavor. The English grow it commercially in spite of its faults.

From across the channel in France comes 'Calville Blanc d'Hiver'. This variety was grown more than three hundred years ago in the garden of King Louis XIII and is still served in some Parisian restaurants. The fruit is slightly lobed and has a skin that is smooth and light, like porcelain. Its tender, spicy flesh, with just a hint of banana, blends well with cheese for dessert.

I am not partial only to old varieties. I also have planted 'Jonagold' and 'Spigold', both introduced about thirty years ago by the New York State Agricultural Experimental Station. 'Jonagold' combines the flavors of its parents, the sprightly 'Jonathan' and the aromatic 'Golden Delicious'. The large fruits are yellow with a splash of light scarlet. 'Spigold', the offspring from a mating of 'Golden Delicous' with 'Northern Spy', surpasses both of its parents in quality. 'Jonagold' and 'Spigold' both have a "cracking" flavor — they are crisp, but when you bite into them, they explode in your mouth with juice and flavor.

Another new variety, 'Mutsu', was introduced by Japanese breeders in 1948. This large, round, yellow apple has a delicate spicy flavor. The texture is pleasantly coarse, reminiscent of biting into a snowball.

The variety 'Melrose', introduced in 1944 by the Ohio Agricultural Experimental Station, is now the official Ohio state apple. In 'Melrose', the tartness of one parent, 'Jonathan', is tempered with some of the sweetness of its other parent, 'Red Delicious'. The trees are productive and reputedly begin bearing at a young age (mine have not begun yet).

From down under in New Zealand comes 'Gala', which I consider one of the best early apples — juicy and sweet. In contrast to most other early apples, 'Gala' stores well until Christmas. This golden yellow apple, with a pink-orange blush, looks as good as it tastes. It is so precocious that it bore fruit the season after I planted it.

To squeeze all these apple varieties into my backyard, I made the trees by grafting branches onto special dwarfing rootstocks. The dwarf trees, only four feet apart in the row, bear full-sized fruits. These plants are not easy to grow. Although the rootstocks keep the plants small, I also have to prune summer and winter to keep them within their allotted space. And I have to spray for insects and diseases. Nonetheless, I expect to be rewarded for my efforts with years of good eating.

October 10

Endive — Pinch your nose with your fingers and say the word *on*. Follow that with a long, drawn-out, *d-e-e-e-e-v*, curling up the corners of your mouth in a smile to get full emphasis on the *e*'s. Endive. Because this vegetable leaves something to be desired in pure, unabashed flavor, it needs the highfalutin pronunciation of its name.

Endive's lackluster flavor is offset by the ease with which it is grown, by its cold-hardiness, and by its attractive, frilly leaves (used in restaurants seemingly only for decorative purposes, where a leaf or two might be found lying beneath anything from a taco to a T-bone). Endive may not add much flavor to a salad, but the lacy texture contrasts nicely with the flatness of most lettuce and spinach leaves.

Before going any further, let's make sure we are talking about the same leafy vegetable, because the common names can be confusing. The endive of present interest is *Cichorium endiva.* This botanical name also applies to a smooth-leaved endive, commonly called escarole.

But the real confusion arises because another plant, *Cichorium intybus*, is known as French endive. To complicate matters further, French endive also is known as Belgian endive and witloof chicory. French endives (or Belgian endives, witloof chicories — whatever you want to call them) are those small, anemic, torpedo-shaped heads of tightly folded leaves flown to our grocers from Europe and sold at high prices. Common endive has another ritzy cousin in that same species as French endive: radicchio.

I planted common endive (*C. endiva)* this summer, and now is the time to start making it palatable. One leaf under a taco tastes okay, but a whole head of dark-green endive is too bitter to eat. Bitterness is removed from the plant by blanching. Once the plant makes a tight rosette of leaves, the idea is to exclude light from the heart of the plant, which turns it pale, succulent, and less bitter.

There are a number of ways to accomplish this blanching, all of which I have tried at various times. Easiest is to just gather together the leaves of each endive plant, then hold them in place with a rubber band. The problem with this method is that if it rains hard and is warm after the heads are closed up, they rot. Sometimes I instead invert a clay flowerpot over each head (clay is better than plastic, because clay breathes), or just lay a wooden board on top of the plants. You would think that laying boards down would flatten the heads. It does, somewhat. Some gardeners blanch endives by digging up and repotting them for growing in a dark cellar, but I do not think this method is worth the trouble.

The amount of time required for blanching depends on the temperature. In warm weather, blanching might be finished in a couple of weeks; in cold weather, longer.

One reason endive is such an ideal salad green for cool weather is precisely because it needs to be blanched. When frost threatens, I scurry out to the garden and cover various plants to keep them from freezing. Well, besides endive's inherent cold-hardiness, it already is covered while it is being blanched!

I prefer to grow endive as an autumn crop only. For autumn harvest, I sow the seeds in flats in early July, then transplant the seedlings out to the garden in late August. Because I was late in sowing endive this year, my plants probably will not produce enough growth to make blanchable heads. I guess I will just use the less elegant, dark-green leaves, and pronounce the plant's name in a similarly less elegant manner, just rolling together the mundane words *end* and *dive*.

October 12

Bittersweet — My vision became blurred with dollar signs as I looked out the car window at mile after mile of bittersweet (*Celastrus scandens*) clambering over trees along a stretch of parkway. That was a few years ago, as I was driving back from a visit to New York City. While there, I had wandered into a florist's shop, where I had been stunned by the price for a few sprigs of bittersweet. A quick mental calculation as I gazed out the car window told me there was gold in them thar' trees.

My financial empire crumbled before it even had a chance to grow. In some states — including New York — bittersweet is a protected plant. Anyone harvesting a protected plant from private property in New York without the landowner's permission is subject to a fine of $25 per plant.

To look at bittersweet, you might very well mistake it for a weed. A rampant, fast-growing vine, it will climb skyward twenty feet or more if given support. Bittersweet can engulf small trees and shrubs, even kill them by twining around, then strangling them. And bittersweet is not found in restricted ecological niches over a small geographic area. The plant grows wild in thickets and along roadsides over an area bounded by southeastern Canada across to the Dakotas, south to Texas, and then back across to North Carolina.

Whether looked on as a weed or as a plant worthy of protection, bittersweet is in its glory now. Neither the leaves nor the flowers (long, whitish panicles in June) are noteworthy. Most seasons the plant is all the more inconspicuous because it gets lost in a tangle of other wild shrubs and small trees.

But now, as the thin, yellow coating of each fruit flares open to contrast and expose the three-lobed, orange capsule within, bittersweet suddenly comes into focus. The bright fruits will last well into winter, cheering up the grays and browns of that season and sparkling against white snow. Indoors, the fruits add color to dried flower arrangements. (The fruit is poisonous, so take precautions with toddlers in the home.)

I now am content to admire and pick just a few sprigs from the bittersweet vines I found growing along the abandoned railroad bed behind my property. But any other gardener who chooses to plant bittersweet must know something about sex. Bittersweet is regarded as polygamodioecious or dioecious. The first botanical mouthful means that each plant has some flowers with male and female parts and some flowers that are partly female or male. Dioecious means that individual plants are either male or female. Only female flowers produce fruit, and to do so they must be pollinated by a male. (In practical terms, this means plant two vines and hope.)

Anyone who has seen bittersweet run wild can correctly surmise that it is not finicky as to site. Full sun or part shade is suitable, although plants bear fruit more profusely in full sun. Soil can be rich or poor. Poor soil and some pruning help keep plants in bounds. Aesthetically, a rampant plant like bittersweet is at home in the same habitat it invades in the wild: rambling over banks and rough stone walls, and up old trees.

Late flash: Visions of my financial empire have come into focus. It turns out that most of the wild bittersweet I see is the *unprotected* Chinese bittersweet (*C. orbiculatus*), which has escaped from cultivation and run rampant in the Northeast. The plants, including their fruits, are very similar in appearance to our native bittersweet.

Birdhouse Gourds — My old birdhouse finally showed signs of decay after about five years, so this past spring I decided to grow another one. That's right: *grow* another one. Gourds have been used by humans for thousands of years for decoration, pottery, musical instruments, and water dippers. So why not a birdhouse?

The seeds I planted five springs ago came from a packet actually labeled "birdhouse gourd." In late May of that year, I planted a few of these seeds in full sun in well-drained, fertile soil. The vines grew many feet long, and soon swellings formed behind each female flower. By season's end, each fruit had developed a thick neck at the stem end and, at the far end, had swelled out into a round bulb measuring almost a foot across. The gourd was very easy to grow, about the same as winter squash (a close relative), except that the gourd seemed less bothered by the cucumber beetles and vine borers that afflict squash.

To become a serviceable birdhouse, a gourd needs to have a hard rind and to be hollow inside. The rind does not thicken until the gourd is fully mature, at which point the stem dries and shrivels where it is attached to the fruit. I delayed harvest as long as possible, but before the first hard frost I cut off all mature fruits, taking care to leave a piece of stem attached and to avoid bruising.

The inside of a gourd dries if the fruit is kept warm and dry. I cut a one-inch-wide hole in the thick part of the fruit to let moisture escape and to provide a future entrance for the birds, then set the fruits in the warm, dry loft above my garage. The gourds dried (I shook out loose seeds and pulp), I coated the rinds with shellac (in retrospect, the rind was thick enough on this type of gourd so that coating was unnecessary), I hung the gourds in trees, and the birds moved in.

Now let's move up to the present season, five years later. Gourds come in all shapes and sizes, and although all gourds are in the same family (Cucurbitaceae), they also represent a few different genera. In addition to birdhouse gourd (*Cucurbita Pepo* var. *ovifera*), there are Turk's turban gourd (*C. maxima*), club gourd (*Trichosanthes Anguina*), serpent gourd (*Lagenaria siceraria*), and hedgehog gourd (*Cucumis Anguria*), to name just a few. Although I used the same seed batch as five years ago, it seems that at least one of the seeds I planted this past spring was not that of a birdhouse gourd. Unfortunately, I thinned my one hill to only two seedlings, one of which grew to shade the other into unfruitfulness.

Throughout this past summer, the one vine grew, eventually reaching about twenty-five feet in length. Yet it produced only one fruit. This one fruit, alone gobbling up nourishment provided by all those leaves, grew rapidly but was not recognizable as a birdhouse, or even a Turk's turban, club, or any other type of gourd. Gourds sometimes hybridize, producing unusual fruits not falling into any defined category, so perhaps this plant was from an accidentally hybridized seed.

My growing monster was round, ridged, and salmon colored, so bore some resemblance to a pumpkin. My gourd also had a large growth, like the navel on a navel orange, on its bottom. (Before seeing the navel, I thought I might accidentally have planted some seeds my brother had given me of giant pumpkins.)

The gourd finally matured and I harvested it last week. The hundred-plus pound giant obviously is unsuitable for a birdhouse, so the birds will have to wait another year before I can set up lodging for them. After I plant seeds next spring, I will allow more seedlings to develop, then watch the developing fruits closely so I can quickly rogue out plants with any fruit shapes I do not want.

This season's giant gourd is not wasted, though. I lugged it into my car and drove it to the home of my brother, who lives nearby, for a birthday present — an ersatz Halloween pumpkin.

October 23

Geraniums — My geraniums are still alive and outside, growing in pots in a sheltered nook where the brick walls of my house and garage come together at a right angle. But before an icy chill turns the geranium leaves to mush, killing the plants, I will lug the pots indoors. Here the plants will spend the winter, and next spring I will put them out again as I have in springs past. Why not keep the plants growing year after year? In faraway Cape of Good Hope, the geranium is a native, perennial shrub; closer to home, old geraniums outgrowing their terra-cotta pots in sunny delicatessen and pizza shop windows attest to the plants' perennial nature.

Before delving into the "how" of overwintering geraniums, let's make sure we have the same plant in mind. Plants usually called geraniums are not really in the botanical genus *Geranium*, but are members of a related genus, *Pelargonium*. My geraniums, and probably yours also, are of the bedding, or zonal, type, characterized by their leaves' fragrance and horseshoe-shaped zone of color. This type of geranium is a hybrid mostly of *Pelargonium zonale* and *P. inquinans*, and is designated *P.* × *hortorum*. Other geraniums include the ivy geranium (*P. peltatum*), a trailing plant with shiny, unscented leaves and usually grown in hanging baskets; and Lady Washington geranium (*P.* × *domesticum*), with large, pansylike flowers and usually grown in Europe (this latter type does not like our hot summers).

With the right conditions, a potted zonal geranium can do more than just survive winters indoors; it can be coaxed to bloom through the winter. All that is needed is to duplicate indoors the bright, dry, and cool conditions of South Africa (or those sunny delicatessen and pizza shop windows). In practical terms, this means the sunniest window of the coolest room — 55 degrees Fahrenheit nights and 65 degree days are ideal. The plants also must be kept on the dry side.

I overwinter more geraniums than I have sunny window space for, so I carry extra plants through the winter in a semidormant state. The traditional recommendation has been

either to knock a plant out of its pot or to dig a plant from a garden bed, then hang the plant upside down, root ball intact, in a cellar. Trouble is, the traditional cellar was dark and very cool in winter — much cooler and darker than mine and a far cry from the linoleum-floored, wood-paneled, heated basements of some modern homes.

The secret to carrying geraniums through winters in this age is to balance the amount of light and warmth the plants receive. The less light on the plants, the cooler they must be. The plants even tolerate a few degrees below freezing, so an unheated attic might suffice.

I have doubts about the "hanging upside down" part of the traditional recommendation. Probably, the basement of yesteryear also was wet, and hanging kept the plants dry. And this brings us to the next part of carrying geraniums through the winter — watering. The more slowed-down a plant is, the more susceptible it is to rotting; therefore, the cooler the temperature, the less water the plants need. I keep geraniums in a fairly dark corner of my basement, with almost no water at all, just an occasional moistening of the soil whenever the stems start to shrivel.

No matter how zonal geraniums are overwintered, near winter's end their sap begins to stir. At this point, unless new shoots are pale and spindly, I clip all stems to within a few inches of the soil line. Pale, spindly shoots indicate a weakened plant, caused by some combination of insufficient light and temperatures that were too warm. Such plants need their leaves and should not be pruned until their new shoots are stocky and dark green.

No matter what the stems look like, I repot all my geranium plants in spring. I scratch away some of the old, worn-out soil from the exposed root ball and firmly tamp new soil around the roots. Then the plants are ready for growth in earnest.

October 29

Cyclamen — I have always liked cyclamens, and when I saw *Cyclamen persicum* 'Dwarf Fragrance Mixed' seeds for sale in a catalog, I knew the time had come to grow them. Almost two years have elapsed since I sowed that packet of cyclamen seeds, and just now two plants are blooming. Cyclamens are fairly difficult to grow, even starting with full-sized plants, but I reasoned that by starting with seeds I would get: (1) a type of cyclamen perhaps otherwise unobtainable; (2) the satisfaction of raising a difficult plant from seed to flowering size; and (3) more cyclamens for my money. And, if anyone thought the plants humdrum, at least they would have the distinction of being grown from seed rather than purchased already in bloom.

Germination of cyclamen seeds is rated intermediate in difficulty ("Some Experience Useful") by Thompson & Morgan, the company from whom I purchased the seed packet. Germination was expected to be very slow, so I sowed the seeds in a flowerpot filled with pasteurized potting soil. I pasteurized the potting soil because I did not want any weeds to grow or hungry bacteria and fungi to gobble up the seeds in the long interim between sowing and growing. I watered the pot, then sealed it in a plastic bag and put it in a part of

my basement where the temperature hovered around 60 degrees Fahrenheit, as per sowing instructions. That was in March.

I had forgotten about the seeds except for occasional peeks when I went down to the basement for some other reason, and in June I was excited to see three pale shoots breaking through the soil. What to do? The seedlings now needed some light, but how much? Cyclamens are shade-loving plants, and tender sprouts just emerging from moist, dark soil in a dark basement would be especially susceptible to sunburn. I decided on a good cyclamen habitat — outdoors, in the shade at the base of my potted fig tree. The fig was in the sun, but evidently cast just the right amount of shade on the pot of cyclamen seedlings, for the seedlings grew, waning only once when I tried to speed their growth by moving them to a sunnier spot. They grew slowly, but they grew, and by summer's end each seedling had graduated to its very own pot.

Before the weather turned cold last autumn, I moved the plants indoors to a sunny eastern window, hoping for blossoms. Instead the plants continued slowly growing only leaves. Unless you are waiting for flowers, cyclamen leaves happen to be quite attractive — a rich shade of green, mottled with a pale-green rim near the rounded edge. They are at least as decorative as the leaves of peperomia, a plant grown for its leaves alone.

Cyclamens, amaryllises, tulips, and other plants with storage roots have an annual dormant period, which often is a prerequisite to flowering. Cyclamens are cool-weather plants, so when hot weather approached this past summer, I decided to let my cyclamens take a rest. When the smallest of my three cyclamens began to flag in the heat, I decided to help nature take her course and gradually withheld water from that plant. Sad to say, that plant still may be in a coma somewhere in my compost pile. It never revived. It was the runt of the lot anyway and, to quote one of my encyclopedias, ". . . a certain percent [of cyclamen seedlings] will not grow, no matter how much persuasion is used."

I did water the other two plants through the summer, and each week a new leaf would emerge . . . until a month ago, when I noticed flower buds, and, now, flowers! They start out light pink, gradually darkening as they unfurl; then they become like scarlet butterflies fluttering a few inches above the leaves. The flowers have a slight, delicate fragrance.

I have learned some things about growing cyclamens beyond the seedling stage. (The Thompson & Morgan rating for cultivation of grown-up cyclamens is: "Needs Understanding and Care.") A cyclamen prefers bottom watering, because water on top of the plant too easily rots its leaves. I let my cyclamens draw water up from the saucers in which the pots sit. The soil for cyclamens should be kept evenly moist, never dry and never sodden. This means giving the plants a bit of water every day while they are blooming.

Cyclamens like moisture-laden air. I leave a little extra water in the saucer below each pot, and this water evaporates and rises around the plant. Cyclamens would not last long in an overheated, forced-air heated house.

Cyclamens like bright, but not intense, sunlight. This means dappled shade in summer, and a thin gauze curtain between the plant and a sunny south window in winter. I keep my plants in the direct light of an east window.

My two blooming plants will never be urged into dormancy; they will have to show their own strong inclinations in that direction.

October 30

Record Keeping — Before the details of this season's garden meld together in my mind with those of previous seasons', I had better start recording what happened. I have to remember where I planted broccoli and tomatoes so that I do not plant them in the same locations for another three or four years. I want to write down that fourteen tomato plants was just the right amount for fresh eating and canning, but that eighteen heads of cabbage — now waiting for me out in the garden — are too many. And those endives — I must write a note to remind myself to sow endive seeds in future seasons in the middle of July rather than in early August, as I did this year.

Any drudgery of garden record keeping is more than offset by the increased enjoyment it brings to gardening. No longer need I feel obligated to plant every seedling I grow (as I did with cabbages this year). No longer need I wonder if it is too early or too late to plant peas. My garden notes remind me to be ready for flea beetles on eggplants in early June and that a five-foot row of parsnips is more than enough.

One type of garden record contains information that remains essentially the same each year. For instance, seed sowing dates need not vary from one year to the next. I tabulate this information on a few sheets of paper, with a heading for each month, then a subheading for the week (OCTOBER, WEEK ONE; OCTOBER, WEEK TWO; and so on) of each month. For each week, I list the seeds to sow outdoors, the seeds to sow indoors, and the transplants to set in the garden. When I look at the list the first week in April, I know it is time to sow peppers indoors and to plant peas outdoors. I include reminders to drape bird netting over the blueberries during week four in June and to bring houseplants indoors the second week in September. My current week-by-week calendar, which changes only as I perfect my timing or change what I grow, is appended.

Notes about varieties also are the type of information that only need updating. For instance, under the heading of tomato varieties, I note that the much-acclaimed 'Bonny Best' and 'Big Boy', which I tried many years ago, are admittedly good tomatoes but do not compare in flavor with great tomatoes like 'Sweet 100', 'Gardeners' Delight', 'Carmello', and 'Belgian Giant'. (And why grow anything but the best tomatoes?)

Another type of garden record, such as the map of the vegetable garden, is never the same from one year to the next. I drew a map of the bare bones of the garden's layout, then made enough photocopies so that I could fill in details each year about planting everything from beans to zucchini.

From here on, my record keeping becomes more chaotic. The little calendar I carry around in my back pocket is where I jot down anything from when I actually planted potatoes, to when the first morning glory blossom opened, to when I have an appointment to visit the dentist. On the wooden stake that marks each garden row, I write the name of the variety I have planted, the planting date, and sometimes even the date I harvest. These inexpensive stakes last just long enough for me to read and jot down the information from them at the end of the season.

Speaking of jotting down information, I also keep a record of when I build and turn each compost pile so that I will know when the compost will be ready to spread. And I record any sprays that I use each season. I also might make note of a particularly successful planting, such as the bed this year in which broccoli, planted in the middle, was flanked on one side by soybeans and the other by carrots.

Sometime in midwinter, I will gather together all these sheets of paper, my pocket calender, and those half-rotted wooden stakes. I will transcribe pertinent information to my week-by-week list of what to do, and start planning for the forthcoming season. JANUARY, WEEK TWO is an appropriate time for this activity.

NOVEMBER

Dry leaves upon the wall,
Which flap like rustling wings and seek escape,
A single frosted cluster on the grape,
Still hangs — and that is all.

Susan Coolidge, "November"

IT IS NOT OVER YET, outdoors. A few hardy vegetables and flowers hang on into November — actually, quite a few in the early part of the month. But one night, before the end of the month, the tops of annual vegetables and flowers will be burned dead by hard frost. The final scene is not elegiac: the garden goes into winter trim and neat, the shrub and flower beds covered with a thick, gray-brown blanket of leaves or wood chips, and the vegetable garden layered with a dark-brown icing of compost.

As everything quiets, I attend to some of the more mundane details of gardening. Before the ground freezes solid, I fill buckets, one each, with compost and garden soil to use for potting mixes as I prepare amaryllis, narcissus, and freesia bulbs for indoor blooms. Shovels get scraped clean of dirt, sharpened, then oiled. Rainfall will meet the water needs of plants in this cool autumn weather, so, in anticipation of winter, I finally turn off outdoor water spigots from inside the house and drain watering cans, then hang them from the garage rafters.

Brussels Sprouts — Today I inadvertently complied with Myth Number One of the Five Myths of Growing Brussels Sprouts — I harvested my first sprouts of the season after the plants had been nipped by frost. Frost reputedly sweetens the sprouts, but I have never tasted a sweet brussels sprout. (Their flavor is admittedly rank in hot weather, though.) Actually, my harvest follows quite a few frosts, and the reason for the delay was because I had to finish attending to squashes, peppers, tomatoes, and other plants that are ruined by frost.

Myth Number Two of Growing Brussels Sprouts states that piling dirt up around the bases of the plants will keep the plants upright. I wish this were true. My brussels sprouts plants always flop to one side before they finally decide to grow straight up, making the plants messy and ruining the sprouts at the bottom of the stem. A hundred years ago, the great French olericulturalist Vilmorin-Andrieux wrote that there was no benefit in earthing up, so I have never tried it. And anyway, this pile of dirt would bury those basal sprouts I was trying to save.

Myths Number Three and Four are better grounded in plant physiology than are the others. Number Three directs to pinch out the growing point of the stem toward the end of the growing season, to force development of the sprouts. Because the topmost growing point of any plant releases a hormone, called auxin, which inhibits development of side buds, and because each brussels sprout is a side bud, this pinching should work. Myth Number Four directs to remove lower leaves as the sprouts they subtend reach almost full size. Leaves also release auxin, which inhibits development of side buds in their axils, so leaf removal should stimulate sprout development. Regardless, I list these two directives under myths because, theory aside, I have never observed any effect of either practice.

The final myth, Myth Number Five, alleges that firming the soil when planting brussels sprouts results in firmer sprouts. I think all this firming business is more misplaced cause and effect: firm the soil, and your sprouts become firm. I may as well (but do not) loosen the soil for loose leaf lettuces.

I am a bit uneasy debunking myths about growing brussels sprouts, because these directives come mostly from England, land of venerable gardeners, where brussels sprouts are held in high esteem. Nonetheless, one has to be careful translating gardening from English conditions to conditions around here. England's climate is very different from ours. I now give brussels sprouts no special treatment, growing them in the same way as I grow cabbage and broccoli, except that I must allot brussels sprouts a whole season of space in the garden.

There were many seasons years ago in which I did not grow brussels sprouts, mostly because of the poor-quality sprouts the plants produced. The past three seasons, though, I have harvested good crops of tight sprouts. I attribute my latterly success not to my adherance to The Five Myths, but to my growing a variety, such as 'Captain Marvel', that tolerates our hot summers.

I also did not grow brussels sprouts in some seasons because I felt ambivalent about the taste of this vegetable. A friend with a wry sense of humor once called brussels sprouts "little green balls of death." Now I am thinking that maybe I misheard her, and she was just pointing out that of all vegetables, this one tastes best cooked as the English cook their vegetables, a "little boiled to death." M-m-m-m-m.

November 13

Garden Cleanup — Now that outdoor gardening activity is grinding to a halt, I begin my cleanup. Cleaning up is a good excuse to get outdoors, and it can be done at a more leisurely pace now than in the spring. But most important, a good cleanup now will decrease weed, insect, and disease problems next year.

Since flowers have faded and harvest has wound down, my attention has been distracted away from the garden; in the interim, weeds have claimed new ground. Ground ivy slowly but surely crept under the privet hedge, and bedstraw appears in what was once a weed-free row of lettuce. Roots of perennial weeds are rushing to establish themselves as freezing weather arrests growth. Time now spent keeping weeds in line will be rewarded in spring.

Insect pests have prepared their winter quarters. Corn borers have settled into old cornstalks from which they will awaken next summer, and apple maggots are crawling out of fallen fruit to find a congenial home in the soil. Shaggy pouches woven by bagworms are hanging from white cedars like drab-colored Christmas ornaments. From the pupae of cabbage loopers now attached to cabbages and broccolis will emerge cabbage-hungry worms next spring. By digging old corn stubble out of the garden, picking up fallen apples, clipping off bagworm bags, and cleaning up the remains of cabbage and broccoli plants, I cut short the careers of borers, maggots, bagworms, and loopers. As a result, I will have less problems with these insects next season.

Diseases also have found suitable niches in which to spend the winter. Old leaves are a favorite haunt. Next season's black spot of rose, scab of apple, and botrytis and leaf blotch of peony come from this season's infected leaves. I gather up the fallen leaves of these plants. Powdery mildew of zinnia spends the winter in infected zinnia leaves and stems. Infected stems also are winter home to black knot of plums (the knots look like blobs of tar on the stems). I go at those stems with pruning shears.

Other diseases spend the winter on rotted fruits and tubers. Black rot of grapes, brown rot of peaches and plums, and blueberry mummy berry will awaken next spring from mummified fruits left hanging on plants this autumn. I also gather these, or bury them beneath a thick mulch. Late blight of potatoes overwinters on potatoes left in the ground. When I dig potatoes, I try to get them *all* out of the ground, even those not fit to eat.

What do I do with the weeds, mummified fruits, and scabby leaves that I gather up? I do not burn them or pack them in plastic bags to be carted off to the dump. I would have a hard time trying to burn succulent cabbage stalks, and burning destroys everything: not only pests, but also beneficial insects or diseases that might be at this moment devouring them. Most important, weeds, diseased plants, even cabbage loopers and other insect pests, are made of organic matter and nutrients. Ironically, the bodies of those same weed, insect, and disease pests that once threatened the garden can be recycled to nourish future crops. I cart all garden debris to my compost pile, where heat and hungry organisms transform everything to nutrient-rich humus that I eventually spread over the garden.

Autumn cleanup is important, but I do not advocate a sterile landscape. A few old stalks and browned flower heads catch swirling snow, the "poor man's manure" of French gardeners, and beautify the winter scenery. Autumn cleanup will not solve all pest problems. Pests with an innate wanderlust still will find their way to my plants from neighbors' yards. But autumn cleanup is one of many cultural practices that keeps inimical weeds, insects, and diseases in check.

November 14

Trees from Seed — Seeds still are clinging to the almost-bare stems of sugar and Norway maples, hornbeams, redbuds, and sycamores. And squirrels must have missed a few acorns and walnuts from beneath oak and black walnut trees. Planted now, these seeds will grow into trees for the next century.

With such aspirations, I dropped an apple seed one autumn day decades ago into some potting soil in an eight-inch clay flowerpot. I wish I could write that that seed now has grown into a majestic old tree. But no. The seed germinated and the tree started to grow, then stalled at about four inches in height. The reason for the abrupt halt was because apple seeds, like those of many other hardy trees, need special pretreatment before they will germinate and grow. (Usually, tree seeds planted as I planted them do not grow at all.)

This behavior is not without logic. If an apple or maple seed grew as soon as it touched the ground in late summer or early autumn, the life of the tender young seedlings would be short indeed, snuffed out with the first frosty autumn night. Tree seeds that ripen in autumn usually have an innate mechanism that prevents them from growing until they have been exposed to a certain amount of cool weather, that is, until the seeds have been convinced that winter is over.

The way to grow such seeds is to keep them cool and moist for a couple of months, thus fooling them into behaving as if winter were over. I have grown many trees from seeds since that false start with the apple years ago. Nowadays, I pack the seeds into plastic bags along with moist sand, vermiculite, sphagnum moss, or even cotton — any material that will envelop the seeds with moisture, without becoming sodden. Then I put the bag into the refrigerator or garage. Creating this artificial winter for seeds is known as stratification, because nursery workers chill large quantities of seeds by packing alternating layers (strata) of seeds and moist sphagnum moss into boxes. Of course, seeds could be sown directly in the ground outside, but this imperils them to squirrels, birds, flooding, and other natural hazards.

Seeds kept cool and moist will germinate as soon as they have accumulated a requisite number of hours of chilling, which varies depending on species. For instance, a sugar maple seed needs three to four months at about 40 degrees Fahrenheit before it will grow. Other tree seeds need different amounts of chilling: two to three months for crabapples and tulip trees, two to four months for hemlock, four months for dogwood. Cool, not cold, temperature awakens a seed from its dormancy, so no time is put into the chilling "bank" when the temperature gets too cold, below about 32 degrees, or too hot, above about 50 degrees.

Some seeds have a hard coating that must be made permeable to water before the seed is stratified. Nick seed coats with a file or soften them in dank warmth before stratification. Redbud, juniper, and hornbeam are examples of tree seeds needing this treatment. To soften such seeds, I pack them into the plastic bags, as directed above, but leave the bags in a warm room for two or three months before stratification.

Not all tree seeds need stratification before they will germinate. Two examples of trees in this class are catalpa and sycamore (although sycamore's relative, the London planetree, does need stratification). Perhaps catalpa and sycamore seeds do not need stratification because they hang on the trees late enough into the winter so that by the time they drop to moist ground, temperatures are too cold for germination. Or else it is spring, and just the right time for germination.

I keep a close eye on seeds stratifying in the refrigerator, because once the requisite hours of chilling are fulfilled, some types of seeds (apple is one of them) sprout suddenly, as if a switch had been turned on. Once I see fat, white roots emerging, I either pot up the seeds or keep them cool enough to hold back growth until it is time for outdoor planting.

Now for the hard part: I try to picture the tree thirty years hence before planting a seedling in a permanent location. One can develop a special affection for a tree raised from a seed, and if I plant the seedling where I will not want a tree in the future, I may not have the heart to cut it down. Remember, "tall oaks from little acorns grow." Likewise for maples, sycamores, junipers, and other trees.

You perhaps wonder why would anyone go to the trouble of planting these seemingly delicate seeds when you can just buy a sturdy young tree at a nursery. Hey, you're reading this, aren't you? You're a gardener; you like to grow plants.

November 15

Turnips — I just sank my teeth into a freshly harvested, crisp turnip. This may not seem like a big deal — unless you have never tasted a turnip grown to perfection.

True, a basketful of even perfect turnips is not nearly as desirable as a basketful of peaches. But the lowly turnip has much to offer. The roots can be sweet and juicy, good either raw or cooked. The plant extends the harvest season from the vegetable garden well into autumn and winter. The roots of my turnips look and taste just as fresh as they did a month ago, in spite of a few nights when the mercury plummeted to the low teens. (The tops are looking a bit ragged.) And turnips are nutritious. Gram for gram, the tops have more than twice the calcium of milk, and almost a third the iron of liver. A turnip root has about the same amount of vitamin C as an orange, and four times that amount of vitamin C is found in the turnip greens.

There is not much to growing turnips — looking in almost any gardening book, I find less said about growing turnips than just about any other vegetable. The secret to

growing perfect turnips is to sow the seed thinly in a reasonably rich soil at the right time. "Inexperienced growers almost always plant turnips too thickly," states one book. Under these conditions, the seedlings must be thinned ruthlessly, or good yield and quality will be sacrificed. I sow just a few seeds every inch of row, then sometimes thin, but evidently not enough, for the bulbous roots always seem to be elbowing each other out of line by the time they reach full size. In my rich, loose soil, a little shoving around does not slow growth enough to make the roots sharp tasting or woody.

AUGUST, WEEK TWO is when my garden records say to sow turnips for a harvest of sweet, crisp roots during the similarly crisp days of autumn. Turnips sown in early spring for a summer crop tend to send up seed stalks before forming full-sized, or particularly good-tasting, roots.

I said the turnip has much to offer, and even this ostensibly bad habit of premature "bolting to seed" has been turned to an asset. The seed stalk that emerges visually resembles, and indeed tastes like, a small broccoli shoot. Some turnips grown in Italy are cultivated specifically for these shoots, called *broccoli di rapa*, raab broccoli, or *cima di rapa* ("shoot of the turnip"). Cooked with a bit of water and garlic, then drizzled with olive oil, the sprouts are delicious. Any turnip will do for broccoli raab, although some varieties have been bred specifically for this use.

Excess turnips maturing in autumn from summer-sown seeds also can be induced to become broccoli raab. The turnip is normally a biennial plant, which means it grows roots one season and then sends up a flower stalk its second season (behavior often gone awry in spring-sown turnips). As winter settles in, a thick mulch can keep turnips fresh. Come spring, unharvested roots will still be alive and, with warm weather, will — lo and behold — send up seed stalks. As with broccoli, harvesting the stalks before the flowers open is important.

Another secret to growing turnips is not to grow too many. They are easy to grow, and an excess soon makes them lose their appeal. I plant about ten feet of row each summer — actually a five-square-foot bed of four rows, each row two and a half feet long and spaced six inches apart — which gives me about ten pounds of roots.

November 20

Holiday Cacti — For years I have been the not-so-proud grower of one of those spineless cacti whose flat, arching stems once a year culminate in brightly colored flowers. I would call my plant a Christmas cactus, or perhaps a Thanksgiving or an Easter cactus, but I really am not sure which it is because it has always bloomed sparsely and sporadically, with total disregard for holidays. Thanksgiving, Christmas, and Easter cacti — "holiday" cacti, if you will — can be beautiful, graceful, and florific. But one needs to find a good variety and then give it the right cultural conditions.

Botanical nomenclature is not much use in finding a good variety, for the nomenclature confuses even botanists. In most books, Thanksgiving and Christmas cacti are referred to as species of *Zygocactus*. The genus *Zygocactus* now has been made defunct by botanists, and Thanksgiving and Christmas cacti have been moved over to the genus *Schlumbergera*. (Friederich Schlumberger was a nineteenth-century Belgian fancier of cacti.) The Thanksgiving cactus, *S. truncata* var. *delicata*, is the one with sharply pointed (but soft to the touch) teeth along the flat margins of its long-jointed stems. There are varieties with rose-brushed white, salmon, or violet flowers. Christmas cacti, now called *S. bridgesii*, have blunt stem margins, and bright purplish pink flowers. The Easter cactus was once also in the genus *Schlumbergera*, but now is called *Rhipsalidopsis gaertneri*. The Easter cactus also has acute teeth on its stems, but the length of its stem joints and its flowers are shorter than those of the Thanksgiving and Christmas cacti. The plants are upright growing with broad, red flowers. Don't expect time of bloom to help in naming these plants. Varieties of Christmas cactus, for example, might be found that bloom anytime from November to March.

Holiday cacti are much easier to grow than to name. Cultural requirements for all are similar, for they have a common ancestral root in moist, tropical jungles of Brazil. There they grow nestled in the duff that accumulates in the forks of trees. Mist-charged air ameliorates tropical heat, and treetops diffuse the tropical sun.

I try to bring these conditions to my potted plants. The plants surely enjoy frequent spritzing from a mister, especially when they are inside the house for winter. They like bright light, but do not need the sunniest windows. These cacti enjoy a potting mixture that is well fortified with organic matter; I use my standard mix (which is about 50 percent organic matter), and it suits them well.

To form flower buds, holiday cacti need a brief period of rest and short days at summer's end. I give them their rest by leaving them outdoors, unwatered, until temperatures drop near freezing, then moving them to a basement window, still without water, until I see flower buds swelling at the tips of their branches. (The plants really need long nights, not short days, so they never should be kept in a room where lights will go on after dusk, even briefly in the middle of the night.)

Last spring a fellow gardener gave me a new holiday cactus, which already has earned its keep over my ten-year-old sporadic bloomer. True, my old cactus suffered neglect, including two drops to the ground in its hanging planter. But neglect was payment, rather than cause, for its poor performance. The old plant was too floppy and messy for my taste, and this new one is neat and relatively upright.

Most important, my new plant is now bedecked with flowers. Each large flower has rose-brushed, white petals, arching back like wings from its floral tube. Inside the base of this floral tube is a pencil line of magenta, and through the floral tube protrudes a magenta style surrounded by yellow anthers. Thank you, Norman K., for a beautiful *Schlumbergera truncata* var. *delicata* cv. 'Bicolor'.

November 23

Three Sisters — The Three Sisters showed up at Thanksgiving dinner today. They are the same Three Sisters that showed up at Thanksgiving dinners in colonial times. But my, how the Sisters have changed!

The Three Sisters are corn, beans, and squash (or pumpkins). These three plants were so important to the Indians that they also were known as Our Life or Our Supporters. The Three Sisters usually were eaten together in succotash, and they maintained a likewise congenial relationship in the Indian garden. Corn and bean seeds were planted on small mounds of soil fertilized with wood ashes and animal offal. Between these mounds, pumpkins were sown. The beans enriched the soil with nitrogen, which they take from the air and turn into fertilizer. The corn plants acted as stakes up which the beans could clamber. And the pumpkins spread over the ground, shading out weeds.

The early settlers no doubt would have starved had they not adopted Indian agriculture. Corn was the best grain crop to grow in the rude conditions of a settler's clearing. Little land preparation was needed, and the ripe ears could be left dangling on the stalks until there was time for harvest. In the kitchen, the settlers did alter the traditional Indian succotash of corn, beans, pumpkin, and chopped dog meat to corn, beans, and pork.

Let's move up a few centuries to today's Thanksgiving table. In front of me is cornbread, but dry beans are nowhere in sight, and pumpkin has suffered an identity crisis. Sweet potato is orange, so has a pumpkin-y, Thanksgiving air to it, according it a prominent position — as pudding — next to the turkey. Ah, the pumpkin pie. Might not be pumpkin here either, because pumpkin pies today sometimes are made with winter squashes. This substitution is justifiable because pumpkin and squash are in the same botanical genus, and in the case of some squashes, even the same species.

How have the Three Sisters changed in the garden? Sweet corn is the corn of our gardens, but most of the corn eaten in colonial times was field corn, ground into a coarse meal for mush or bread (Hiawatha's "yellow cakes of Mondamin"). The first record of sweet corn did not even show up until 1779, and those early sweet corns could not match today's hybrids for sweetness (less than 10 percent sugar then, over 35 percent now). Dry field corn was a staple in colonial times because it would keep through the winter if it was protected from rodents and kept dry. Sweet corn, or immature field corn, sometimes was preserved for the winter by roasting fresh-picked ears until they were dry.

We now grow beans in our gardens to eat as green beans, rather than as mature, dry bean seeds, as they were grown by the colonists and Indians. Also, most gardeners now plant bush beans, rather than pole beans, perhaps because bush beans have a shorter period from sowing to first harvest.

I do not know many gardeners who grow pumpkins. Pumpkin vines strew themselves widely enough to engulf most modern gardens, and part of the lawn, too. Large pumpkins usually are grown for Halloween rather than for eating. Today's gardeners wanting pumpkins of more manageable size could grow a newer variety, such as 'Jack Be Little', which produces cute three-inch pumpkins. Squash often turns up as the pumpkin substitute in the garden as well as in the kitchen. The trailing habit has been bred out of a squash variety like 'Golden Nugget', so ersatz pumpkins could be accommodated even in a postage-stamp-size garden.

This year I decided to experiment with an almost-traditional planting of the Three Sisters, using sweet corn, pole green beans, and zucchini squash. I knew my planting could suffer from two potential pitfalls. First, if the timing was wrong, the corn might grow so fast as to shade the climbing beans, or the beans might grow so fast as to strangle the growing cornstalks. By planting the beans and squash just after the corn leaves appeared aboveground, I was able to grow all Three Sisters together in harmony.

The second pitfall — unavoidable in my planting — was harvesting. A planting of field corn, dry beans, and pumpkins needs to be harvested only once, at the end of the season; not so for a planting of fresh corn, fresh beans, and fresh zucchini, which need picking every few days. Uncurling bean vines from around ears of ripe(?) corn while stepping gingerly about to avoid squashing squashes and the itchy squash foliage that grabbed at me was no easy task.

Next spring I will plant for a one-time, end-of-the-season harvest of dry beans, mature corn (maybe popcorn), and winter squash. Followed by a harvest festival, of course.

November 25

Groundnut — I do not mean to be discourteous to the Three Sisters, but it is time to recognize an unsung hero of Thanksgiving — the groundnut (*Apios americana*). The Wampanoaga Indians introduced this plant to the Pilgrims, and the Pilgrims' diet during one of those first winters was supplemented by an Indian cache of groundnuts and corn discovered by Miles Standish. The Pilgrims soon coveted groundnuts for themselves, to the extent of issuing an edict in 1654 ordering that "if an Indian dug Groundnuts on English land, he was to be set in stocks, and for a second offense, be whipped."

So why didn't the groundnut queue up along with turkey and cranberries for Thanksgiving fame? Perhaps the reason was the inherently weedy nature of this plant, which has grown wild for centuries throughout eastern United States, reaching as far west as Colorado. American Indians never really cultivated this plant, but merely encouraged it, then reaped harvests. Even today, groundnuts are a common weed in — of all places — cranberry bogs.

Right after I planted groundnut, I discovered it growing profusely in the shade along the old railroad bed nearby my house. In this moist soil, the twining stems sprawl over the ground or opportunistically clamber up other plants for support. In some places, groundnut cohabits with poison ivy, which is unfortunate because groundnuts' compound leaves bear a superficial resemblance to those of poison ivy. The groundnut's leaflets usually appear in fives or sevens, however, and the whole character of the plant is much softer and finer than that of poison ivy. In July and August, groundnuts bear drooping clusters of purplish to chocolate-colored flowers which, on some plants, suffuse the air with their sweet fragrance.

Below ground is where the groundnut should achieve its fame. Its edible, golfball-size roots are strung together like rosary beads. Comparisons with the white potato are unavoidable, and the groundnut — nutritionally rich, with three times the protein of potatoes — holds its own. The groundnut is a legume, which means that it can gather some of its nitrogen from the air rather than only from the soil. Thomas Hariot, in *A briefe and true report of the new found land of Virginia* (1590), may have been the first to write of the groundnut, and his opinion was that "boiled or sodden they are very good meate." In 1602, a correspondent from New England wrote to Sir Walter Raleigh that groundnuts were "as good as potatoes." Dr. E. Lewis Sturtevant, in *Sturtevant's Notes on Edible Plants* (1919), reported an eighteenth-century horticulturalist writing that the "Swedes ate them for want of bread, and that in 1749 some of the English ate them instead of potatoes." He also quotes a nineteenth-century writer who wrote that the Pilgrims "were enforced to live on ground nuts." Moving up to the twentieth century, Euell Gibbons, who enjoyed everything from cattails to milkweed pods, was reserved in his praise of groundnuts.

Now, finally, there are efforts to rescue the groundnut from obscurity, to bring into the garden this plant heretofore sought after in modern times only by Euell Gibbons types. Agricultural scientists are studying cultivation of the groundnut and combing the woods for superior plants to use for breeding. We are still in the discovery stage with this plant, though. How far apart should they be planted in a garden? Maybe two or three feet. What kind of yield can one expect? Maybe four to eight pounds per plant. What kind of soil is best? Judging from their native habitat, the plant likes, or at least tolerates, soils that are moist and acidic. I actually am more worried about the plant being too easy to grow in my garden. I dug beneath a plant today and found the chain of swollen roots sneaking across the ground two feet from the mother plant. And aboveground, the twining stems have reached over and insinuated themselves among the branches of a nearby bush cherry.

If the groundnut ever becomes a common denizen of cultivated fields and gardens, it may even acquire its own common name. Groundnut, you see, is in some places another name for the peanut. The groundnut has acquired other common names over the years: bog potato, Indian potato, and potato bean. The Indians had their names for it: *makoosit, nu nu*, and *chicamins*.

Anyone wanting to grow groundnuts cannot expect to thumb through a gardening catalog to G and then find 'Big Boy', 'Beefsteak', or some other named varieties of groundnut. A few companies mail-order "wild" tubers or seeds (Conley's Garden Center, Boothbay Harbor, Maine 04538; Forest Farm, 990 Tetherow Road, Williams, Oregon 97544; Tripple Brook Farm, 37 Middle Road, Southampton, Massachusetts 01073), or tubers for planting could be dug from the wild. The plants are herbaceous perennials, so a one-time planting will provide year after year of harvest as long as a few roots remain in the ground.

I boiled my recently harvested groundnuts, tasted them, and found them to be almost as good as potatoes, although less distinctive. The texture was dry and mealy. Like Euell, I am reserved in my praise of the roots, but other groundnut plants might have better or worse roots. (After all, not all potatoes taste the same.) I do think that groundnut, even in its present primitive state, is good enough to deserve a place at the Thanksgiving table. How about calling it one of its Indian names — *nu nu*, perhaps — and making *nu nu* stuffing standard Thanksgiving fare?

November 26

Popcorn — I was surprised at the different colors of my ears this autumn (popcorn ears, that is). 'Strawberry' popcorn lived up to its name, yielding stubby ears with dark-red kernels. But peeling back each dry husk of 'Papoose' popcorn revealed an ear of a different color, or, rather, of different colors, since each ear had white, yellow, red, and blue-black kernels. Some ears were almost all yellow, dotted with a few dark kernels; other ears had these colors in opposite proportions. There even were ears with almost all mahogany-red kernels.

I brought some of these popped kernels to Thanksgiving dinner, just as Indian chief Massasoit's brother, Quadequina, brought along a sack of popped popcorn to the first Thanksgiving feast three and a half centuries ago.

Popcorn actually predates that first Thanksgiving in America by thousands of years. Kernels have been found in the remains of Central American settlements almost seven thousand years old. The Quichas of Peru and the Aztecs of Mexico grew red, yellow, and white popcorns. Even after that first Thanksgiving dinner, settlers in the Northeast ate popcorn as a breakfast staple with milk and maple sugar, or floated on soup (very good!). In this century, movie and television viewing caused a resurgence in popcorn consumption.

I can just hear some "rational" person explaining to me why popcorn is not worth growing in a backyard garden. After all, you can drive to the grocer's and pick up a whole pound of popcorn for about a dollar. And not just any popcorn, but "gourmet" popcorn that makes tender and large (expansion ratio of forty-four to one, for the technically minded) popped kernels.

If you grow popcorn, you must set aside a separate portion of the garden for it, isolated from sweet corn, so cross-pollination does not make your popcorn less poppable and your sweet corn less sweet. In my garden, a distance of thirty feet was enough to keep popcorn and sweet corn chaste.

The trouble of weeding and keeping pests at bay is another rationale against growing backyard popcorn. I did weed, but had no pest problems.

And, if you grow popcorn, you have to go to the trouble of harvesting the ears and preparing the kernels for popping. On a recent dry, sunny day, I went out to the garden and snapped each ear off its stalk. I sat down on an overturned crate next to my basketful of popcorn ears, and as the low autumn sun warmed my shoulders, I pulled back the dry husks to expose the ears, then tied together the ears in bundles by their husks. All this is not what I would call unpleasant activity. Most of the bundles now are hanging in the garage, and the rest are in the kitchen.

To ready the corn for popping, I snap off a few kernels to make some empty space on an ear, then grasp the ear in both hands and twist it the way friends and I used to give "Indian burns" on each other's wrists when we were children.

Water — just the right amount (13 to 14.5 percent by weight, once again, for the technically minded) — is the secret to getting popcorn to pop. I have heard of gardeners trying to get their harvested popcorn to the right moisture level by either sprinkling the kernels with water or spreading the kernels on trays to dry in the sun. The *Farmers Cyclopedia of Agriculture* (1914), by E. V. Wilcox and C. B. Smith, recommended letting popcorn "dry in a loft for a season or two. Dry two-year-old corn pops best"! I have never let fear of nonpopping dissuade me from planting popcorn. If I leave ears on the stalks late into the season, then hang them to dry first in the garage, then in the kitchen, my popcorn's poppability matches that of store-bought.

I admit that my popcorn's expansion ratio is only a measly twenty to one, but this ratio depends more on what variety is grown than on my horticultural skill. Taste differences between popcorns are subtle, but I believe that my popcorn tastes better than store-bought. I also noticed that yellow 'Papoose' kernels have a richer, "cornier" flavor than the other kernel colors. I plan to save some yellow 'Papoose' kernels for planting next year. I also plan to try some other old varieties, mostly on the basis of name: 'South American Dynamite' and 'Squirrel Tooth' are two likely candidates.

All in all, it seems to me that the main rationale against growing popcorn is having to decide whether to pop it up or just to let the colorful ears hang from the kitchen rafters, where I can admire them through the winter.

DECEMBER

Through the hush'd air the whitening Shower descends,
At first thin wavering; till at last the Flakes
Fall broad, and wide, and fast, dimming the day
With a continual flow. The cherished Fields
Put on their winter-robe of purest white,
'Tis brightness all.

James Thomson, "Seasons. Winter."

WHETHER THE REST IS WELCOME or not (it depends on my mood), December offers respite from gardening. Even houseplants, although warm and indoors, respond to these shortest days of the year. They hardly budge and are undemanding as to water or fertilizer. If I am so inclined, I might pot up a few more freesia or hyacinth bulbs. Outside, the garden could use a bit more tidying — again, only if I am so inclined. Nothing *has* to be done. I might straighten up the compost bins, spread more mulch, or prune the hardiest plants. The first snowfall of winter hides any remaining disarray in the garden, unifying the landscape into a glistening harmony of white. If only that first snowfall would last!

December 6

Winter Ornaments — Thoughts of the drab grays and browns that lie ahead outdoors have stirred in me a desire for flowers, or at least some kind of plant ornamentation indoors or out. My potted amaryllis and freesia bulbs are ready to begin growth; their flowers will not appear until late winter, though. There is not much left in the garden, but while meandering along the edges of woods, I have come upon bits of decoration that I can bring home and indoors.

Two plants in the garden still provide a bit of visual divertissement. Usually I forget about lilies once their fragrant, white trumpets fade, but yesterday, as I walked past the clump of them snuggled against the giant willow, their seedpods caught my eye. The large capsules, flared open at their ends along longitudinal sutures, are arranged atop short stalks like a candelabra. Even my cat finds them interesting, perhaps because of the loose seeds that rattle within the capsules.

Interesting can grade to the bizarre, and perhaps the seed heads of purple coneflowers belong more in the latter category. They look like prickly little balls and are the source of coneflower's botanical name, *Echinaceae*, from the Latin word for hedgehog. Whether the seed heads are truly attractive matters no more. Since I began looking on them as little hedgehogs, a warm fondness wells up inside of me as I am reminded of Beatrix Potter's cozy Mrs. Tiggywinkle.

As long as I am looking to seed heads for decoration, I should include the ears of red, yellow, brown, and white popcorn festooning the kitchen ceiling. And strawflowers, still ruddy and perhaps a bit dusty from last year, also hang from the ceiling. The garden could yield more winter ornament — maybe next year I will plant some ornamental grasses to furnish tawny decoration indoors and out throughout the winter.

For now, I must roam farther afield for decoration. One of the first plants I stumble on is a wild clematis, Virgin's Bower. Its seed heads look almost like flowers (which I do not recall seeing anyway), each with gray, silky threads radiating out like a shaggy mane from the end of the stalk. Even brighter are the contents of milkweed pods, although the shiny, white down escaping from the pods would be messy indoors. And, of course, there are pine cones and cattails.

I think I need some color. But no, I do not have to condescend to spray painting pine cones or purple coneflower seed heads. I do not have to look far for real color outdoors — staghorn sumac is ubiquitous. The leaves just finished their fiery autumn show, and now the staghorned branches are capped by plumes of fuzzy, red berries.

Other fruits also are providing color. Small red or yellow crabapples still hang from some trees. Looking more closely, I see that the berries have become shriveled and mushy — pretty outdoors on the trees, but not very attractive viewed up close indoors. Bittersweet still looks fiery red, although the fruits have lost some of their charm now that many have shed their yellow coatings.

One of my favorite decorative fruits for this time of year is that of multiflora rose. Sprays of these fruits brought indoors belie the exuberant, rank nature of the plant from which they came. The sprays are delicate and refined, consisting of fine twigs, not densely packed, but open and loose and capped in a dignified manner by small, dark-red fruits. They are hardly noticeable outdoors, but very attractive indoors plunked into a glass bottle.

December 12

The Well-Dressed Tree — All my young trees are now decked out in their winter finery — arboreal attire, perfumes, and cosmetics to protect the trees through the winter. With insects and diseases dead or dormant outside, from what would a tree need protection? Larger animals, for one thing. Stems, bark, and roots have become enticing food for deer, rabbits, and mice, now that leaves have either frozen or fallen. And with winter cold comes the potential for desiccation and sunscald of plants. Sunscald, caused by fluctuations in bark temperature, is most likely to occur where the bark is last warmed by the sun each day, on the side facing the southwest horizon.

Evergreens are most at risk of desiccation, because they lose water through their leaves all winter long.

Here is what my well-accoutered young trees are wearing this winter:

Mulch as "footwear" is de rigeur. Leaves, hay, and straw insulate the soil against low temperatures and wide swings in temperature. Evergreens are especially thankful for mulch, which keeps soil water unfrozen and thus available during the winter. I keep mulch a couple of inches back off tree trunks, though, or the trunks will rot and mice will have sheltered living quarters and bark to nibble on right at home.

There is a choice of "furnishings" for keeping animals at bay. Down around a tree's "ankle," a legging of a twelve- to eighteen-inch-long cylinder of quarter-inch hardware cloth pushed an inch or so into the ground prevents mice and rabbits from gnawing at tree crowns and bark. To keep deer at bay, I dangle a bar of deodorant soap in the branches of some trees — one bar per tree. A mesh bag containing a wad of human hair is equally repulsive to deer. The efficacy of either hairballs or soapbars depends on the number of deer and how hungry they are. Last winter, olfactory affronts notwithstanding, deer chewed side branches on some of my young trees back to the trunks.

Moving on in the perfume department of winter tree wear, we find sprays to deter animal feeding on trees. Commercial sprays are appropriately named: Deer-Away, Chew-Not, and Hinder. Thiram is another, and some gardeners make homemade sprays from egg whites. Spraying must be repeated periodically through the winter, especially as animal feeding gets worse as winter wears on.

None of my well-dressed young trees would think of going into winter without their "makeup," a coating of white latex paint on the south side of their trunks. It protects the bark from sunscald by reflecting the sun's rays so the bark does not heat up during the day, only to rapidly cool at sunset. Paper or plastic tree wraps that serve the same purpose are sold. I added bone meal to the paint that I used last winter after a friend suggested that rabbits and mice, being vegetarians, would not gnaw on bony tasting bark. They didn't.

A few other measures also avert winter animal damage. In November, I gave the lawn one last mowing, not only for the lawn but also so that mice, exposed to the hungry, searching eyes of owls and hawks, would be less brazen about scurrying over to my trees. The surest cure for a deer problem is a fence, but I am not about to surround my yard with an eight-foot-high barrier (deer playfully leap over a fence less than seven feet high) or a specially designed electric fence. My efficient alternative is Mike, a hulking, black Labrador retriever, whose gentle ways deer have yet to come close enough to learn; his companion, Nicky, is a rust-colored cat who polices the grounds for any mice missed by the hawks and owls.

Final decor for trees this season is lights. These are not functional, but Christmassy.

December 15

Old Bulbs — On a shelf in my garage sits a box that arrived in September's mail and is full of autumn bulbs still patiently waiting to be planted. There also is a bag of similarly forgotten bulbs that I had carefully selected from store bins during the first hint of cool weather in late summer. It does seem a bit late for planting bulbs, but there still is time. The rule for planting bulbs is: better late than never . . . with some caveats.

Plants that make bulbs tolerate being out of the soil for a period of time because they go dormant for part of their life cycle. While dormant, leaves and roots dry up and wither away, which is ideal behavior for a plant shipped all over the world. Yet all the while the bulbs are sitting out adverse conditions, their flower buds are preformed within, waiting for a brief period of cold, followed by moisture, to arouse them from slumber.

"Better late than never" applies to all fall-planted bulbs except lilies. Lily bulbs never like being without their roots, and their roots never like being out of the soil (although they will tolerate it for a short while). I did not buy and forget to plant any lily bulbs back in September, but if I had, I would now throw them out.

Although most bulbs can tolerate an extension of their natural dormant period, with time they will suffer out of the soil. The flower bud might die, in which case the bulb will grow but will not bloom. Even if the flower bud survives, a late-planted bulb is weakened by lack of sufficient time to develop roots in autumn.

These are not reasons to forgo planting, but are reasons to expect a poor show from autumn bulbs planted this late. As a frugal gardener who cannot toss out even a piece of string (I will find some use for it in the garden), I surely cannot toss out these forgotten bulbs if they have any spark of life still in them. With good growing conditions, the bulbs will recuperate after a season and in years to come will thrust their colorful blossoms skyward each spring.

One by one, I examine my forgotten bulbs and select for planting only those that appear sound. Any that are not firm or show signs of rot I relegate to the compost pile. Fortunately, the bulbs stayed cool and moist on my garage shelf; if I had left them outdoors, they would have frozen to death, and if I had left them in the house, they would have dried out.

The actual planting operation is more of a problem than deciding which bulbs are worth planting. Depending on how frozen the soil is, I may need either a trowel or a pickax. Any mulched ground is still unfrozen. No matter how or where I plant, I ensure intimate contact between the bulb and the soil.

As an alternative to planting directly in the ground, I could plant the bulbs in pots. They will then need one good watering, then storage where temperatures are cold yet protected from the full fury of winter. Good spots for storing pots of bulbs are on the ground beneath a thick pile of hay or leaves, in a corner of an unheated garage or garden shed, or in an unheated basement. Potted, forgotten bulbs are not the ones I will force indoors for bloom. These weakened bulbs should be held back from growing as long as possible; then, with ideal growing conditions in spring, I will slide them out of their pots with their root balls intact into their permanent sites in the ground.

Next autumn I will try to remember to plant all autumn bulbs as soon as I get them. If I cannot plant immediately, I will keep them cool and dry. The unheated entrance foyer to my house should be a suitable spot, because it is cool and dry, and because the bulbs, sitting there, can constantly nag me until I plant them in the ground.

December 17

Flowering Maple — Maple trees, having shed their dazzling autumn raiment, no longer command my attention. In their stead, I turn my eyes indoors to admire my "flowering maple" (*Abutilon* sp.). Right now, salmon-pink flowers hang like Lilliputian hoop skirts from the branches. The petals are each about an inch long, and a column of powderpuff yellow stamens protrudes from the center of each flower. In other varieties and species — and there are many hybrids — the flower color is white, yellow, or various shades of red.

Even a casual glance at the flowering maple's blossoms brings to mind the similar blossoms of okra, hibiscus, and rose of Sharon — all in the mallow family. The flowering maple is not a flamboyant plant. Just like okra, which in my garden has only a few flowers (and pods) at any given time, the flowering maple is never dripping with flowers. Then again, it does blossom reliably year-round, and any and every blossom is welcome in winter.

Besides reliable bloom, the flowering maple has the quality of being easy to grow. This time of year, my plant leads a life of luxury, basking in the sunniest possible window in my house. The plant is almost too easy to grow, and it can be so exuberant that it outgrows its bounds. I bridle my plant's growth by repotting it every spring, not into a larger pot, but back into the same pot in which it has grown for the past four years. Before putting it back in its pot, though, I slice off an inch or so of the outer layer of roots from the root ball. I also cut back the branches severely, to balance root loss during repotting and to induce the fresh new growth needed for flowers.

As a member of the mallow family, the flowering maple is not really a maple at all. The name derives from the plant's maple-shaped leaves. Actually, I consider the maplelike leaves to be the plant's main defect. In common with other members of the mallow family, large leaves and a rank growth habit make for a coarse plant. After all, how pretty is a hibiscus plant without flowers? Some varieties of flowering maple — mine for instance, which I believe is *A. megapotamicum* '*Variagata*' — are jazzed up with splashes of yellow on their leaves. But the flowering maple would be greatly improved if someone made or found one with smaller leaves.

Training can counteract the plant's ungainly growth habit to some degree. Pinching out the growing point induces branching. For plants in hanging baskets, repeated pinching of the growing tips is a must so plants can spread and fill the baskets.

I have coerced my plant into growing a single stem, straight upward. I did this by pinching off all side branches as they developed. When the plant finally reached a couple of feet in height, I also pinched off the tip of the main stem, causing side branches to break. When I prune the plant each spring, I do not cut into the main stem, but shorten the side branches and their laterals, sublaterals, and so on. With all this pinching and pruning, my plant has developed a trunk crowned with a head of leafy shoots — not unlike the real maples outdoors.

December 20

Flower Talk — The garden outdoors has barely quieted, and already a few seed and nursery catalogs have appeared in my mailbox. I plan to wile away some of winter's hours circling with a red pen flowers that I might need to grow for the purpose of delivering messages next year. *The Household Guide, or Practical Helps for Every Home (including Home Remedies for Man and Beast)* (1893), written by Professor B. G. Jefferis, M.D., Ph.D., serves as my reference on the language of flowers. "Say it with flowers," suggests the florist of today. After reading Dr. Jefferis's treatise, I am more careful to make sure I know what I am saying.

Everyone knows that a rose represents an expression of romantic love. But watch out! According to my little book, you had better heed what kind of rose you pull out from behind your back to present to a lover. In the early stages of a romance, a moss rose in bud is a confession of love. Or a white rose might be appropriate, to say "I am worthy of you." If you feel your lover glancing astray, a yellow rose will express your jealousy. For the relationship becoming stagnant, Doctor Jefferis prescribes a damask rose, meaning "beauty ever new."

There is no better way to cement that budding romance than with an outstretched hand clasping a four-leaf clover, the plant that says "be mine." Because you could spend all day on hands and knees looking for a four-leaf clover, and still never find one, you might substitute a leaf of oxalis (*Oxalis deppei*, sometimes called the shamrock plant). Although not related to clover, oxalis leaves bear a close resemblance to those of clover, except that *all* oxalis leaves have four leaflets.

Because it can be grown as a houseplant, shamrock plant provides "four-leaf clovers" for year-round use.

Later, if an amorous relationship turns sour, it is time to send (do not hand-deliver this message) sweet-pea flowers. The message: depart! Anyone in a rush for this message should make sure to sow sweet pea early in the spring.

Sentiments represented by other flowers may or may not be obvious. Forget-me-not, as expected, means just that. As suspected, witch hazel represents a spell and dead leaves of any kind represent sadness. But who could have guessed that pansy represents thoughts . . . red clover represents industry . . . ferns represent fascination . . . goldenrod represents caution . . . and orange blossoms represent chastity? One can only imagine what "dangerous pleasures" meant in 1893, but they were represented by the fragrant tuberose.

Dr. Jefferis further instructs that flowers can be combined for greater depth of meaning. For example, a bouquet of mignonettes and colored daisies means "your qualities surpass your charms of beauty." Yellow rose, a broken straw, and ivy together mean "your jealousy has broken our friendship." And, a white pink, canary grass, and laurel mean that "your talent and perseverance will win you glory." I close with a combination of my own: a bouquet of red clover, fern, and pansy ("I hope my industry has stimulated a fascination for thoughts about plants").

December 21

Holiday Gifts — How about this for a holiday gift for a gardening friend or relative: an electronic moisture detector that "plays a musical tune when your plants need water"? Not for me, thanks. A nursery full of plants tended by "Dry-N-Cry" might turn me into a computer programmer.

There is a surfeit of horticultural gadgetry that one might be tempted to buy as gifts, but too many are sure to end up tucked away in the back corner of a garage or closet. I saw a magazine advertisement depicting a woman standing upright in a garden, power drill in hand, drilling holes into the soil with a special auger (the item for sale) for planting bulbs. She might have been better advised to get down on all fours, and stay there for the complete job of planting, rather than to bob up and down "drilling" holes, planting, then covering each bulb. And I didn't even mention the electric cord she evidently was dragging around the garden. Consider buying a cordless drill to go along with this gift.

On the premise that a picture is worth a thousand words, a gardening video would seem to be a great educational tool for the beginning gardener. But compare a video with a good gardening book, which can be skimmed, or pored over in detail, according to the gardener's mood. And come April 15, when a question arises during the frenzy of pea planting, which will be more useful: a book index or a fast forward button?

What is a good gift for a gardener? How about a watering can? Even a cheap one, which gushes water out its holes, is fine for watering newly planted trees and shrubs beyond the reach of a hose. A watering can with an upward-pointing spout shoots water upward before settling it gently on the soil — just the thing for delicate seedlings. A rain gauge is useful for confirming whether a summer downpour really was a downpour (did an inch of rain fall, so watering can be forgone for a week?). A thermometer that records minimum and maximum temperatures might help explain why tomatoes died one night in late spring, or help a gardener brag about lettuce still growing in the fall, even though it "got down to 19 degrees last night."

Seed packets, some opened and some unopened, seem to turn up everywhere around the house and garage by midsummer. A couple of plastic freezer containers can keep seeds organized and will store them so they remain viable longer than if left lying around on shelves and in cardboard boxes.

Tools like shovels, hoes, and trowels are indispensable in the garden, and therefore good candidates for gifts. To me, though, the fit or style of these tools is very personal, so presenting a shovel to me as a gift would be as chancy as giving me a pair of shoes. Stools and cushions for garden work are useful only to the gardener who likes to stay put and pull every weed from a square foot of soil before moving on. A gardener like me who hops about the garden — pulling a weed here, pinching off a tomato sucker there, then sowing a short row of radishes — would be encumbered by such paraphernalia.

Necessary, yet expendable, items make good gifts for gardeners. A stack of current seed catalogs is a good gift, especially to a beginning gardener. Inexpensive wooden labels and a pencil would be appreciated in spring to mark rows where vegetable and flower seeds are planted. Gardening gloves, cheap or expensive, never last more than one season, at least for me. A new pair of gloves is my impetus to toss out the old pair.

A ball of string tops my list of good gifts. I never forget to buy seeds and transplants in spring, but I never even think to buy the string I will need for tying tomato vines, marking rows, and making bean trellises. Natural fiber string is best, so that it can be tossed, along with entangling vines, onto the compost heap at season's end.

December 25

Christmas Trees and Mistletoe — In the darkness of the deep forest there glowed the great Thunder Oak tree, decorated with gilded apples and lighted candles. Around the tree shone the candlelit faces of the Druids. On this Christmas day in eighth-century Germany, the god Thor was to be appeased with a human sacrifice. Enter Wynfred, an English Christian missionary later to be known as Saint Boniface. With one stroke of an ax, he split the giant oak into four parts, revealing a small fir tree nearby . . . the first Christmas tree, perhaps.

For centuries, people have had the urge to decorate trees at this time of year. In ancient Rome, decorated trees were part of the festival of Saturn, celebrated beginning December 17. The Paradise Tree of the Middle Ages, a fir tree hung with red apples, was a prop used in the biblical play telling the story of Adam and Eve. The play was performed on the supposed birthday of Adam and Eve, December 24. The tradition of Paradise Trees was moved into homes after "miracle plays" were banned in the fifteenth century. Today, Christmas trees are still called the *Paradeis* in parts of Bavaria.

Germany is probably the original home of the Christmas tree as we know it. A written record of 1604 describes trees decorated with paper roses, apples, and, recalling the Paradise Trees of the Middle Ages, figures of Adam and Eve, and a serpent. From Germany, the custom of decorating trees at Christmas spread south through Austria and north into the Scandinavian countries. The custom did not spread through the British Empire until the Christmas of 1841, when Prince Albert and Queen Victoria celebrated the birth of their first son with a decorated tree at Windsor Castle.

The technology of lighting the Christmas tree began, according to one story, when Martin Luther was struck by the beauty of the nighttime stars around a fir tree as he trudged home one night. He sought to recapture the image with lighted candles on an indoor tree. In the late nineteenth century, gas jets, and then electric lights, were tried as replacements for the candles. Safe lighting came when a New England telephone employee, Ralph Morris, lit his tree with a string of low-voltage light bulbs like those then used on telephone switchboards.

That great Thunder Oak tree may have had growing among its branches another plant associated with Christmas, mistletoe. Kissing under the mistletoe also harkens back to the Druids, and is practically all that remains from the many mistletoe legends of the old European cultures. A sprig of mistletoe seems fairly innocuous, but it was not always so. The ancients saw mistletoe as having supernatural powers, sometimes evil and sometimes beneficent. Two thousand years ago, mistletoe was known by some as "all heal," an herb that was brewed as an antidote for poisons and epilepsy, or worn as an amulet to ward off all diseases. Evidence of mistletoe's ominous nature is found in Scandinavian mythology, which credits mistletoe with the destruction of the sun-god, Balder the Beautiful.

Mistletoe is only a small wisp of a plant, so why would the ancients embody it with such awesome powers as healing, or overpowering gods? The reason is because mistletoes are capable of killing large trees, even the Thunder Oak.

Mistletoes are parasitic plants that nestle into the branches of a host tree, penetrating the bark and sapping nutrients and water. The host tree is weakened and, in some cases, killed. The effect on the tree is conveyed in the generic name for Christmas mistletoe, *Phoradendron*, which means tree thief in Greek. Gazing up into tree branches, the ancients recognized that the tufts of mistletoe, although intimately associated with the tree, were nonetheless different from the rest of the tree. Hence our word *mistletoe,* a derivation of the Saxon word *mistl-tan,* meaning different twig. Not that mistletoe always was a mere sprig, dependent for survival on its parasitic nature. Ancient Christian legend relates that mistletoe once was a forest tree itself, but it was dwarfed for shame after its wood was used to make the cross at Cavalry.

European legends were based on their native mistletoe, known as true mistletoe, *Viscum album.* As the Americas were colonized, European customs were carried across the Atlantic and applied to one of our indigenous mistletoes: Christmas, or true American, mistletoe (*Phoradendron flavescens*). Christmas mistletoe is relatively rare, occurring in isolated pockets south of New Jersey, and then west to New Mexico. It lives mostly on deciduous trees, to which it is rarely life-threatening. In fact, Christmas mistletoe could be considered an agricultural crop, as it supports a Christmastime industry.

Not all our mistletoes are innocuous. There is another kind of mistletoe in this country, the dwarf mistletoe (*Arceuthobium pusillum*), that is a serious pest mostly of pine forests in the West.

Notice the white berries of mistletoe. Within the berries are sticky seeds, just right for sticking to the bark of a tree. Birds and other animals carry the seeds from tree to tree. In the case of dwarf mistletoe, the ripe seeds are shot out of the berries, often as far as fifty feet. Where mistletoe is cultivated, gardeners take the sticky seeds and sow them in the bark of a suitable host tree. I prefer to get my mistletoe from the florist — it's a plant for the doorway, not the garden.

December 27

Poinsettia — Christmas has passed, and a friend already has asked me to care for her poinsettia until next November. The unspoken request, I know, is, "Could I please have the plant back ready to bloom again?" I am not adverse to caring for an extra plant. The problem here is that I don't really like the looks of poinsettias. Fortunately, though, I do like them as botanical curiosities.

The first interesting aspect of poinsettia is its milky sap, evident when I nick the stem. Poinsettia, *Euphorbia pulcherrima*, is a member of the spurge family. All plants in this family, when cut, exude a milky sap, often poisonous and sometimes used medicinally as a purge (hence *spurge,* from the French word *espugier*, meaning to purge). The sap of one member of the family, *Hevea braziliensis*, is tapped as the commercial source of rubber.

The second curious thing about this plant is the way stores always manage to have *blooming* poinsettias for the holiday season. Poinsettias, along with holiday cacti, chrysanthemums, and most strawberries, are short-day plants. Short days induce such plants to form flower buds. (Plants are actually responding to long nights, but the phenomenon was originally thought to be *day*-length dependent, and the term *short-day* has persisted.) The poinsettia can be fooled into blooming at any time of the year merely by exposing it to artificially shortened days.

To return my ward blooming to its owner next November, I will first have to give the plant a rest. As the "flowers" (Why quotation marks? Read on.) fade and leaves drop, the plant is entering dormancy. When it becomes dormant, I will move it to a cool place and give it just enough water to keep its stems from shriveling.

Around April, the plant will be ready to start growing again. I will cut the stems back to a few strong shoots, each about six inches long, and spur on growth with sun, warmth, and water. When warm weather has settled, the plant will go outside.

The short-day treatment begins when I bring the plants back indoors at the end of the summer. I will put the plant at a sunny, warm window, but it will have to spend time each day in a closet to make sure it gets its required daily dose of fourteen-hour nights. After two months, it can stay at its sunny window. Flower buds will soon be evident, and the plant should be blooming within a month.

My favorite poinsettia lore concerns the flowers themselves. To appreciate this, set your blooming poinsettia on a table in good light and look closely at its flowers. I say "closely" because the flowers are *not* those large, red, leaflike structures. The large, red, leaflike structures are just that — leaves, albeit modified leaves called bracts. The bracts attract pollinating insects to the plant. The actual flowers of the poinsettia originate within the cyathiums, which are the little greenish, cup-shaped structures you see above the bracts.

Each cyathium contains a single female flower surrounded by a harem of males. Pluck a cyathium from the plant and slice it in half from top to bottom. A magnifying glass helps here. You will see that the inner wall of the cyathium is lined with numerous tiny flowers. These are all male flowers. If you look carefully, you also will see a stalk attached to the very bottom of the cyathium, protruding up through the cup opening and capped by what looks like a turban. That is the single, female flower. In addition to the male and female flowers, on the outside of the cyanthium is a single yellow gland that looks like the mouth of a fish poised to ingest food.

Next time a friend comments on the beauty of a poinsettia flower, I will take out a magnifying glass and examine a few cyathiums before looking up and agreeing nonchalantly.

December 28

Identifying Trees in Winter — No need to stay indoors all day long. Trying to identify leafless trees this time of year is a nice game to play alone or with a companion as I wander outdoors enjoying the brisk winter air. (I did say "leafless," for identifying evergreen trees quickly becomes too easy.) The game also forces me to look closely at the more subtle details of plants, so I can appreciate them even now when they are stripped of leaves and flowers. The transition from autumn to winter has brought trees from their most ostentatious to their most subtle beauty.

Of course, some trees are hardly a challenge. Everyone recognizes the paper birch by its peeling white bark. (Watch out, though, the gray birch has similar bark.) The catalpa tree is quickly identified by its long, brown pods. And the pin oak by its growth habit: lower branches droop downward, midlevel branches are horizontal, and upper branches turn upward.

Most deciduous trees do not have such obvious signatures this time of year. Then, what is needed is an observant eye and a good book to describe trees in words and pictures. Particularly helpful are those books that follow a logical sequence of steps in identification (such as *Fruit Key & Twig Key to Trees and Shrubs* [1959] by William Harlow, or *Master Tree Finder* [1963] by M. T. Watts).

One of the first things I look for when confronted with an unknown, leafless tree is the arrangement of the buds on the young twigs. Are the buds "opposite" (in pairs, on opposite sides of each twig) or "alternate" (single and separated from each other along the length of the stem)? Most deciduous trees around here have alternate buds (and most shrubs have opposite buds). So if I see opposite buds on a tree, the choice immediately is narrowed to dogwoods, maples, or ashes (also horsechestnut, although it is not very common here).

Other features will further narrow the choices within each of the two categories (opposite- or alternate-leaved) of trees. The shape of the buds can be telling. For example, flowering dogwoods have flower buds that look like little buttons capping short stalks. The pawpaw's buds are rusty brown, and fuzzy like velour. Also telling is twig color. Purple twigs covered with a cloudy coating identify a tree as boxelder.

I look to see if a tree has thorns. If so, it is most likely black locust, honeylocust (watch out again, though, for most cultivated forms of honeylocust are thornless), hawthorn, or wild plum. The black locust has short thorns, the honeylocust has long thorns, often branching, and the plum's thorns have little buds along their length.

Fruits are another guide. Prickly gumballs hang almost throughout the winter on sweetgum trees. Magnolias still have their fruits, which look like little pineapples with red seeds popping out. And looking on the ground for help in naming a tree is within the rules of the game. There you still will find some nuts of the shagbark hickory (identified also by its shaggy bark) and acorns (but there are many oak species, so the trick is to identify which one).

Sometimes the bark is a giveaway. Patches of pale green and brown immediately identify sycamore, as do the red-brown, fine papery curlings peeling from the trunk of the river birch. The gray bark of beech is fine enough to appear uniformly smooth, but rough enough so there is no gloss. It looks like elephant hide, an effect enhanced by the folds and creases at its limb "joints." Long, vertical strips of shagbark hickory bark remain attached to the trunks at their middles, their upper and lower ends curling away from the trunk — a shaggy trunk from top to bottom. The little blocks of the bark of persimmon and flowering dogwood give the trunks the texture of alligator hide. American hornbeam, a small under-story tree common in our woodlands, has a bluish gray bark that resembles muscle — close fitting, with the smooth surface broken by sinewy ripples. Another common name for this tree is musclewood.

If I am still at a loss as to a tree's identity, I break off a twig and make a slanting cut on it to expose the pith. If the pith is chambered, rather than continuous, the tree is either a black walnut or a butternut. Butternut trees have chocolate-brown pith; black walnut trees have toffee-brown pith.

The taste of a twig sometimes is the giveaway. Black cherry tastes like bitter almond, and yellow and river birch tastes like wintergreen (no taste to paper birch twigs). Slippery elm twigs become mucilageneous when chewed.

It is within the rules of the identification game to look for a few dead leaves still hanging on deciduous trees. The leaves will be dead, dry, and twisted, but often still readable. The very presence of leaves can be the giveaway. Oaks and beeches are reluctant to lose their lower leaves. Throughout the winter and even at a distance, I can identify either of these trees by their full skirts of dry leaves.

JANUARY

These Winter nights against my window-pane
Nature with busy pencil draws designs
Of ferns and blossoms and fine spray of pines,
Oak-leaf and acorn and fantastic vines,
Which she will make when summer comes again —

T. B. Aldrich, "Frost-Work"

JANUARY IS the pivotal point in both the calendar and the gardening year. It is the month when I summon together my memories and notes from the season past and dream of the season hence. As with any change in direction, the pivotal point brings a temporary lull in activity. January is a time to wait, a time to read about gardening, a time to thumb through plant catalogs, and perhaps a time to travel south far enough to where, outdoors, new leaves still are unfurling and fruits are ripening.

Indoors, there is but one sign of exuberant plant life: freesia, amaryllis, and hyacinth bulbs I am forcing have been fooled, and are pushing up new leaves as if it were spring.

Outside, the garden is draped in a hoary, frozen silence. The scene, though, is nonetheless pretty, even cheery. On bright days, the low sun sparkles on bare branches; on snowy days, each branch is like a dark shelf, decorated and slightly bent under its small, white load of snow.

January 7

Labels — Outside, the garden is deathly still except for the almost lifelike rustling of plant labels playing in the wind. I have affixed labels to many of my trees and shrubs because I cannot always remember what variety I planted. I also have a nagging fear that the next person to live in my house will one day wander out to the garden, pluck from a tree an apple, bite into it, and not know what variety it is.

I need permanent labels, not the temporary plastic ones that come with purchased trees and shrubs and become illegible after a season or two. So last year I bought labels from a nursery supply company. With a pencil, I embossed the plant names on the thin aluminum strips and attached each to its appropriate tree or shrub.

What attractive playthings these labels became for my cat. The tags, dancing in the slightest breezes, made what I suppose to the cat were mouselike scratching sounds. Needless to say, some of those thin aluminum strips are already torn to shreds.

Looking through some good, old-fashioned gardening encyclopedias, I found whole discourses under the subject heading of "Labels." For instance, here's an idea for eking a few extra seasons out of a cheap, wooden label: Instead of writing a name on a single label, write it on two labels, then wire the labels flat together with the writing facing the same direction. When the writing on the outside-facing label weathers away, the writing that was sandwiched between the two labels still will be legible.

Years ago, sheets of zinc were commonly used for labeling — the metal cuts easily with scissors and resists decay. One suggestion for a long-lasting label was to coat a zinc strip with paraffin, scratch the plant name through the paraffin, then immerse the strip in dilute hydrochloric acid to etch the zinc.

A number of permanent inks could be used to write a plant name on a strip of zinc. A once well-known concoction, developed by the French chemist Brainnot in 1837, consisted of verdigris, sal ammoniac, lampblack, and water. Copper or mercury chloride also made good inks. One of the blackest inks for zinc was made from platinum chloride — an indication of the low price of platinum and/or the high importance of

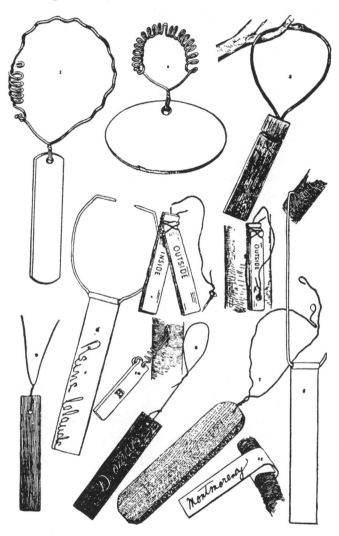

labeling in times past. In spite of my quest for permanent labels, I would not mess around with any of these inks — all are poisonous.

One suggestion I particularly liked was writing a plant name on a stiff piece of paper, then inserting the paper into a stoppered glass vial or test tube. Such a label potentially could outlive most plants. And the idea of those vials hanging one per tree seems almost as fanciful to me as a stoppered bottle, message enclosed, bobbing in the ocean.

Any label — no matter what type — has to be attached to the plant to be identified. Nailing is unsatisfactory because a nail might damage a plant. More important, the bark of a tree eventually will overgrow a nailed label. I have seen more than one old apple tree whose bark had just about swallowed up its metal label, leaving exposed only a two- or three-letter hint of the variety name exposed. Attaching a label with a wire loop around a branch is satisfactory if the loop is occasionally loosened so as not to girdle the limb. Of course, decay-resistant wire such as copper or aluminum is needed.

My old gardening encyclopedias even have some clever suggestions for attaching labels to trees. Why not affix them with spring-held screws to allow for bark expansion? And instead of a wire loop needing constant adjustment, why not use a wire loop, part of which is wound into a spring that expands with plant growth? No matter how labels are attached, they are easier to find if put at the same height and facing the same direction on all trees.

I am going to replace my purchased labels with homemade ones hung on the branches with springy loops of copper wire. For the labels themselves, I will cut disposable aluminum trays, such as those used for frozen foods, into strips — a suggestion from an old *Popular Mechanics*. This aluminum is thin enough to be embossed with a pencil, yet thick enough to be, I hope, cat-proof.

January 12

Siting Houseplants — "Nothing adds more to the beauty of a home than a few well-selected houseplants. It makes the long bleak winters pleasant, and there are no pictures or furniture that can add so much beauty and interest as the natural flower." I'll wager these two sentences are as true today as when Professor B. G. Jefferis, M.D., Ph.D., penned the advice in his *Household Guide, or Practical Helps for Every Home* in 1893. This advice is perhaps more true now, given our increasing synthetic environment: plastic clothes, plastic toys, even plastic plants!

Dr. Jefferis rightly points out that each houseplant has its preferred window. A geranium revels in the scorching sunlight that floods through a south-facing window, yet in that same light a Chinese evergreen would, well . . . scorch. Conversely, the geranium would languish in a dim, north-facing window, whose light makes the Chinese evergreen feel as if it were back in the shaded depths of a tropical forest floor it once called home.

North windows receive only diffuse sunlight, except for a glancing slice of direct sun early in the morning and late in the evening when days are long. North windows also are the coolest windows in a house. Nowadays, with airtight and double-paned windows, at least we don't need to stuff newspaper between the pane and the plants each night, as was recommended in Victorian homes of Dr. Jefferis's days. A north window is ideal for foliage plants like ferns, cast-iron plant, philodendron, and peperomia. Any of the ivies (English, German, Swedish, or devil's) can be trained to trail around the molding.

The full force of the sun in south windows brings light and heat. This calls for attention to watering. One missed watering and plants are apt to wilt beyond recovery (unless they are succulents or cacti, which thrive in south windows). Where watering is attended to, exotics like bougainvillea, bromeliads, calla lily, and lantana can be brought to flower. More mundane — except this time of year, when no flower is mundane — is a pot of petunias or alyssum. I fruit a few pots of alpine strawberries in a south window. Coleus leaves also need bright sunlight to encourage their colors.

The climate at an east or west window is intermediate to that between north and south windows with respect to temperature and light. Even so, east and west windows are not the same. An east window brings friendly, morning sun, which floats up and away before hardly warming window plants. This combination of bright light and equable temperature suits plants such as gardenia, cyclamen, and begonia, which are finicky about holding onto their flower buds before they open.

A west window is also bright, but hotter than an east window. Such conditions are better suited to African violets, gloxinias, and hoyas. Many foliage plants requiring medium amounts of light, such as rubber tree, weeping fig, dracaena, and asparagus fern, do well at either east or west windows, although more water is needed at the west window.

One final bit of houseplant advice from the wise Dr. Jefferis: "Do not attempt to grow too many plants. It is better to have one healthy, well-grown plant, than a dozen sickly ones which have neither beauty nor blossom." Periodically, I force myself to purge the house of unsightly plants, freeing up window space for new ones.

January 15

Kumquats — Year-round warm weather does not attract me to the tropics. Yet the thought of plucking sun-warmed oranges from a backyard tree has appeal. I feel no need to move south, though, because I can enjoy the snow here and still pick fresh citrus simply by growing a citrus plant in a pot, where it can wait out cold weather indoors. This idea is not new. A whole wing at Versailles — the orangerie — was built expressly for overwintering potted orange trees.

A potted citrus tree would be worthy of window space even if its fruit were inedible. The orange or yellow berries (yes, they are berries, botanically speaking) make a festive contrast to the luxuriously green leaves, and the fragrance of the flowers rivals that of gardenia or jasmine. The beauty of the plant is attested to by the fact that the citrus plants most commonly grown as houseplants are the Calamondin orange and the Otaheite orange. The robust-flavored fruits of either plant are unpalatable, except perhaps diluted to flavor an ade.

I reason that if I am going to grow a potted citrus plant, it might as well also bear edible fruit. Oranges or grapefuits are a possibility, although a pot-sized plant cannot hold many fruits. And a small orange or grapefuit tree festooned with large fruits looks clumsy. Lemons or limes are good choices, since the juice of only one fruit will flavor a whole bowl of guacamole or a few servings of fish. I get the most out of one citrus plant by growing a type that has lush foliage, fragrant flowers, edible fruit — and more. I am growing kumquats, whose skin is even edible!

Just about any citrus plant can be started readily from seeds. Volunteer orange seedlings have sprouted at the base of a dracaena next to a rocking chair in my living room, evidently from seeds discarded as someone sat rocking and eating a orange. (How do I know it's an orange? Crushed

citrus leaves smell much like the fruit.) The seeds germinate readily if sown fresh, before they dry.

Whereas seedlings of most fruit plants do not bear fruits that are identical to the parent plant, this is not the case with citrus. Many citrus exhibit apomyxis, which is the ability to form seeds without fertilization of the flower. A plant grown from such seeds is genetically identical to the mother plant. Simply put, a 'Valencia' orange seedling eventually will bear 'Valencia' orange fruits. Not so for 'McIntosh' apples or 'Bartlett' pears.

Last year, I finally gave away a four-year-old tangerine seedling and bought my present kumquat plant. The tangerine seedling could have taken a decade to bear fruit, and, like other juvenile citrus plants, it was armed with undesirable stout, inch-long thorns.

I bought my kumquat plant at a nursery, but had I known someone with a plant, I could have started the plant from a cutting. Most citrus root easily, and the cuttings usually flower and fruit at a young age. I once rooted a lemon cutting that was smothered with a half-dozen blossoms before the plant was more than a half-foot tall.

Growing and fruiting potted citrus trees require no special techniques. The plants will grow in any potting soil suitable for houseplants. Sometimes, especially in midwinter, the young leaves yellow, indicating a need for iron. The way to cure or avert this problem is by periodically using an "acid plant fertilizer." For quick response, a plant can be dosed with a spray of "iron chelate."

For best fruit production, citrus plants need sun. My kumquat is now in a cool room at a south window. The plant shows no signs of life, but I am not concerned. Kumquats and other citrus just sit when the average daily temperature drops below 60 degrees Fahrenheit. But while the shoots and buds are quiescent, the roots are growing. Soon the tables will be turned, and the roots will rest as new shoots and, I hope, flowers will push out from the buds. As soon as the weather settles in the spring, I will move the kumquat outdoors to a site almost in full sun.

I have a confession: My kumquat — all kumquats — really are in the genus *Fortunella*, not *Citrus*. But *Fortunella* and *Citrus* are closely related, even to the point of freely interbreeding and producing such strange-named fruits as limequats and citrangequats. And botany aside, kumquats taste and look very much like little oranges.

January 16

Exotic Fruit Plants — Exotic fruits are turning up on the grocer's shelves these days: dates, papayas, tomatillos, guavas, and others. I look on these fruits opportunistically, for within each lies dormant seeds that can be coaxed to become exotic, if not beautiful, indoor plants. Such plants provide a break from the humdrum of spider plants, philodendrons, and Swedish ivies.

Seeds of tropical fruits usually germinate best if planted as soon as the fruits are eaten. All that is necessary to grow most tropical fruits is to wash their seeds, then sow them in potting soil, using the old rule of thumb of burying a seed to twice its depth. And then wait.

The waiting period can be long if the seed is from a date fruit. But stop for a moment and think about deserts, where dates are native. Should a date seed send up a leafy shoot with the first hint of moisture? Of course not. The dry desert air would dehydrate the sprout in short order. When a date seed germinates, it sends a thick taproot straight down into the soil seeking permanent moisture, long before even a small sprout appears aboveground.

I once planted some date seeds (first making sure they came from unpasteurized dates). Knowing that I would have a long wait before the first sprouts emerged, I planned to abate my impatience by watching the roots grow. I put an inch of water in the bottom of a peanut butter jar, slid a tube of rolled-up blotting paper into the jar, and then "planted" the date seeds halfway up the jar, pressed between the glass and the paper.

As predicted, the roots appeared and thrust downward before there was any sign of a shoot. When I eventually became bored watching the progress of the roots, I planted the seedlings in potting soil. Leaves finally did poke up through the soil, but the event was far from dramatic. Each emerging seedling looked like a green toothpick stuck into the soil. In time, the "toothpicks" unfurled into a succession of fanlike leaves that would match any ordinary houseplant for beauty and tolerance of neglect.

Fruit production from a homegrown date palm is well-nigh impossible. The plant grows slowly even under ideal conditions of brilliant sunshine and a long, warm season. And because only female plants produce fruit, enough plants must be grown to flowering size to ensure at least one male (for pollination) and one female.

A couple of years ago, I planted some seeds from a papaya I had just eaten. Having seen papayas growing wild throughout the tropics, I assumed they would not be hard to grow. I scooped the seeds from the fruit, washed them to remove their gelatinous coating, and sowed them immediately.

Growing papayas proved as challenging as growing dates. In this case, not only were the seeds slow to germinate, but the young seedlings were extremely fragile and subject to damping-off disease. I nursed a single survivor beyond this frail toddler stage, and, in time, it began to grow robustly.

In the tropics, papayas are short-lived trees that often bear their first fruits as early as eleven months after seed is sown. My papaya tree was outgrowing its one-foot-diameter pot when warm weather arrived, so I planted it outside in the ground and hoped for fruit. Imagine the astonishment of my neighbor, who grew up in Florida, when he saw a tropical papaya tree in my garden!

As summer progressed, I decided it was do-or-die for my now-very-large papaya: either the plant would fruit by late summer, in which case I would somehow bring it indoors to be nursed through the winter; otherwise, I would let it succumb to the first autumn frost. Frost struck down my barren papaya. I was consoled by the knowledge that fruiting would have been chancy anyway, because papaya plants come in various combinations of sexes. Some plants have only male flowers; others only female flowers; still others have bisexual flowers. Papaya plants even have been known to switch their sex under certain conditions. To fruit, my single plant would have needed bisexual flowers that remained so.

I do expect a crop someday from one plant that I have grown from the seed of a grocery store fruit. This is the pineapple guava, also known as feijoa (pronounced *fay-shó-a,* from the generic part of its tongue-twisting botanical name, *Feijoa sellowiana*). The fresh seeds, scooped from the fruit, germinate and grow readily — my year-old plants are now about a foot high.

The feijoa seems to me an ideal exotic fruit to attempt in the North. The bush should not mind being kept small enough to cart indoors during our frigid winters, because even in equable climes it never grows much larger than a head-high bush. The plant is subtropical rather than tropical, so can stand a bit of cold, down to about 10 degrees Fahrenheit.

Feijoa is a pretty plant, with leaves that are shiny and dark green on their upper surfaces, and feltlike and silvery on their lower surfaces. The flowers' stamens are arranged in a tuft like a red bottlebrush, and the petals are thick, purple and white, and edible. Best of all is the fruit itself. Beneath the thin, green skin is a gelatinous center whose flavor is a commingling of pineapple, mint, and a dash of spice.

I saved three feijoa seedlings, planted together now in one pot for cross-pollination, and I hope for fruit in about three years. Until then, the feijoas will be yet more nonfruiting fruit plants in the indoor jungle, among avocados, prickly pears, date palms, kumquats, and soursops.

January 22

Bay Laurel — I managed to pack lightly on a recent journey to the West Coast, toting along only one extra pair of pants, a couple of shirts, and a few other essentials. But on the return trip, how could I resist lugging back such bits of California as orange-flavored olive oil and chestnut-fig preserves? The most obvious bit of California that came back with me was a potted bay laurel plant (*Lauris nobilis*), whose single stem poked out of my small backpack, brushing fragrant leaves against the faces of my fellow travelers.

Not only does the bay laurel bring a bit of California to my home, but also traditions dating back thousands of years from its native home along the Mediterranean coast. Ancient Romans crowned victors with wreaths of laurel and bestowed berried branches on doctors passing their final examinations (the word *baccalaureate* comes from *bacca laureus*, Latin for laurel berry). Bay laurel, sacred to Apollo, was planted near temples.

Although bay laurel can grow fifty feet tall, my plan is to develop my plant into a small tree about four feet high, having a single, upright trunk capped by a pompom of leaves. The plant is hardy only to about 15 degrees Fahrenheit, so I will keep it indoors until spring, and in a pot. The plant is a rich feeder, and will need abundant fertilization from spring through fall, less so now. This potted tree will decorate the house in winter, the terrace in summer, and provide fresh bay leaves for soup and the like year-round.

I am trying to emulate the Mediterranean climate of hot, dry summers and cool, moist winters for my bay laurel. Our summers are hot and dry enough to keep the plant happy, but cool, moist winters — indoors — are a harder proposition. Because a cool room has a higher relative humidity than a warm room in winter, I am keeping the plant in a cool room. (Light is not so critical, now that the plant is resting.) But if the leaves begin to scorch or drop excessively, I will move the plant to a window in my unheated basement. I never before thought of my basement as having a Mediterranean winter!

Bay laurels can be trained to a number of shapes — pyramids, cones, and globes, with long or short trunks. In the early part of this century, hundreds of thousands of bay laurel plants were propagated and trained in Belgium and Holland, then shipped to America and throughout Europe for "decoration of open-air or exposed restaurants, esplanades, architectural appurtenances, and the like." For my lollipop-shaped tree, I am allowing only one stem to grow straight upward, and I pinch out any side shoots that develop. When the trunk reaches three feet in height, I will pinch out the top to cause branches to form high on the stem. Then I will keep

pinching these branches to cause further branching, thus forming a dense head.

All this pinching is going to yield leaves, which will find their way into the kitchen. The fresh leaf has a strong flavor, and one cookbook suggests (and I now confirm this) that just one fresh leaf is sufficient for a dish to serve four people. The aroma of the fresh leaf is more than just strong; it actually has a different quality from that of the dried leaf. The fresh aroma is almost oily, to me somewhat reminiscent of olive oil — how California!

January 23

Nourishing Houseplants — A jar of houseplant fertilizer is sitting on the table in front of me. The instructions read: "Mix ¼ teaspoon of [Brand X] per one quart of water and water plants normally. Feed every two or three weeks." It sounds simple enough. Too bad it's wrong. Plants are not machines; they are living things, and, just now, they're not hungry.

Even though shielded from the outdoor environment by insulated walls, panes of glass, artificial lighting, and heated air, houseplants are nonetheless influenced by changing seasons. Plants respond to the present season by shutting down growth and taking a rest. We gardeners must respond accordingly in our care, by slackening the amounts of fertilizer and water the plants receive.

A little extra fertilizer won't hurt, you say. At best, extra fertilizer is merely wasted as it leaches through the drainage hole in the bottom of a flowerpot. But a more serious problem often occurs: the extra fertilizer accumulates in the soil, making it salty enough to burn plants' roots. A white crust on the soil surface and browning of leaf margins are symptoms of this problem. The cure is to soak the whole pot in water a few times to wash the salts out of the soil.

I don't fertilize houseplants at all this time of year, because the soil and compost in my potting mix naturally release small but sufficient — for now — nutriment. In a couple of months, plants will begin to grow in response to the lengthening days of approaching spring, and then I will increase fertilization accordingly. Some commercial potting mixes lack nutrients, or have just a small amount that is soon expended. For such mixes a general rule is to fertilize at half strength in winter. But I never fertilize blindly — I look at my plants. If old leaves are yellowing and dropping off, I feed the plants a little more.

Similarly, plants need the least amount of water this time of year. On the porch this summer, my weeping fig required almost daily watering as it grew rapidly, basking in sunlight and warm breezes. Now this same plant is growing slowly, if at all. In the cool, still air and reduced light of my living room, once-a-week watering is adequate.

The surest way to determine when a plant needs water is to poke a finger into the soil. But who wants dirty fingernails every day? I lift small pots, and experience tells me how much water they need by their weight. This technique doesn't work so well for my weeping fig, which is six feet tall and growing in a fifteen-inch clay pot. I have heard of gardeners who can rap on their pots with a stick or their knuckles and determine, from the sound, the water content of the soil. There also is an electronic device with a metal probe that you slide into the soil, then read the soil moisture from a dial. These water meters work well, but are somewhat influenced by fertilizers and types of potting mixes. No matter how I figure out when to water, after a while I get a feel for the needs of each plant through the seasons, and then poke and probe the soil only as a periodic check.

Bulbs are the exception to the rule that plants should not be hastened in their growth this time of year. Hyacinth, freesia, and amaryllis bulbs that I potted up for indoor blossoms a couple of months ago are raring to grow. I force the growth of these potted bulbs with food and water, and let the rest of the houseplants plod along for now.

January 24

Plant Names — Since there is not much else to do gardenwise this time of year, why not muse about plant names — their common names and their sometimes intimidating-looking botanical names? Dawn Redwood, for example, reads more easily than this tree's botanical name, *Metasequoia glyptostroboides*. But speak the botanical name aloud slowly: *me-ta-see-kwoý-a glyp-to-stro-boy-dees*. It is a delight to intonate, a smooth dance of the lips, the tongue, and the upper palate.

Sensual pleasure aside, there is a practical side to botanical names. Whereas there are a hundred or so common names for that woolly leaved plant that sends up a candelabra of creamy yellow flowers each summer (I call it mullein; other names include Aaron's rod, Adam's flannel, bullock's lungwort, and velvet plant), this plant has only one botanical name: *Verbascum thapsus*.

Each plant has only one botanical name, and that name is recognized worldwide. If I want a packet of marigold seeds, I could ask for *Tagetes minuta* whether I am in Andorra or Zanzibar. In the case of plants like petunia, chrysanthemum, rhododendron, and fuchsia, at least part of the botanical name is the same as the common name in English.

A botanical name can tell a story about a plant: its discovery, its origin, its form. Adalbert Emil Radcliffe Le Tanneur von Saint Paul-Illaire discovered the African violet growing among the lush vegetation in the mountain jungles of East Africa; in his honor the plant was given the Latin epithet *Saintpaulia ionantha*. *Juniperus virginiana* is a juniper native to eastern North America; *Juniperus chinensis* hails from China. The tulip tree, *Liriodendron tulipfera*, has a particularly descriptive name. *Liriodendron* was the ancient name for this plant, meaning lily tree. And *tulipfera* means tulip bearing. (Tulip is a member of the lily family.)

Botanical names can tell about plant relationships. The apparent similarity between peaches, plums, and apricots is confirmed in the similarity of their names, *Prunus persica*, *Prunus domestica*, and *Prunus armeniaca*, respectively.

Note that the botanical name of each plant is two words, a Latin binomial. This system of plant classification was set forth in *Species Plantarum* (1753), by Carl von Linne (who is usually known by the latinized form of his name, Linnaeus). The first word in the binomial is the genus, and each genus is subdivided into one or more species, which is the second word of the binomial.

I have a pet peeve about botanical names of plants that finds root in a challenge issued years ago when I took high school English. Mr. Mehegan gave the class detailed information on the correct way to list bibliographic references at the end of our term papers: punctuation, underlining, capitalization, ordering. Then he predicted that no one would list all their references exactly right. Now it irks me when the rules are not followed in writing plant names.

Rules for plant nomenclature are simpler than Mr. Mehegan's rules for referencing. The genus and the species always are underlined or italicized. The genus is always capitalized whereas the species is not, unless it commemorates a person.

Also, the species is never written by itself; if the genus is obvious, it may precede the species in abbreviated form.

In some cases, a species might be subdivided into botanical varieties. For instance, cabbage and its close relatives all are *Brassica oleracea*. But cabbage itself is the botanical variety *capitata* (head), brussels sprouts are *gemmifera* (little gems), broccoli is *botrytis* (clusterlike), and kale is *acephala* (without a head). The correct way to write broccoli is *Brassica oleracea* var. *capitata*.

In the garden, we grow cultivated varieties (sometimes these two words are shortened to *cultivar*) of species and botanical varieties, plants like 'Yellow Boy' marigold, 'Red Delicious' apple, and 'Big Boy' tomato. The correct way to write out the full name of the last-named cultivar is either as *Lycopersicon esculentum* cv. Big Boy, or *Lycopersicon esculentum* 'Big Boy'. Green Comet Hybrid broccoli becomes *Brassica oleracea* var. *botrytis* cv. Green Comet Hybrid.

What about hybrids between different species or genera? The common strawberry, for instance, is a hybrid of *Fragaria chiloense* and *F. virginiana*. Suffice it to say that by early June my mouth will be salivating for the first *F. × anannassa* of the season. Occasionally, hybrids have been produced between two genera. In this case, the "×" is put before the name, as in × *Guzviesa*, a bromeliad hybrid.

Gardeners put off by botanical names for plants should take heart — things used to be worse. Before the days of Linneaus, baby's breath was the Latin mouthful *Lychnis alpina linifolia multiflora perampla radice*. Catnip was known as *Nepeta floribus interrupte spicatis pedunculatis*. Thanks to Linneaus, the scientific names of these two plants now are the manageable and descriptive *Gypsophila elegans* and *Nepeta cataria*, respectively.

January 25

New Varieties — What is wrong with me? The lists of "New Vegetable Varieties" for this year are beginning to appear in gardening magazines, yet I am not excited. Last year I had the same affliction: probably a dozen new tomato varieties were introduced, and I didn't grow even one of them.

No, I'm not immune to horticultural hype. Each year I am lured by horticultural promises of productivity, flavor, and pest resistance. One year I compared a bevy of broccolis: some produced slightly bigger heads, others made a few more side shoots, and still others matured a few days early. These nuances perhaps would be important to a commercial grower, but they seemed unimportant to a farmer (me) whose "back forty" is more on the order of forty square yards than forty acres.

Even when new varieties really are different, improvements that make an introduction noteworthy in one garden may be superfluous in my garden. A recent introduction, 'Salad Bush' cucumber, had almost everything a gardener would want from a cucumber variety. The plants bear early, are compact, and tolerate five important cucumber diseases. Unfortunately, it is a sixth disease, bacterial wilt, that spells the death knell to my cucumber plants each year. I continue to grow the old 'Soo Yow' cucumber because it is less prone to wilt, although not quite as tasty as 'Salad Bush'.

I am not saying that new varieties are never substantially different and better. This year, a pole bean called 'Kentucky Blue' is in the limelight. I will try this variety, and if it does indeed live up to the press release claims that it combines the best of its renowned parents, 'Kentucky Wonder' and 'Blue Lake', 'Kentucky Blue' will become an annual summer resident of my garden. 'Golden Crown' watermelon is another contender this year. It is tasty, disease resistant, blah, blah, blah . . . most important, though, is the way it signals ripeness. The skin turns yellow. (I never have mastered the art of thumping watermelons for ripeness.)

In spite of all the hullabaloo over new vegetable varieties, scores of noteworthy, albeit non-new, varieties have been nestled for years in quiet greatness on the pages of gardening catalogs. 'Gardener's Delight' is a tomato that has been around for a while. It might look like any other cherry tomato, but 'Gardener's Delight' is so good that the fruits rarely make it past my garden gate.

This annual midwinter ballyhoo of what's new in the plant kingdom not only may narrow the number of kinds of beans, broccoli, and tomatoes that gardeners might try, but also might further divert interest from lesser-known vegetables, most of which are not worth a breeder's time. *Mâche* — a salad green with a delicate, floral flavor — is relatively unknown in America in spite of its many aliases. Yet it is cold hardy enough to reliably survive the winter in my garden, even growing during mild spells in midwinter. You are not apt to find 'Dunkelgrüner Vollherziger' or 'Ronde Maraîchère' *mâche* in any list of "What's New." Nor any fennels, cardoons, scorzoneras, groundnuts, ground cherries, or mustards.

Another danger in this ballyhoo over "varieties" is that it might lead one to believe that choice of variety is the end-all for acquiring a green thumb. Not so. 'Ha Ogen', 'Earlidew', and 'Chaca' all are ambrosial melons, but bringing them to fruition in my garden is the culmination of a carefully ordered sequence of events that starts with seed sowing and soil preparation and ends with timely harvest.

The frenzy over new varieties reaches its peak with the midwinter lineup of each year's All-America Selection (AAS) winners. These are new varieties that have been judged superior in test gardens at more than twenty-five locations scattered throughout the country. The folks of AAS perform a valuable service, encouraging breeders and facilitating press coverage of "what's new." In one form or another, AAS press releases reach more than eighty-five million people.

At the same time, the focus on a few varieties tends to overshadow, especially for beginning gardeners, the true diversity available. Red, savoyed leaves made 'Red Sails' lettuce an AAS winner one year. But if I wanted to eat red lettuce, I also could grow bronze-tinged 'Pirat', red-tipped 'Lolla Rosa', deep-red 'Ruby', or deepest-red 'Red Salad Bowl' — whatever intensity of red suits me. These lettuces can never be AAS winners simply because they are not new introductions, and AAS contenders are limited to varieties that never have been sold previously.

Imagine what might happen if the yearly national hype of new flower and vegetable varieties became a rousing success. Just as a McDonald's stand in Alberquerque looks like and serves the same Big Macs as one in Boston, every backyard garden would have the same broccoli and tomato varieties, yet no cardoons or tomatillos. Remember, those AAS test gardens are scattered throughout the country to find varieties adapted nationwide.

We need more variety, not just new varieties, in our gardens. What the doyen of American horticulture, Liberty Hyde Bailey, said at the beginning of this century about apples applies equally well today to vegetables: "Why do we need so many kinds . . .? Because there are so many folks. A person has the right to gratify his legitimate tastes . . . [and] should be accorded that privilege." As I sit by my wood stove perusing gardening catalogs, I *am* going to select new varieties to grow this year. But "new" means any of the hundreds of varieties I have not tried yet. I will try to look at, then beyond, this year's horticultural hype to find what is worth growing, whether it is new, old, common, or uncommon.

FEBRUARY

Wintry boughs against a wintry sky;
Yet the sky is partly blue
And the clouds are partly bright.
Who can tell but sap is mounting high,
Out of sight,
Ready to burst through?

Christina G. Rossetti, *"Spring signals to Winter"*

BRIGHTENING SUN — made more so as it reflects off the snow — streams in the windows, stirring houseplants not only to grow, but even to produce flowers. Amaryllis, cyclamen, and freesia blooms were expected, and perhaps I can coax a few from a geranium plant. Flowers on potted alpine strawberries foretell of a few tasty berries out of season.

Outside, frigid air and snow maintain a quiet stillness over the landscape. But wait! If I watch closely, I see that even trees and shrubs have begun to stir, as their buds fatten ever so slightly with each little bit of warmth. Nature is doing all the moving; there still is little for me to do, except to watch, to wait, and to enjoy.

February 1
What's in a Name? — Garden catalogs are neatly stacked, and it is time for a final run through them to decide what to grow.

With only a name to go on, which tomato would you choose to grow: 'Supersonic' or 'Oxheart'? If the name 'Oxheart' seems a bit too gruesome, make the choice between 'Supersonic' and 'Ponderosa'. My guess is that most gardeners would choose 'Oxheart' or 'Ponderosa' for a tomato, 'Supersonic' for an airline. What compels a contemporary plant breeder to give a tomato a name like 'Supersonic'? Many old-time names of vegetables — 'Oxheart' and 'Ponderosa' are examples — are a lot more appealing than some of the newer names. A good name may even be part of the reason a vegetable of yore still appears in today's catalogs among all the new hybrids.

Many old-time varieties had interesting names, interesting sometimes only because the rationales behind the names are not immediately obvious. As I thumb through a catalog of vegetable varieties, I cannot help but wonder why anyone would name a parsnip 'The Student'. The same goes for 'Old Bloody Butcher' corn and 'Missing Link' apple. Such names surely were not chosen as marketing ploys. In the case of the 'Lazy Wife' string bean, the rationale behind the (sexist) name is not at all obscure (old-fashioned string beans had to be de-stringed). Compare such clever names with those of today's varieties — 'Superhybrid' eggplant, 'Green Duke' broccoli, or 'Bounty' green bean.

Some of the old variety names have a nice ring to them. Who can resist growing a corn called 'Country Gentleman', or a bean called 'Red Valentine'? Such names are more appealing than cutesy names like 'Kandy Korn' corn or 'Tasty Hybrid' pepper. (At least the pepper is not 'Tastee Hybrid'.) Which variety name sounds more appealing to you: 'Red-Cored Chantenay' carrot or 'Six-Pack' carrot? 'Calabrese' broccoli or 'Packman' (or is it 'Pac-Man'?) broccoli?

Some old names might have had appeal in their day, but just would not do today. With metropolitan New York City looming closer than ever, 'Hackensack' melon cannot evoke the bucolic tang it did back in 1929. And I doubt that any plant breeder today would name a beet variety 'Detroit Dark

Red'. Nothing against Detroit, but the name is better applied to an automobile than to a beet variety.

Before you lovers of 'Supersonic', 'Jetstar', and 'Ultra-Boy' tomatoes get your hackles up, remember that I am not knocking the quality of these varieties — only their names. In fact, appealing names often were assigned to varieties of dubious merit in the past. The name 'Sops of Wine' makes my mouth water more than did the actual apple. The same goes for 'Maiden Blush' apple — beautiful name (and beautiful fruit), but mediocre eating quality. On the other hand, the luscious modern apple with the vapid name of 'Jonagold' was derived by simply combining the names of its parents, 'Jonathan' and 'Golden Delicious'.

As I peruse garden catalogs in the coming days, I must stop and think about what makes me choose one cultivar over another.

February 4

"Garden" — The continuing lull in gardening activity prompts me now to ponder etymology. (Etymology, not entomology; aphids, mealybugs, and whiteflies will be crawling around soon enough.) What exactly do we mean when we talk about a "garden" or "gardening"?

"Gardening" is pretty much synonymous with "horticulture," the latter word from the Latin *hortus,* meaning a garden, and *cultura*, to culture. According to Webster, horticulture is the "art or science of cultivating fruits, flowers, and vegetables." The word "horticulture" was given official recognition in *The New World of English Words* in 1678 by E. Phillips, although the Latin form, *horticultura*, first appeared as the title of a treatise in 1631.

Note that horticulture concerns fruits, flowers, and vegetables; nothing is said about cultivating a field of cotton or wheat. These latter crops are in the ken of agronomy, from the Latin root *ager,* meaning field. Once again quoting Webster, agronomy is the "science or art of crop production; the management of farm land." Horticultural crops are more intensively cultivated than are farm crops — and are more apt to be threatened by neglect.

In fact, gardening and horticulture are not exactly synonymous. Horticulture usually is associated with growing plants for a livelihood, and is broken down into pomology (fruits), olericulture (vegetables), floriculture (flowers), and landscaping. Gardening usually implies something more homey and intimate.

Over the centuries, there have been numerous spellings of "garden." The fourteenth-century lyric poem *King Alisaunder* relates that "samytes and baudekyns Weore contined in the gardynes." Later in that century, Chaucer wrote the word a bit differently: "Yif me a plante of thilke blessed tre And in my gardyn planted it shall be." We find yet another spelling early in the sixteenth century: "My lord you have very good strawberries at your gardayne in Holberne." Finally, by the time of Shakespeare, we have: "Ile fetch a turne about the Garden." Here, "garden" at least is spelt the moderne way.

The root of the word comes from the Old English *geard*, meaning fence, enclosure, or courtyard, and the Old Saxon *gyrdan*, meaning to enclose or gird. These words are closely related to our modern words "yard," "girth," and "guard." Medieval gardens were physically enclosed. Mine is too, but mostly as protection against raccoons that relish my sweet corn and rabbits that love my peas and beans, not against knights practicing jousting or wild pigs roaming the fields. The medieval garden was against the house and protected by a high wall or, perhaps, a wattle fence.

Over the centuries, garden and gardening have come to mean more than the fenced medieval garden. The archetypal Persian garden is dominated by refreshing pools or fountains of water. In the Italian garden, we find trees and shrubs, and stone stairways, balustrades, and porticos. Grand parterres characterize the French style of gardening. About a hundred years ago, the increasingly grand style of gardening fell from favor as an Englishwoman, Gertrude Jekyll, came forward to laud and design gardens that emulated intimate, colorful, and informal cottage gardens. She wrote that the "first purpose of a garden is to give happiness and repose of mind, which is more often enjoyed in the contemplation of the homely border . . . than in any of the great gardens where the flowers lose their identity, and with it their hold on the human heart."

What do garden and gardening mean today? A few tomato and marigold plants, separated from the house by an expanse of lawn? A woodland glen of ferns and bleeding hearts? Or a knot garden of herbs within a white picket fence — in the medieval style, one might say?

February 11

Purple Broccoli — Keep your eye out for seeds of purple broccoli and cauliflower, for these are vegetables well worth growing. Sometimes they are listed with cauliflowers, other times with broccolis, but this is all right because some broccolis are the same genus, species, and botanical variety as cauliflower (*Brassica oleraceae* var. *botrytis*). The purple broccolis and cauliflowers — aw, why not just call them purple broccoflowers or cauliccolis? — I have grown behave more like cauliflower in that there is no sprouting of side shoots after the large head is cut. The purple heads also are a bit more loosely packed than white cauliflower curds. The name broccoli is justifiable on the grounds that the purple heads turn emerald green when cooked.

I think of this vegetable now as a reminder to get seeds for a spring sowing. The seeds are uncommon on seed racks in stores, but are offered by most mail-order vegetable seed specialists. There is still time to order the seeds if they are not available locally.

Purple broccoflowers are delicious, a bit more delicate in flavor than either cauliflower or broccoli. They also are very tender — too tender to be widely grown on a commercial scale. The heads are a regal purple, attractive enough so that I regret having to cut them. Last season, I even interplanted some of these purple beauties with red zinnias and blue delphiniums.

Purple broccoflowers are grown in essentially the same manner as regular cauliflower or broccoli. For a summer crop, I sow seeds in March, then transplant plants into the garden in early May. For autumn harvest — which, with cool days, makes for especially tasty buds — I sow seeds either directly in the garden or in seed flats, about mid-June.

Purple broccoflowers are easier to grow than white cauliflower, being less finicky as to weather and not needing their leaves tied to blanch the curds white. Also, the quality of the purples does not suffer if harvest is held off a couple of days, which is not the case for white cauliflower.

It is alleged that purple cauliflower and broccoli are more pest resistant than regular cauliflowers and broccolis. The cabbageworm is the only cauliflower or broccoli pest in my garden, and this insect seems equally fond of purple as green or white flower heads. True, the velvety green worms do stand out prominently in the purple heads, making it easier for me, and perhaps birds, to pick off the insects. At any rate, cabbageworms are easily controlled with a spray of *Bacillus thurengiensis*.

These purple-headed beauties really are not all that new. They were mentioned in seed catalogs a hundred years ago. Perusing local seed racks and mail-order sources, I find the following varieties available today: 'Green Ball Chartreuse', 'Purple Head', 'Burgundy Queen', and 'Purple Giant' cauliflower; 'Sicilian Purple', 'King Purple', 'King Robert Purple', 'Purple Sprouting', and 'Violet Queen' broccoli. In my experience, some varieties head up sooner than others, and some make larger heads than others. Vilmorin-Andrieux wrote a hundred years ago that some of these purple broccoflowers needed two seasons to make heads, which is fine in France, where the plants will overwinter, but not in my garden. Some varieties I have grown never headed up, and I suspect these were such varieties. The other varieties I have tried are well worth growing, most notably 'Purple Sprouting' and 'Violet

Queen'. I even may give up growing any green broccoli; definitely any white cauliflower.

February 13

Amorphophallus — In retrospect, I am not sure whether the plant from the fellow up the street was meant as a neighborly gift or as chicanery. I had never spoken to him before, but he stopped to chat as I was outside spreading leaves over my vegetable garden one autumn day. He began to describe and soon offered me what seemed a most fantastic plant — one that would flower reliably every winter without even being planted in soil! He returned later that day with a warty tuber somewhere between a softball and a basketball in size.

I resisted the urge to plant the tuber in soil, and set it on a saucer to prevent it from toppling. Sometime in February,

as I recall, a dark, pointed shoot began to emerge atop the tuber. In a day, any skepticism I may have had about whether this tuber would grow without soil dissolved. The shoot grew noticeably each day — to one foot, two feet, three feet, and four feet. Then, at five feet, an inverted, plum-purple skirt unfurled beneath the chocolate-brown shoot. The flower actually was more eerie than beautiful, and made more so by its being perched atop a five-foot stalk that was poking out of the top of a naked tuber.

Now for the possible joke: my neighbor, perhaps purposely, had said nothing of the flower's aroma. The whole room reeked like an abandoned fish market. The plant was not admired long before I whisked it into the basement and sealed its head in a plastic bag.

One day soon after, I stumbled on a picture of this flower as I thumbed through Volume A of a gardening encyclopedia. There was no mistaking it; my plant was in the aptly named genus, *Amorphophallus*, probably *A. Riviera*. The genus *Amorphophallus* is in the Araceae family, which also includes plants like jack-in-the-pulpit and calla lily. As with the jack-in-the-pulpit and the calla lily, the true flowers are on the phalluslike, pointed spadix. The inverted "skirt" is actually a modified leaf.

Delving more deeply into other horticultural texts, I learned that *Amorphophallus* plants have achieved newspaper headlines in their day. In 1932, the New York Botanical Garden received from Sumatra a sixty-pound tuber of *A. titanum*. The tuber grew only leaves for a few years, but on June 8, 1937, a flower stalk emerged. The tuber at this time weighed over a hundred pounds, and the flower unfurled to a width of four-and-a-half feet(!) across after the shoot attained a height of more than eight feet. A *New York Times* clipping from that time showed the great botanist Hugo de Vries perched on a stepladder, peering into the giant flower. How could he have tolerated the stench? (Incidentally, the odor of these plants attracts carrion insects, which pollinate the flowers in native habitats.)

I learned from my reading that the show was not over when my plant's flower finally wilted. (It was over for the specimen at the New York Botanical Garden; that species dies after flowering.) Each year after flowering, my plant needed to grow leaves to feed the tuber for next winter's bloom.

So when the soil warmed in the spring, I planted the tuber in the garden under cover of a few inches of soil. Shortly thereafter, a stalk emerged, this time pale olive green with dark-brown splotches. A single leaf unfurled when the snake-like stalk reached a couple of feet in height. This single leaf divided and spread out like three radii of a circle, with each of the three sections further subdivided. At this stage, the plant was quite attractive, although still eerie.

At the end of the growing season, I dug the tuber, which had enlarged considerably, for storage. As a tropical plant, even the dormant tubers must never be exposed to temperatures below 50 degrees Fahrenheit. My plant also had grown offsets, which after a few years of growth also would reach flowering size.

Amorphophallus is not likely to be found among the bins of gladiolus, begonia, and dahlia bulbs at garden supply stores in spring. *Amorphophallus* does periodically turn up in mail-order catalogs, under such names as Voodoo Lily, Snake Palm, or Devil's Tongue. I no longer grow and do not recall what I did with my plant or its progeny. But I do not think I passed them on to any (unsuspecting) fellow gardeners.

February 19

Wardian Cases — In 1827, a London physician with an interest in caterpillar metamorphosis built small glass boxes to contain the cocoons and emerging butterflies. Peering into the dirt in one of the boxes, Dr. Ward one day noticed that a fern spore had germinated. Enthralled with the way the developing plant flourished without care in the box, Dr. Ward changed his course of study. In 1836, he published a book entitled *On the Growth of Plants in Closely Glazed Cases*.

Wardian cases, as the glass boxes were called, became the rage in Victorian England. Plants were protected by their cases from chilling drafts, dry air, and gas fumes of Victorian homes. Plant explorers also found a use for Wardian cases. Live plants from exotic lands could be transported by ship to England, protected within these cases from salt air and changing climatic conditions.

Whether in the home or on ship, plants in Wardian cases need little care. The small amount of water that the leaves transpire in their humid environment condenses on the glass and dribbles back to the roots; oxygen released each day from photosynthesis is used each night in respiration. Dr. Ward reputedly grew ferns in one of his cases for fifteen years without any care at all!

A Wardian case full of lush green plants is still a year-round oasis, even if my home is less drafty and the air is cleaner than that of the homes of Victorian England. Today we call such plant cases terrariums. Aside from decorative value and ease of care, a terrarium provides the moist, boggy environment essential to the cultivation of certain plants.

Any of a number of types of containers can serve as a Wardian case. I have made my own, using glass and silicone glue. Other possibilities include five-gallon water jars, one-gallon canning jars, aquariums, and oversize brandy snifters. Large plastic soda bottles can be converted into small terrariums. Pry the plastic piece off the bottom of one of these bottles to reveal the domed bottom. Then cut the bottle in half crosswise and invert the dome over the base you initially pried off. Once you have settled on a container, wash it thoroughly, for you will not get another chance once it is planted.

When ready to plant my Wardian case (I think I'll use this appellation, which has a more exotic ring than does terrarium), I put a layer of charcoal down first, to keep the soil sweet. I top this with a layer of gravel, then potting soil, the amount depending on the container, the plants, and the type of landscaping I plan. Finally . . . the plants. Dexterity with chopsticks helps in planting.

Plants that thrive in high humidity and do not grow too fast are best for a Wardian case. A spider plant in a terrarium I made for my brother a few years ago has pushed off the wooden lid and now is climbing out the top. Good plant choices for larger terrariums are dracaena, diffenbachia, and palms. Low-growing plants include English ivy (small-leaved varieties), prayer plant, ferns, and mosses. The climate within a closed container allows cultivation of insectivorous plants like Venus's-flytrap, pitcher plant, and sundew, all of which need moist, boggy soils and very humid air. (And perhaps a fly every now and then.)

The final step, watering, is the most critical. I add enough water to moisten the soil without making it sodden, pouring it in slowly enough so puddles do not form. Then I set the Wardian case in its permanent location, in bright light but out of direct sun, and watch for condensation. If I have added the right amount of water, some will condense on the glass each morning. If I have overwatered, I let the case dry out a few days with the lid off.

The succession of plants, and perhaps other organisms, that thrive in the unique ecosystem created within a Wardian case is fascinating. Something always thrives. My first case was far too sodden, but it did grow an attractive and interesting crop of mushrooms in addition to the few plants that survived.

February 23

Experiments — Here are four easy plant experiments for inside the house. These timely prologues to spring are sure to provide amusement and spark botanical interest.

First Experiment. This experiment allows close observation of the development of seedlings from seeds. Buy a bag of dry kidney beans at the grocery store. Soak one seed about fifteen minutes to soften it, and then split it open. The seed splits easily along the line that separates the two large halves of the seed, the cotyledons. (Cotyledons provide food for developing seedlings or humans.) A little hooked shoot capped with two tiny leaves will be pressed against the inside face of one of the cotyledons.

Now that we have looked inside a seed, let's see what a seed can do. Roll up some blotting paper and slide it into a drinking glass so it presses against the glass. Slide four new beans around the glass between the paper and the glass, a couple of inches from the bottom. Pour a half-inch of water into the glass, replenishing the water as it soaks into the blotting paper and evaporates. Cover the glass with a plate for a couple of days, until the seeds germinate.

The beans will swell as they imbibe water. The first sign of life will be the small rootlet that will poke out the end of each seed, followed by lateral and sublateral roots. Developing seedlings must begin life by sending out roots to search for a reliable water supply. Once awakened from its dormancy, a seed will die if redried.

After the roots have made some growth, the small hooked

shoot within the seed will expand and straighten out, catapulting the whole seed up. The tiny leaves will unfold to become the first foliage leaves, and the cotyledons will wither, their usefulness past. In some seeds — corn, for example — the cotyledons stay below ground and the shoot pushes upward alone.

The experiment teaches: (1) Make sure seedlings in flats or in the garden do not dry out once they have swelled with water (but do not drown them — they need oxygen also). (2) In the garden, make sure the soil is soft enough so that seedlings can break through the surface. Help by covering the soil with a thin layer of peat, sand, or compost, or lightly sprinkling the surface with water.

Second Experiment. Plants that are hungry for light become etiolated. Etiolated plants are stretched out, with small pale leaves, as compared to stocky, green plants grown in bright light. The same beans-paper-glass setup can be used to demonstrate etiolation. Set up two jars, one in a bright window and one in a closet. After a week or two, the plants will look as if they came from different types of seeds.

Etiolation increases the survival value of plants. Imagine a germinating seed buried in the dark soil, pushing its way upward. Underground, which seedling has more chance of reaching the surface: the thick, stocky seedling with large leaves, or the one with small leaves and a slinky stem, str-r-r-etching for the light?

Once an etiolated plant is exposed to light, it turns green, with large leaves and thick stems.

The experiment teaches: (1) Do not plant seeds deeper than suggested on seed packets. (2) Give your plants more light if they appear to be stretching in the direction of light and their leaves are small and pale.

Third Experiment. Growing plants bend toward light in a response called phototropism. This phenomenon fascinated Charles Darwin and his son Francis to the extent that they wrote a book entitled *The Power of Movement in Plants* (1881).

Once again, use your bean-paper-glass setup to get three plants growing. When the plants are a few inches high, wrap only the growing tip of the first plant with aluminum foil. On the second plant, leave the growing tip exposed and wrap aluminum foil around the stem. Do nothing to the third plant. Now put the glass where it gets light from one side only — a sunny window, for instance.

The completely exposed plant will bend toward the light, and the plant with the covered tip will grow straight up. The plant with the covered stem will grow straight up, except for the new growth above the foil, which will bend toward the light.

The Darwins concluded from this same experiment (they used oat seedlings) that "when seedlings are freely exposed to lateral light some influence is transmitted from the upper to the lower part, causing the latter to bend." About fifty years later, that "influence" was determined to be a plant hormone, called auxin, which is produced and carried downward from the growing tips of plants. The hormone causes cell expansion, and when one side of a stem is illuminated, the auxin migrates to the opposite side. Thus the plant bends toward the light because cells on the darker side of the stem grow larger than those on the lighter side. The tip does need light to produce auxin.

The experiment teaches: (1) Give plants in sunny windows a turn every couple of days to keep them straight. (2) Be careful with herbicide. A common ingredient of lawn "weeders" is 2,4-D, a concentrated, synthetic auxin that can twist plants out of shape. Tomatoes and grapes are especially sensitive.

Fourth Experiment. Tree buds swell, almost imperceptibly, by the end of this month, as they prepare to burst open with growth in spring. These buds are dormant, restrained now *only* by cold temperatures. These same buds would not have budged if given warmth and water in early December, for hardy plants have built-in protection mechanisms against the cold. Until they have been exposed to a minimum amount of cold, they will not respond to warmth. The requirement for chilling has now been fulfilled, and buds will advance as weather turns warm.

The experiment teaches: (1) Keep fingers crossed that warm weather does not tempt the blossoms of peaches and apricots too early, whereupon they are liable to be killed by subsequent freezes (no blossoms, no fruit). (2) Cut branches of flowering trees and shrubs to put in jars of water around the house. Anticipate spring with the fragrant white plum blossoms, pink peach blossoms, yellow forsythia blossoms, and furry pussywillow blossoms.

February 25

Gardenia — Next time I come across a gardenia plant for sale, I will buy it, as much for the challenge of growing it as for its deliciously fragrant, camellialike blossoms. I have grown — or I should say, *tried* to grow — the plant before, but each time I eventually admitted defeat and the plant ended up in the compost pile.

The gardenia is an acknowledged difficult houseplant, and this gives me some consolation for past failures. Gardenias are prone to chlorosis (leaf yellowing) and lack of flowers. By paying close attention to the causes of these problems, I predict success with my next gardenia.

Chlorotic leaves are unsightly and cannot properly nourish a plant. Actually, the glossy, dark-green leaves of a healthy gardenia make the plant attractive even without blossoms (but not enough to warrant the trouble of growing it solely as a foliage plant).

Leaf chlorosis usually indicates a deficiency of iron in a gardenia plant. An obvious cure is to dose the soil with iron, and the best "Geritol" for plants is iron "chelate," available in garden stores. This chelate can perk up a plant even overnight if sprayed on the leaves.

More commonly, a soil has sufficient iron, but the plant is iron poor because improper soil conditions prevent the roots from absorbing adequate amounts. Gardenias need soil that is acidic, rich in humus, moist, and not too cold. The ideal soil pH for gardenias is 5.5 to 6.0, which is more acidic than that required by most other plants. Sulfur, acid plant fertilizer, or watering occasionally with vinegar solution (one-half teaspoon vinegar per quart of water) will make a soil acidic.

Although gardenias need a constantly moist soil, a sodden soil will bring on iron deficiency. Therefore, the potting mix should drain freely and be rich in moisture-holding humus. My standard potting mix, without added limestone, should suit a gardenia. Water should be applied at room temperature so as not to chill the roots.

Getting a gardenia to flower presents a more challenging problem than keeping its leaves green. If environment conditions are not just right, flower buds drop off or do not form. The plants need bright light, an even temperature in the low 60s by night and 10 degrees warmer by day, and high humidity. Once buds start to form, a gardenia resents being disturbed and will respond to being turned or moved by dropping its buds.

Gardenia blossoms are most welcome in winter, and the botanical variety *Gardenia jasminoides Fortuniana* (also called *G. Veitchii*) is the species that flowers at this time. Unfortunately, bright light and, to a lesser extent, equable temperatures are at a premium in winter. Plants housebound year-round and exposed to artificial lighting may not flower unless they go though a three-week period of "short days," which means no light at all from 5 P.M. to 8 A.M. If I buy this winter-flowering variety, my plan is to summer the plant outdoors, then winter it indoors in a south window in a cool room. I will set the plant on a tray filled with pebbles and water, with a "Do Not Move" sign.

G. jasminoides, commonly called the Cape Jasmine, is easier to flower. Blossoming begins in late spring and continues through the summer, so the plant can be kept semidormant indoors through the winter, then put outside in spring. The idea is to hold back growth in winter by keeping the plants cool (about 45 degrees Fahrenheit) and the soil dryish.

The plants need light in winter, but not a great deal, since they are semidormant.

By late winter, semidormant plants will look ragged, with many yellowing and falling leaves. But the plants should perk up in spring as soon as they are pruned back a bit, then given warmth, water, and food. Once warm weather settles in the spring, a position outdoors in slight shade will provide the light and humidity plants need for flowering.

Given my druthers, I will face the challenge of growing the more difficult *G. jasminoides Fortuniana*, not so much for the challenge but for the flowers in winter. I will probably not be given my druthers, and will impulsively buy a small gardenia plant from among those I commonly see offered for sale in the local supermarket. Although these lush, green plants are spruced up with a few paper flowers, I nonetheless am attracted by the foreshadowed fragrance of the fat, real flower buds nestled among the leaves.

A friend's mother acknowledges little skill or general interest in growing plants. But she does have an enormous, old gardenia that has flowered regularly for years in her living room window. To her and anyone else who grows gardenias successfully, I suggest that you ignore any advice I offer and just continue doing whatever you are doing.

February 26

Wood Ashes — I wonder if my neighbors suspect that I am engaging in some sort of occult ritual as I take my biweekly winter rounds through the garden followed by puffs of grey smoke. Perhaps I am entreating tiny gnomes living within the soil to keep weeds at bay next season? Or begging garden gremlins to make my soil fertile? No, and again no! I am merely spreading wood ashes about.

I must be careful with my terminology: I am not disposing of wood ashes; I am fertilizing my soil with them. Wood ash is a rich source of potassium, a nutrient required by plants in amounts second only to nitrogen. Potassium helps build strong stems and helps plants resist disease. It also regulates the opening and closing of the tiny pores in leaves, through which gases pass for photosynthesis.

The close connection between potassium and wood ash is reflected in a traditional source of, and the root of the word, potassium — "potash." Potassium compounds once were extracted by mixing wood ashes with water in iron pots. Go to a nursery and ask for a potash fertilizer, and you will be handed a bag of potassium sulfate (sulfate of potash), potassium chloride (muriate of potash), greensand (a mined mineral), or — if the time were a half-century ago — wood ash. "Potash" technically means potassium oxide, but sometimes also refers to potassium carbonate or hydroxide.

Wood ash contains from 1 to about 10 percent potash. (Since potash includes the weight of potassium and oxygen, the raw potassium concentration is always less than the potash concentration — 17 percent less, to be precise.) Ashes from hardwood trees are at the top of this range and softwood ashes are at the low end. Because rain will leach much of the nutriment from ashes, I store my ashes in a metal tub under cover of the garage.

I am not overly precise in my spreading of these ashes. I start at one end of the garden in the beginning of wood heating season, then work my way across the garden, aiming to spread five to ten pounds of ashes over every hundred square feet. When finished with the garden, I spread ashes over the lawn.

Wood ash is good stuff, but not to be overused. Plants need adequate, not excessive, potassium. Too much potassium upsets the balance of other nutrients in a plant. Wood ashes also make the soil more alkaline, so I never use them under my blueberry or rhododendron bushes. Nor should wood ashes be used on azalea, pin oak, mountain laurel, or other plants that enjoy very acidic soils.

I do not dump — whoops, spread — all my wood ashes on the garden and lawn. I save some for use in potting soils, mixed in at the rate of a half-cup of ashes per gallon of mix (except in potting mixes destined for acid-loving plants, of course).

And some I sift, then save, to use in the garden during the summer for pest control. Plants sprinkled with dry ashes become unpalatable to rabbits, bean beetles, and onion and cabbage maggots. A thick line of dry ashes on the soil becomes a Maginot Line against slugs, until washed away by rain. Conversely, alkalinity washed into the soil from wood ashes spread over the ground kills cutworms. Cucumber beetles are repelled (or killed?) by a spray made from a handful each of wood ash and hydrated lime mixed into two gallons of water, then sprayed on the leaves. A sprinkling of wood ashes into which has been mixed turpentine, at the rate of one tablespoon turpentine per gallon of wood ash, repels squash bugs. And a paste of wood ashes and water on the trunk of a peach tree keeps borers at bay.

Squash bugs have never been a serious problem in my garden and my cabbages rarely get maggots, so I cannot personally vouch for all these pest-deterring and -killing properties of wood ashes. But wood ashes are nontoxic and the above suggestions come from reputable sources, so the treatments are worth a try when needed. The main drawback to using wood ashes for pest control is that they usually must be applied again following rain. Also, keep wood ashes off tender seedlings, or they will be burned.

Perhaps there is indeed some sort of gnome or gremlin in these ashes, after all, to impart them with such a myriad of uses.

February 27

Garden Structure — This may sound crazy, but winter is not a bad time to admire the garden. With herbaceous plants, flowers, and leaves a memory of the past season and a hope for the future season, the garden is reduced to its bare bones. But the present wintry scene need not be dull or bleak. Good bones give structure to the landscape, knitting it together in some places, dividing it up in others, framing vistas, and providing firm footing for the eyes (figuratively) and feet. Even now.

Three-dimensional forms give structure to a landscape. A house usually is the most obvious mass jutting up into space on a property. Too often it is the only structural element, feebly tied to the landscape with gumdrop-shaped junipers or yews along the foundation. I have effected a relationship between my yard and my house by building out from the rear wall a grape arbor, then enclosing the ground beneath this arbor with a low hedge of potentilla. Similarly, the stone wall framing slopes at the front and side of my house flows into the landscape with a contiguous stone wall sweeping out across the yard.

Plants add mass and definition to the landscape only if they are evergreen, or sufficiently large or densely twiggy. Although the privets dividing my property from my neighbor's are now leafless, their twigs are dense enough to make

a billowing, brown swatch in the landscape. Around the other side of the yard, an old boxelder's contributions are massive limbs and a trunk four feet in diameter. My long, double row of dwarf fruit trees, with four feet between the trees and fifteen feet between the rows, makes a small *allée* that curves out of sight. The thick trunks of the small trees draw me along like highway markers to the back of the yard.

Unlike annual plants, which leave no legacy at the end of the season, trees, hedges, and stone walls make strong, permanent statements, so must be planned as part of the overall design. Every structural element needs a clearly defined purpose before it is built or planted. It took me five years to realize that my vegetable plot needed to be more physically and aesthetically connected to my house. I finally knocked a hole through the back wall of the house, then put in a glass doorway. Through this doorway, I can see or walk out under the arbor, then continue straight along a path up to and through the vegetable plot. On the other hand, I have planted more than my share of trees on impulse, and later have had to cut them down or move them to more suitable locations. And that arbor: it is less than a decade old but already has suffered numerous readjustments as I added, removed, or just shifted plants, posts, and crosspieces.

An *allée,* a billowing hedge, or an arbor does not come into its full glory overnight. Even if almost full-grown plants are set in the ground, some seasons must pass before plants snuggle into their surroundings and look truly at home. With time, frost and rain and sun lend a patina to tree trunks, stone walls, and fences; near the ground, creeping plants lend a gentle embrace. There is no way around it — age is needed to bring character to these weighty garden elements. Some aspects of gardening should be long-term propositions.

Epilogue

EVEN AS I committed to paper, at the end of February, those final thoughts for the gardening year, change occurred. My garden — every garden — is like a living organism, bearing the imprint of growth and decline left by time measured not only month by month through the seasons, but in terms of years. The garden also changes with the gardener. Yellow flag irises, a mental image in my garden when I wrote of them last June 9th, were subsequently planted and by autumn developed into strong growing clumps. The decades-old willow that aesthetically anchored my lilies last July 25th also threatened the house, so now is gone, remembered for a few more years by the broad, flat stump that remains.

Through this ebb and flow of a garden's growth and decline, and continual planting and rearranging, there emerges a scene that increasingly approaches a personal vision of paradise. In my garden, that vision is of a plot of land that pleases the senses, nourishes the body, and stimulates the mind. This may seem like too much to ask from a plot of land, but the road to this paradise is an end in itself, along the way offering understanding and pleasure.

A garden is something to start, but not necessarily finish. Our next visit will be different from our last.

Appendix:
My Weekly Gardening Schedule

NOTE: *While "My Weekly Gardening Schedule" is specific to my growing conditions and what I like to grow, it may be useful to other gardeners as a model for record keeping.*

March

WEEK 1: *Sow indoors:* statice; larkspur; lettuce; impatiens; petunia

WEEK 2: *Sow indoors:* strawflower; lavatera; cosmos; snapdragon; bachelor's button; aster; allysum; bells of Ireland; celery; fennel; celeriac; cabbage; broccoli; brussels sprouts; parsley

Sow outdoors: greens in cold frame

Transplant: lettuce to cold frame

WEEK 3: *Sow indoors:* ground cherry; heliotrope; stocks; gazania

Sow outdoors: allysum; California poppy; Shirley poppy

Transplant: overwintered perennials

Other: clear garden beds; fertilize; force branches of spring flowering shrubs

[*249*]

WEEK 4: *Sow indoors:* dahlia; cauliflower; lettuce

April

WEEK 1: *Sow indoors:* tithonia; calendula; scabiosa; pepper (warm water); eggplant (warm water); annual herbs
Sow outdoors: peas; radishes; onion sets; spinach; sweet pea; cleome
Other: spread compost

WEEK 2: *Sow indoors:* tomatoes (warm water); marigold; zinnia
Sow outdoors: spinach; *mâche*; mustard; arugula
Transplant: lettuce
Plant: potatoes

WEEK 3: *Sow outdoors:* onion; carrot; parsley; radish
Transplant: cabbage; broccoli; cauliflower; brussels sprouts
Spray: gooseberries

WEEK 4: *Transplant:* onion; leek; larkspur; pansy
Other: take black currant cuttings

May

WEEK 1: *Sow indoors:* cucumber, squash, and melon (warm water); basil
Sow outdoors: aster; bachelor's button; calendula; larkspur
Transplant: allysum; statice; calendula; snapdragon
Other: mow hay; watch for curculios on apples, peaches, and plums; watch for frost on strawberries

WEEK 2: *Sow outdoors:* corn; beans; okra; basil

WEEK 3: *Sow outdoors:* squash
Transplant: tomato; celery; celeriac; tender annuals
Other: watch for caterpillars on fruit trees

WEEK 4: *Sow outdoors:* corn; cardoon
Transplant: ground cherry; pepper; eggplant
Other: cut back tansy

June

WEEK 1: *Sow outdoors:* corn; squash; okra; parsley
Transplant: melons
Other: bag grapes; cut off tulip foliage; trim hedges
WEEK 2: *Sow:* perennial flowers
Other: watch for gooseberry mildew
WEEK 3: *Sow outdoors:* corn; cabbage; broccoli; cucumber;
summer squash
WEEK 4: *Sow outdoors:* carrot; soybean
Other: renovate strawberries; net blueberries; place
maggot traps in apple trees

July

WEEK 1: *Sow:* cilantro; parsley; bush beans; endive
WEEK 2: *Sow:* lettuce; fennel; *mâche*
Transplant: cabbage; broccoli; cauliflower
WEEK 3: *Sow:* beets; calendula
Other: prune gooseberries; take privet cuttings

August

WEEK 1: *Sow:* biennial and perennial flowers; lettuce (sixty
plants)
Other: harvest garlic and some onions; watch for
gooseberry fruitworm
WEEK 2: *Sow:* spinach; turnip; *mâche*; Chinese cabbage;
winter radish
Transplant: endive
WEEK 3: *Sow:* lettuce
Plant: garlic
Other: watch for fleas on dog

September

W E E K 1: *Sow:* lettuce; small radishes; greens
Other: blanch cardoon and endive
W E E K 2: *Other:* Bring houseplants indoors; dig celery and
set roots in pots of soil in garage

October

W E E K 2: *Other:* move fig into basement; clean up garden;
pick all tomatoes; turn off water; set mouse-
traps
W E E K 3: *Other:* dig carrots; make sauerkraut; move onion
and garlic braids to basement

November

W E E K 1: *Other:* plant bulbs for forcing
W E E K 2: *Sow:* spinach in cold frames
Other: spread wood ashes and lime; harvest cab-
bage for storage

December

•   •   •

January

•   •   •

February

W E E K 1: *Sow indoors:* pansy; onion; leek; lettuce
W E E K 2: *Other:* take geranium cuttings

Index

Index

Index

Index

Index